BUSINESS FLYING

The Profitable Use of
Personal Aircraft

AOPA/McGraw-Hill Series in General Aviation
General Editor: Robert B. Parke

Hansen: BUSINESS FLYING
Newton: SEVERE WEATHER FLYING (1982)

PAUL E. HANSEN

BUSINESS FLYING
The Profitable Use of
Personal Aircraft

McGraw-Hill Book Company

New York   St. Louis   San Francisco   Auckland
Bogotá   Hamburg   Johannesburg   London   Madrid
Mexico   Montreal   New Delhi   Panama   Paris
São Paulo   Singapore   Sydney   Tokyo   Toronto

Library of Congress Cataloging in Publication Data

Hansen, Paul E.
  Business flying.

  Includes index.
  1. Airplanes, Company.   2. Private flying
I. Title
TL722.H36   629.133′340422   81-4544
                                        AACR2

ISBN 0-07-026071-0

1 2 3 4 5 6 7 8 9 0   DODO   8 9 8 7 6 5 4 3 2 1

The editors for this book were Jeremy Robinson and Chet
Gottfried, the designer was Elliot Epstein, and the production supervisor was Paul A. Malchow. It was set in Melior
by York Graphic Services, Inc.

Printed and bound by R. R. Donnelley & Sons Company.

Unless otherwise credited, all the photographs in this book
are by Paul E. Hansen.

For my friend Richard Bach, who first introduced me to the idea that flying is a great deal more than getting an airplane from one place to another.

CONTENTS

The bookshelves are loaded with volumes explaining the various aspects of airmanship, weather, aerodynamics, and the intricacies of operating in the IFR environment. Therefore, *Business Flying* passes over most of these to deal with the problems of acquiring, maintaining, and operating a general aviation airplane profitably, safely, and efficiently within the goals and structure of a business enterprise.

No attempt has been made to provide a series of shortcut, ready-made answers to the myriad problems confronted by the business pilot. To do so would be impossible, as each individual and company has unique needs and, therefore, requires unique answers to those needs. Instead, *Business Flying* works to develop the proper questions to ask and suggests alternate courses which may be followed to generate answers that will fit the particular needs of the individual surveying the potential and the compromises involved when starting to fly for business.

The answer for a company with unlimited funds and a multi-thousand-hour instrument pilot on the staff will require a differing set of compromises than will the business owned by a private pilot with a desire to put a 10-year-old Skyhawk to work in a profit-producing capacity. The situation will be different again when the person in question is one with an extremely high income from his profession who is looking for some way to ease the tax bite and do it with something he finds interesting and enjoyable, such as an airplane.

Although the masculine pronoun has been used in the preceding paragraph and will be used throughout the remainder of this book, the choice was made simply for its ease of expression. "The pilot . . . he" reads smoother than "the pilot . . . he or she." This convention should not be interpreted as a wish to exclude women from either the use of this book or participation in business flying.

Considerable time and effort were expended in covering the financial and tax aspects of owning and operating a business aircraft, yet there are no magic, something-for-nothing formulas here to appease the individual who wants to *play* at being a pilot and "take it off his income tax." This book was written for the business person who seriously wants to use a general aviation airplane as a profit-producing business tool for his company.

Unfortunately, during 1980, business profits were squeezed by the high cost of borrowed funds when the "prime rate" established a historic high of more than 21 percent. Many experts in the fields of economics and finance believe the wild gyrations of the interest rates were caused by manipulation of the money supply by the federal government and by its heavy demands upon the credit market to supply the monetary needs of legislated deficits. If these experts are correct, perhaps what we have witnessed and suffered through during 1980 can be categorized as an anomoly, and the future will be brighter.

This optimistic view has been taken while preparing the various charts, tables, and calculations presented in this book. The interest rates selected are representative of those one might expect to see when we return to a more stable economic climate. The various values are necessarily "nominal" in nature, but they serve well to present the financial principles and procedures under examination.

Business Flying should be of interest to anyone who travels or plans to travel extensively by general aviation aircraft. But, it is directed primarily to the entrepreneur, to the business owner, who not only charts the course for the financial success of his business but also takes the left seat in the company airplane. This is a complex and demanding job even for the person who is already an experienced pilot. For the low-time private pilot or the nonpilot who aspires to "fly for business," the path will be long, time-consuming, and probably expensive. It is, however, an attainable goal and one which can provide many rewarding experiences. In the opinion of one who has struggled down that "long path," it is well worth the effort.

Paul E. Hansen

BUSINESS FLYING
The Profitable Use of
Personal Aircraft

CHAPTER ONE

General Aviation

The World of Business Flying

OF TIME AND TOOLS

Individual freedoms coupled to abundant resources have allowed us, the American people, to build a nation of unparalleled industrial capability and economic strength. Our growth has been pushed forward by the tremendous technological advances made by our scientists and engineers in the areas of manufacturing, communications, and transportation. As each new invention moved from the mind of its creator into solid reality, imaginative business executives found ways to bring these new entities together with capital and labor to generate profits, jobs, and a standard of living unmatched elsewhere in the world.

Ours is a dynamic and highly mobile society in which the highest rewards of the marketplace have historically gone to those who were the most productive, efficient, and adaptable. Today's competitive business atmosphere makes these capabilities more important to success than ever before. As members of the business community, we must work our skills and resources harder just to stay even. We must do more, do it better, and do it in less time.

Time, of course, is always a vital consideration to the business person. In every problem he faces, time is an element in the equation. It is the unrenewable resource. Each of us is allotted only 24 hours in a day, and how much we accomplish is totally dependent upon how productively we use that time. We cannot effectively slow the passage of time. But, with the use of tools, we can increase the productivity of every hour and expand the effectiveness of each day's efforts.

Our choice of tools will often dictate our method of operation. As surely as the installation of automated machines will alter the procedures on the factory production line, the use of a company airplane will affect the planning and procedures of the entire business enterprise. The decision to become involved in business flying is more than just the acquisition of another capital asset. It is a commitment to a different way of doing business.

New tools invariably lead to new opportunities. Many of the things that we do in life we do simply because we have the capability. When a business person can *conveniently* call on prospects in formerly out-of-the-way places, he will do so. His market penetration will increase and his marketing area will be enlarged. Ultimately, his sales and his business will grow.

For the business executive, a general aviation aircraft can offer flexibility of travel scheduling and routing which can result in literally weeks of productive time being saved during the course of a year. Out-of-town meetings which once required overnight stays can become one-day situations, allowing the business person to spend more nights at home. Airport security checks and baggage searching are avoided when traveling in a business aircraft. This results in additional time savings and much lower levels of personal frustration. The business airplane also avoids the hazards of terrorist hijackings and bomb threats which have become so common to airline travel in recent years.

A couple of more mundane considerations for the traveling business executive are those pertaining to cigarette smoke and luggage. Both these items are usually handled in a less-than-satisfactory manner by the airlines, so a company airplane offers a meaningful alternative form of air travel.

In a private business aircraft, the nonsmoking executive can avoid the discomfort and annoyance resulting from hours spent in the confined and polluted atmosphere of a typical airliner. Although "nonsmoking" sections are available on most flights, they are practically meaningless since the airline aircraft is a "pressure vessel" with a totally homogeneous atmosphere. To the smoker, concern over this will seem an extremely trivial matter, but for the business person with a deep aversion to smoking or an allergy to airborne irritants, this single consideration may provide sufficient justification for the purchase of a private business aircraft.

There are few regular airline travelers who have not been touched by the system's ability to "misplace" passenger luggage. Even on the temporary basis that this usually occurs, it can either be a minor inconvenience or a major disaster depending upon the individual's circumstances. It is one thing to be in Kansas City without a clean shirt, but it is a far more impactful event to be a "sample-line" salesperson enroute

Business flying is not a recent phenomenon. This Lockheed Vega, which received its original type certificate in April 1929, was one of the first "business aircraft." In 1931, Wiley Post flew his Vega, the *Winnie Mae*, around the world in 8 days, 15 hours, and 51 minutes, proving the viability of business flying in a single-engine airplane. The Vega was also pressed into service by some of the first operational airlines of the day. This five-passenger machine was a remarkable design for the period since its speed and performance rival those of comparable aircraft in today's business fleet.

to a week-long tradeshow in Chicago and find that the airline has misplaced your samples. In either case, the situation is a nuisance which costs time and money. The "temporarily misplaced" samples, however, could easily result in lost sales equal to the operating costs for a general aviation airplane for a year. When the business executive travels in his own airplane, he is assured that when he arrives at his destination, his luggage will be there too.

Of the 14,746 landing places in the United States at the end of 1979, only 477 were being serviced by scheduled airlines. That figure is dropping daily as the airlines cut back in an effort to increase the number of revenue passengers and shave costs in the face of escalating fuel prices. The Civil Aeronautics Board (CAB) reported that during a recent 1-year period the domestic trunk airlines scheduled 5 percent fewer departures and aircraft miles from that of a previous period. Moreover, 1980 was an extremely bad year for the airlines, and these cutbacks are likely to continue, particularly on low-density, short-haul routes. At the same time, business will probably continue to decentralize, moving away from the cities to the suburbs or even rural areas. These two factors will make the general aviation airplane increasingly important to the business traveler.

Attempting to make comprehensive direct comparisons between general aviation travel and travel by the airlines would be an extremely complex and lengthy undertaking. In fact, there can be no valid comparisons of cost-benefit relationships unless each specific case is examined in all areas of need and past history pertaining to travel costs. The appropriate selection of company equipment and proper planning for asset utilization can make the figures run from a fraction of comparable airline travel costs to multiples of three or four times those costs. If prudent judgment is used, however, and planning is done with an eye to cost-effectiveness, a small general aviation aircraft can be a most valuable travel tool for business since it is directly under the control of those people with the travel needs.

EFFICIENT, SAFE, AND ECONOMICAL

Since the original Arab oil embargo in late 1972, the efficiency of fuel used by air transportation has proved to be much higher than that of other forms of transit. And general aviation has demonstrated more favorable fuel specifics than either the airlines or automobiles. In 1975, general aviation consumed a total of 454 million gallons of avgas, which is less than 0.4 percent of all gasoline used in transportation. Yet, this segment of air transportation moved more than 100 million passengers between various American cities.

According to a report from the Aircraft Owners and Pilots Association (AOPA), the fuel economy of the typical general aviation aircraft is much better than that of an automobile. To illustrate this point a comparison was made between various aircraft and automobiles covering the distance from Baltimore to St. Louis. The report shows that a twin-engine Beech Baron would use 81.4 gallons of fuel for that trip, while a Cadillac would consume 102 gallons, or 25 percent more. Comparing a six-place Beech Bonanza traveling at 198 mph with a Volkswagen sedan, AOPA points out that the Bonanza will produce 88.8 seat miles per gallon (smpg) of fuel consumed, while the VW will provide only 83.6 smpg.

General aviation not only provides an extremely fuel-efficient mode of air travel, it is also the most flexible and convenient means of meeting the travel needs of many business executives. The airlines, of course, provide the fastest and least expensive travel from Los Angeles to New York, for example, but when your office is in St. Louis and your customer is in Waterloo, Iowa, it is a completely different story. Unless your departure and arrival points are *both* on the list of twenty-four major terminals, which receive 54 percent of all scheduled airline flights, you will be in the classic position of "you can't get there from here." Attempts to use the airlines in such circumstances become an exercise in utter frustration.

The American business person is a pragmatist. He eagerly accepts that which works. When the telephone and computer were introduced, the more progressive and adventuresome entrepreneurs hurried to utilize these technological advancements as a means to gain an edge over their competitors. They struggled and faltered occasionally, suffering the frustrations and growing pains attendant to any new tool as methods and procedures for its effective use were being developed. The long-term record, however, shows the valuable contributions made by these business tools and justifies the faith placed in them by early supporters.

Like the telephone and the computer, the business aircraft is a valuable time expander, and it has followed a similar path, fighting every step of the way to gain acceptance as a meaningful business tool. Unfortunately, due to its history, its nature, and the mystery surrounding the environment in which it works, the airplane has been stigmatized in the minds of many. Although jet travel is an accepted part of daily life in our country, "little airplanes" remain unsafe, uncomfortable, unreliable, impractical, and hellishly expensive toys to a great number of otherwise well-informed people.

This problem, of course, is perpetuated and compounded by the irresponsible actions of television networks which produce and air blatant distortions on the subject of aviation safety. For example, using the tools of editing and camera angles, a highly rated TV show manipulated the facts in such a way that the average viewer would be led to a false conclusion and a prejudice against general aviation. It is impossible not to question the intent of the producers and speculate on what correlation there might be between such material and airline advertising budgets.

Sensationalism and a total disregard for facts seem to offer temptations too great to resist for many members of the general press when they are reporting on aviation safety. This is particularly true when little airplanes are involved. Currently, some of the most reprehensible examples of this journalistic malignancy are being produced by a self-styled expert in the field of air safety. This "expert," a nonpilot, has authored several articles, appearing in the popular press, which depict general aviation pilots as uneducated, undisciplined, and irresponsible fools who in large measure cause grievous aerial accidents which have happened or will happen.

That the author's "facts" are occasionally faulty and his conclusions are based on ill-informed assumptions does not alter the damage that he and others like him do to the image of general aviation in the eyes of the public and our legislators. Capitalizing on fear, of course, is not a new tactic; but it is a powerful one. And widespread publication of such misinformation pertaining to air safety creates enormous problems for the business executive who is trying to convince a fearful spouse or stockholder of the practicality of business flying.

Regardless of the propagandizing of the media, general aviation is a safe and viable form of air transportation. A comparison of the 1975 records of the National Transportation Safety Board (NTSB) shows that the airlines conducted 99.9999996 percent of their flights without a fatality, while general aviation followed very close behind by completing 99.9999888 percent of its flights without a fatality. When you consider that the general aviation figures include fatalities resulting from hazardous operations, such as crop dusting, air racing, and the use of experimental or antique aircraft, this difference of 0.0000108 percent seems of questionable significance. During the 10-year period from 1969 to 1979, general aviation averaged 4.67 fatalities for each 100,000 hours flown, while the air carriers recorded a 3.71 rate. This amounts to a difference of only 0.96 fatalities per each 100,000 flight hours. Certainly, these figures will support a conclusion that *either* method of air travel is reasonably safe. To develop a perspective on the relative safety of travel by general aviation aircraft to other modes of transportation, however, consider the fact that school buses are involved in 1.68 accidents for every 1 million vehicle miles, while the rate for private planes is only 1.13 accidents per million vehicle miles.

Not only is general aviation a relatively safe and fuel-efficient form of transportation, it can also be very attractive in a purely economic sense. In fact, it can be less expensive to own and operate a high-performance, single-engine airplane than a family sedan on a basis of cost per mile.

According to a report by a national research firm, as announced on the October 31, 1977, edition of the *Today* show, the average cost for ownership and operation of a 1977 mid-sized automobile was running 30 cents per mile. When this figure is compared to the 27 cents per mile it cost during the same year to own and operate an airplane valued at more than $94,000, the cost-effectiveness of a general aviation airplane becomes very clear. That 27 cents included *all* direct, indirect, and capital costs pertaining to the acquisition and operation of the airplane. Operational costs have increased considerably since 1977, primarily due to increased fuel prices. The impact, however, has been proportional to both automobile and aviation fuels. Therefore, the cost-effectiveness differentials between the car and the general aviation airplane continue to be valid.

THE INVISIBLE GIANT

Although the safety, efficiency, and economy of general aviation can be factually demonstrated, the average person has no concept of the vital role that little airplanes play in the scheme of our national economy. Few are aware that airplanes are one of the major export items of the United States. As such, they have a meaningful impact on our balance-of-payments problems. Most people know that our farms provide food for hungry nations all over the world, but they rarely consider the fact that our tremendous food-growing capability is in large measure dependent upon little airplanes.

To the general public, the word *aviation* is synonymous with *airlines*. In daily life, the TV commercials and overhead sounds of jet engines see to it that people are constantly aware of this segment of our air transportation system. Full-page advertisements incessantly tout on-time arrivals, wide-bodied legroom, low-cost gimmick fares, and airborne conviviality at 40,000 feet. Boasting about millions of accident-free passenger miles, airline public relations departments have convinced the public that theirs is the *only* way to fly, but it just isn't so.

In the United States, general aviation offers the business person another way to fly. With 210,523 aircraft in the fleet at the close of 1979 versus only 3609 pieces of active airline equipment, general aviation is numerically a much larger component of the air transportation system in this country than the airlines are. Flying 5.3 times the number of hours that the airlines do, general aviation annually logs almost twice as many miles as the combined total for *all* the airlines in the United States. Although it is not well known, general aviation is, in fact, the largest single air carrier in the world!

The use of general aviation aircraft for business travel breaks down into three distinct segments: (1) commercial charter and air-taxi opera-

The single-engine general aviation airplane in the foreground is more fuel-efficient than the commercial jet which shares the ramp with it at Bakersfield, California. This Piper Lance is one of the more than 210,000 aircraft in the general aviation fleet. As such, it belongs to the *largest* single air carrier in the world. In the United States, general aviation carries more people each year than the next three air carriers combined.

tions, (2) corporate flight operations, and (3) business flying. It is estimated by the General Aviation Manufacturer's Association (GAMA) that during 1977 these three groups will fly 72 percent of the 38 million flight hours forecast to be flown by general aviation.

The safety record of these three segments is superior to that of general aviation as a whole. The statistics for corporate and business flying show these operations to be even safer than the heavily regulated Part 135 air-taxi operations.

Corporate flight operations are currently the safest segment of general aviation, having a record which rivals that of the airlines. Like the airlines, corporate flight operations employ professional pilots who are paid to fly. It is this one factor which separates corporate flying from business flying. In the latter category, business flying, the aircraft is *owner-flown.*

But why would anyone in his right mind wish to fly a little airplane, being bounced around by winds and weather, when he could be making the trip in martini-soaked splendor high above the clouds? If the previously given facts concerning economy, fuel efficiency, convenience, and travel flexibility don't provide a satisfactory answer, then there must be something else. In some cases, of course, there may be no other choice. As it has been pointed out before, due to departure points and destinations, the option of travel by the airlines may not be available. But even if it is, for some people, there will always be the compelling consideration of *control*.

The entrepreneur is an uncommon person. He has the need to determine his own fate. This fact is evident in his decision to become an independent business executive. It is difficult for this type of personality to relinquish control, either in business or in travel. The owner-flown business aircraft is the *only* mode of air transportation which allows the entrepreneur to satisfy this need.

Business flying offers the business pilot the opportunity of almost total control over his airborne travels. It is a fascinating, demanding, multidimensional activity that is constantly challenging and one which can be richly rewarding both economically and personally. Without proper planning and preparation, however, it can be an expensive and frustrating addition to the complexities of running a business enterprise. In the pages that follow, we will look at the choices, decisions, and problems facing the individual who elects to enter the world of business flying. The various options available and considerations of utility and safety will be explored, seeking always to find answers which provide an optimum balance between risks, rewards, benefits, and costs.

CHAPTER TWO

The Price of Admission

BASIC CONSIDERATIONS

Flying for business is an entirely different game than flying for pleasure. Although the basic skills pertaining to aircraft control remain the same, the overall flight operation becomes a great deal more complex. There are financial and tax considerations which are considerably different than those of the pleasure pilot. And due to the "bottom-line" demands for cost-effectiveness, the pressure to "get there" is probably felt more often and more acutely by the business pilot than any other member of the pilot population.

Business runs on schedules. Appointments are made, and it is expected that they will be kept. Everyone is busy, and no one likes to be kept waiting. It is both a matter of self-esteem and recognition of the fact that, in business, time is indeed money. Therefore, the pilot who wants to fly for business must be able to do so on a basis which allows him to make and keep appointments. "On-time arrivals" become just as important to him as they are to the airlines. If he didn't have the need to be at some specific place at some specified time, his company should not have invested all those dollars in an airplane.

Weather, of course, is the constant variable in the flyer's world. Conditions are difficult to predict with a high degree of accuracy for more than a few hours at a time. Even if long-term forecasts were more reliable, making appointments with out-of-town customers contingent upon the weather is an untenable procedure. This means that the pilot who would fly for business must have "weather capability."

For the experienced instrument pilot, weather capability simply requires the appropriate equipment. For the novice or nonpilot, however, the problem takes on much larger dimensions. There is not only the problem of acquiring the proper equipment but also the need to obtain the necessary skills, ratings, and experience required to function safely in the IFR (instrument flight rules) environment. During this "start-up" period, the company's mission capability will be significantly compromised. And every compromise of mission capability, of course, has an unfavorable impact upon the cost-effectiveness of the company airplane.

THE INSTRUMENT RATING

The pilot with only a VFR (visual flight rules) rating *can* operate his airplane for business, but he must be willing to accept being constantly delayed. Making and keeping appointments will be impossible. Stratus layers will prevent early morning takeoffs, and all too often, he will be forced to sit on the ground because his destination is below VFR minimums. Under such conditions, the rate for mission completion falls so low that analysis would lead to the conclusion that business was being conducted *in spite of* the use of a general aviation airplane, not because of it. Unless you are an Arizona rancher who uses a Super Cub to fly around the ranch and tend to the needs of your cattle, there is no practical, cost-effective way to engage in business flying without an instrument rating.

Perhaps the greatest danger for the business pilot who lacks instrument capability comes from the temptation to press on into darkness or deteriorating weather conditions. Attempting to continue VFR operations into marginal weather conditions with a high-performance business aircraft is toying with suicide. Such aircraft simply cover too much ground too rapidly for this type of activity. The National Transportation Safety Board (NTSB) statistics state quite emphatically that *scud running* is one of the most deadly operations conducted by non-instrument-rated pilots.

The instrument rating is probably the most expensive and difficult of all the Federal Aviation Administration (FAA) pilot ratings to obtain. For the business executive, however, it can easily prove to be even more expensive not to have it. When a big-dollar asset like an airplane sits unproductively on the ground, it becomes a liability. The more expensive the airplane, the more it costs to have it sit idle while you are waiting for the visibility to increase or a cloud deck to dissipate. The positive impact that instrument capability will have on aircraft utility will make the instrument rating one of the most economical aviation investments available to the business person. As an additional bonus, your insurance company will probably reward you with better rates once the word *instrument* has been added to your ticket.

Although the Federal Aviation Regulations (FARs) require a minimum of 40 hours of IFR training, the national average is currently 59 hours when the rating is issued. It can be done in the minimum number of hours only if the project is approached in a logical and well-organized manner. If your training sessions are too far apart, your chances of getting the instrument rating in the minimum 40 hours are very slim. The best approach would probably be to establish a schedule that puts you in the air for an hour or two every day. Remember also that some of those 40 hours can be in a simulator which is less expensive than an airplane and in many ways is a better instrument trainer.

Selecting a school and an instructor for your instrument training is extremely important. For a business person, time is money. Therefore, it is imperative that you get the absolute maximum out of every hour that you spend in training. Remember, not only will you be paying an instructor for every hour of dual that you take but you will also be taking time away from your own money-making activities. This is no small part of the overall cost for your instrument ticket, so you won't want to show up at the airport for a lesson only to find that your instructor has just taken off with a charter flight. The best way to prevent such an unpleasant surprise is to enroll in one of the several aviation schools that do nothing but flight training. Their hourly costs are usually a bit higher than the average flight school, but in the end, this route may well work out to be cheaper.

Once you have earned the instrument rating, use it. Use it at every opportunity. Build your IFR experience and confidence on every flight. Get comfortable with the Air Traffic Control (ATC) system by filing IFR in VFR weather conditions. Any mistakes you make under those conditions will result in nothing more than minor embarrassment and some lasting insights about the IFR system. If the going gets too tough and you want some time to reflect upon the cause of your confusion, simply push the mike button and say, "Cancel my IFR flight plan."

Plan your first solo IFR trips to occur under "easy IFR conditions." The rule for easy IFR is "Always fly into improving weather conditions." At first, that will mean a takeoff and departure in actual instrument meteorological conditions (IMC) for a destination that is clear. Preferably the IFR conditions at the departure airport would be the result of a stable stratus situation which will provide you with smooth, nonturbulent air. The enroute portion of such a flight would then be made either above a cloud deck or in the clear, ending in an approach at your destination in good VFR weather.

As your experience and confidence grow, you will then want to plan your flights to provide greater and greater challenge. For example, your travel plans call for a 3-hour cross-country flight. Your departure airport is currently IFR and your destination is forecast to be 3500 overcast with 5 miles at the time of your arrival. The overcast extends along your entire route, but the tops have been reported to be about 8000 feet. You can file for 9000 and be "on top" all the way, but that's too easy. The conditions are perfect for getting some really good IFR experience for an extended period. If you file for 5000 or 7000, you will be in the clouds for the entire trip from takeoff until perhaps 15 minutes before touchdown. You will have had the opportunity to work almost an entire flight, covering departure, enroute, and arrival procedures completely on your flight instruments. This kind of experience goes a long way toward building the self-confidence needed to be proficient and comfortable in the IFR environment.

Night flight in good visual meteorological conditions (VMC) is another example of easy IFR. The air is generally smooth at night, the ATC frequencies are quiet, and operations away from the major metropolitan areas provide very little in the way of visual cues. Therefore, these conditions are ideal for IFR-procedure practice for the neophyte instrument pilot. You will want to be especially careful about the temperature-dewpoint spread, however, when practicing this nighttime variant of easy IFR in coastal areas or around lakes and rivers. When that spread drops below 4 degrees, the chances become very good that your destination or your alternate could become enshrouded in fog. Given the right conditions, fog can drop an airport below minimums in a matter of minutes. Then it will often stay that way all night. So always have several alternate plans.

When operating on an IFR flight plan in VMC at night, you will learn that ATC will invariably say, "Cleared for the visual approach." This is probably done to expedite your flight and get you out of the controller's hair. Acceptance of such a clearance, of course, does nothing to add to your instrument proficiency. So when "center" hands you off to your destination approach controller, let the person know what you want. Tell "approach" that you would like to shoot the ILS (instrument landing system) and do the full procedure. Generally, he will be most obliging, offering the option of radar vectors or your own navigation. It is probably a good idea to accept the opportunity to use your own navigation whenever it presents itself. This is extremely good practice, as you will rarely get the chance to do this under actual conditions.

THE NONPILOT

Since a private pilot certificate with an instrument rating is the basic requirement for admission into business flying on a safe and cost-effective basis, the nonpilot is faced with a long-term project. Even if he is able to complete all the FAA requirements in about the minimum time, his logbook will still contain almost 250 hours of flight time. During his training, he will, of course, be able to use his newly acquired aeronautical skills on a limited basis. After his private license has been obtained, he can probably combine some of his business travel with portions of his advanced training, provided that an agreeable instructor can be found.

The calendar time involved will be dependent upon the dedication of the individual and the number of hours each day that can be devoted to the required study and training. Although it might be possible to rise from a nonpilot to a private pilot with an instrument rating in as little as 6 months, to do so would be highly improbable and would require making flight training a full-time occupation. Few business executives would be able or willing to do this. Even for the individual who was willing to make this type of commitment, such an accelerated program would probably produce less than optimum results. Flying skills take time to mature. Therefore, the nonpilot should probably plan on spending at least a year or perhaps even 2 years in his quest for the instrument rating. He should also remember that once obtained, this is just another "license to learn."

IS IT DEDUCTIBLE?

This is a question of constant concern to every business person: "Is it deductible?" When applied to pilot training, this question can gather a variety of answers. Depending upon the circumstances, the answer might be "Yes," "No," "Maybe," or "It depends."

According to the Internal Revenue Service (IRS) regulation 1.162-5, *education expenses are deductible if the education: (a) maintains or improves skills required in the taxpayer's employment or trade or (b) is required by the employer or the law.* There are some exceptions to this, however. Education expenses are not deductible if such education is needed to meet the *minimum requirements of the job* or if it *qualifies the taxpayer for a new trade or business.*

Applying this rule to getting a pilot's license or a new rating for a business person gets into one of the many "gray areas" in the law. Certainly, a private pilot certificate does not prepare anyone for a new business or trade, but ratings such as commercial or airline transport pilot (ATP) most assuredly would. If a private pilot owned a business with a company airplane, for example, and in the interest of increasing asset utilization he decided that an instrument rating was necessary, it would appear that this training would be deductible. The circumstances *seem* to fit the IRS requirements and avoid the exclusions, but an IRS agent might disagree.

In fact, an IRS agent did disagree on a situation like this. The taxpayer upgraded to an IFR-equipped aircraft and then proceeded to learn to fly it. The IRS allowed the deductions for the business use of the airplane but denied the deductions for the advanced training. The taxpayer believed he was right and functioning within the tax law. The tax court agreed with the taxpayer (Knudtson, TC Memo: 1980-455) and restored the deductions for training which had been disallowed by the IRS.

If you and your tax advisor decide that your circumstances fit the requirements of the law, go ahead and deduct your pilot-training costs, but be prepared to defend your position, perhaps even in court, should this item come up in an audit.

POCKETBOOK POWER

The decision to fly or not to fly for business requires a great deal of introspection and soul-searching on many levels. To become a novice in a discipline which requires years to advance to the expert level, at a time in life when an individual's position in the business world is secure and unquestionable, can be an extremely difficult thing to handle emotionally. In hiding from that factor, many will try to advance more rapidly than it is possible to do safely. They will use their business-world power and wealth to press beyond their personal capabilities in terms of aeronautical skill and experience. If some incident does not put such a person back on the right track, the chances are good that he will eventually become an NTSB accident statistic.

The stereotyped candidate for this situation is usually a medical doctor. One does not have to be around the aviation field very long before he is informed of the extremely poor safety record of the flying physician. The general wisdom proclaims that doctors have more money than sense, are always in a hurry, feel that they have a special relationship with the gods, and very often trade up their equipment faster than they build flying expertise. The net result, according to the airport pundits, is the disproportionate accident rate for those of the healing arts.

Without entering into a comprehensive defense of the validity of the above assertion, there is a definite problem associated with "pocketbook power," and this problem is *not* the exclusive territory of doctors. All the ingredients for this particular brand of trouble assemble very readily around anyone who is highly motivated and intelligent and functions as a high-level achiever. Usually, the scenario begins when a professional man with a lot of money decides a high-performance twin is befitting his station in life. It doesn't seem to matter that he only has 65 hours of flight time and most of that is in a Cessna 150. He can afford a King Air and that's what he wants.

Somewhere along the line, before a salesperson gets his money, a friend or a flight instructor will talk him out of this folly. But, he still wants "twin-engined" safety, so he settles for a Cessna 310 or a Baron.

Business flying makes different demands than pleasure flying, both in pilot skills and equipment sophistication. The delightful simplicity of the instrumentation of this homebuilt "Breezy" is a large part of the charm of pleasure flying, but a panel with just airspeed, altimeter, and compass would be woefully inadequate for the business aircraft. Flying for business requires an "all-weather" mission capability, just like the airlines. This means there must be appropriate equipment in the aircraft and the proper level of pilot skills to operate safely in the IFR environment.

After getting his multi rating on his ticket, he flies off in his new air-plane, a machine that can carry him into more demanding situations *faster* than his low-level skills can accommodate. Even when this pre-mature transition is only to a Cessna 210 or a Beech Bonanza, it can still be a problem.

In order to achieve a proper level of safety and utility, there must be a balance between pilot proficiency and equipment sophistication. In terms of mission capability, there is just as much compromise in a situation where an experienced ATP-rated pilot is flying a J-3 Cub as there is with a low-time private pilot standing beside his new Cessna 421. In the first instance, we have the experience but lack the equip-ment. In the second, the reverse is true. We have the equipment, but lack the experience to operate it to its fullest capability. In either case, the mission capability is compromised.

If we were to switch the equipment, the ATP would enjoy a quan-tum leap forward in his mission capability. The private pilot, however, would have gained little in this area, but he would probably be in a much safer operating envelope. It is imperative to match the pilot and the equipment to achieve the optimum in terms of a balance between mission capability and operational safety. Expensive equipment is sim-ply no substitute for experience and skill.

PROFESSIONALISM

Business flying is not for everyone. For example, the individual who can't fulfill the time demands of his business itself can hardly under-take the additional time demands created when he decides to be his own pilot. How can someone who always runs out of hours before he gets his workday tasks completed even think about taking on more obligations? On any reasonable basis, he can't. But is his problem one of time or is it rather one of time management?

Time management, of course, is the rightful subject of another book, not this one. But the reader should give some thought to this subject and do a little reading on it if he honestly finds that he does not have time to do those things which he really wants to do. Perhaps the prob-lem is simply a matter of poor priority establishment or an inability to say "No" when coworkers or circumstances confront you with "just one more thing."

We have all met the person who has always wanted to fly, but his spouse won't let him do it or he must "think of the family," not just himself. He is probably the same individual who can't find the time to do so many things that he wants to do in life. Someday, he will "write a novel," but more likely he will die of old age reiterating excuses concerning all the things he really wanted to do, but just couldn't find time for.

These are self-deceptions, pure and simple. Perhaps we all play this game from time to time in greater or lesser degrees. Maybe it is just easier to see in someone else. Still, it is extremely rare when a person *really* can't make the time available to do what he really wants to do.

The real world doesn't accept excuses about not having time to study or practice or some other such nonsense. Once you have launched yourself and your airplane into the weather and the IFR system where the turf belongs to the "big guys," you had best be able to function to their standards. If you can't, you are a threat to them, to yourself, and to the people on the ground. You have committed an irresponsible act.

If you are seriously going to fly for business, you are going to have to be a better-than-average pilot. You must be a better-than-average decision maker. You will have to leave the ranks of the "Sunday flyers" and become a professional. That doesn't mean that you must obtain an ATP with a bundle of type ratings. It means you must develop a professional attitude toward flying. Overlearning and recurrent training must become a way of life for you just as it is for the airline captain. You owe this to yourself, your family, the stockholders of your company, the controller with whom you will work, and the other pilots with whom you will share the sky.

In many respects the business pilot has even greater demands made of him than the airline types do. He shares the need to go, and he must do so in generally less sophisticated equipment and without the aid of additional eyes, hands, and minds of other crew members. He must handle the chores of the captain, the first officer, and the flight engineer. He will be functioning in the same demanding weather and complex ATC system. He flies the same approaches, fulfills the same communication and navigation requirements, and he is doing it alone.

The fledgling airline pilot is fortunate. His job provides him with the opportunity to grow into his responsibilities under the guidance of a more experienced pilot. This apprenticeship system allows a depth of understanding to be built which is difficult to gain any other way. Although there are abundant flight schools available which will enable the business pilot to meet the requirements of the various FAA certificates, his accumulation of practical experience will generally be done without the aid of a mentor. This is a serious handicap, but circumstance and economics rarely allow it to be different.

Just like any other "handicapped" person, the business pilot has to work harder to achieve comparable results. The task is not *easier* because you must "go it alone." It is more difficult. Weather systems don't play preferential games. They couldn't care less that you don't have a copilot, weather radar, or a flight director. That's your problem, and if you intend to keep appointments when the ceilings and visibilities are down to minimums, then your skills had best be of a professional level.

For the better part of 20 years, I earned a living as a free-lance photographer. During this period of life, I found that every customer I worked for had a friend or relative that was a photographer. Every model who worked for me had either a husband or a boyfriend that was "an excellent photographer."

In many instances, these amateur photographers had pictures that would have made any professional proud to have claimed as his own. So what's the difference? How can a professional make it in such a world? With so much talent readily available, why do photographic clients continue to pay professionals $500 to $1000 a day and many times even more to do what the amateur can do? The answer is really very simple. The client understands that the friend or relative, the amateur who has produced some beautiful pictures, cannot *consistently* do what the professional photographer does. The professional can produce those beautiful pictures on demand—every day. If the conditions are not perfect for the required shot, the professional will either be able to cope with the conditions existing or will alter the conditions to fulfill the requirements. He may even use the unfavorable conditions to produce something more exciting than the photo first envisioned by the client. He will also do this within the confines of limited time and budgets.

The mark of a professional in any field is the ability to perform to a high level of competency under a variety of conditions and the stress of both time and monetary limitations. The professional delivers the product, not excuses or rationalizations for his limitations.

In few fields is the demand for professionalism of more serious consequence than it is in flying. If you are not willing to spend the time and money necessary to acquire and maintain the skills of a "professional" pilot, then you should enjoy your Sunday flights with the family; and when the need for serious business travel occurs, take the airlines and leave the flying to a professional.

CHAPTER THREE

The Tools
of the Trade

THE PURPOSE IS PROFIT

Buying an airplane can be either an answer to the problems facing a company in terms of transportation costs and expanding markets for the company's product or a horror story leading to financial disaster. The difference is made by the amount of time and effort put into the prepurchase study of the company's needs and allowable budget for the acquisition. To buy an airplane without proper analysis and planning is nothing more than acting out a fantasy of flight and power. It is an ego trip. It will quickly turn into an expensive daydream if the profit motives are not kept in full view at all times.

Unfortunately, there is probably nothing more emotionally derived than the "reasons" for taking a lover or purchasing an airplane. Hence, acquiring and profitably using a company airplane is one of the most difficult and complex jobs that a manager can be faced with. The first part, buying an airplane, is surprisingly simple. Making such a purchase a profitable investment, however, is a far more challenging task. In large measure, this difficulty stems from a lack of prepurchase planning and the inability of some pilots to overcome the emotional nature of an airplane acquisition. Even the most prudent business pilot may have some trouble in being totally objective in this area.

It has been said that the human being is a rational animal. It might be more accurate, on a general level, to say that the human being is a *rationalizing* animal. We seem to have an unending ability to rationalize just about anything we wish to do, particularly when it involves airplanes and members of the opposite sex. If the level of desire is high enough, the mind will create all manner of seemingly logical reasons to justify whatever actions we take to fulfill our desires.

Richard Bach, author of *Jonathan Livingston Seagull,* has elevated this ability into a fine art with his thinking concerning one of his previous flying machines, a Canadian T-33 jet trainer. He points out that the T-33 cost less to buy than a Bonanza or an Aerostar. Therefore, he is getting jet speeds at bargain prices. Conceding that the T-33, however, uses fuel in tremendous quantities, he figures that he can afford to pay his fuel bills with the money he saved by not buying a Bonanza, an Aerostar, or a Lear Jet. Never left without an alternate plan, Bach has a real winner to cope with his airplane's voracious appetite. If the money saved by not buying those expensive airplanes is insufficient to cover the T-Bird's fuel, he will simply use the money saved by giving up bowling, tennis, golf, fancy clothes, high-priced sports cars, motorboats, and expensive women. Certainly any airplane lover would find it difficult to argue with such well-structured logic.

Bach, of course, looks at the world with the eyes of an incurable romantic, and he probably drives his business manager nuts. His approach to cost justification would be unacceptable to most business executives and their accountants. Although Bach's approach to airplane economics, as he presented them in the fiftieth anniversary issue of *Flying,* was completely facetious and is totally untenable in view of the current fuel shortage, it demonstrates the rationalizing mechanism used by many pilots when contemplating a new airplane.

Understand from the beginning that the purpose of your company is to show a profit, and the airplane is like any other asset. It should be subjected to the same tests of cost-effectiveness, pay-back, and profit contribution as any other asset. A smart business person does not buy an expensive production machine and then let it sit idle just to be able to collect the investment tax credit or heavy depreciation deductions. The equipment must work. It must be able to pay its own way or the purchase will not be made.

This same thinking should be applied to the acquisition of a company airplane. The primary reason for its purchase should be to contribute to company profitability. How well it does this will depend upon how well you have done the job of fitting the airplane purchased to your company's mission requirements and budget. A solid plan for asset utilization is also imperative if the machine is to become a cost-effective investment. If your airplane gets you to more places faster and you do nothing that adds to company profits when you arrive, then you have a very expensive plaything. It should be showing upon the liability side of the balance sheet rather than in the asset column. The crux of the matter is one of planning. You must plan ahead in order to make a company airplane pay.

LOOK INSIDE FIRST

Before you can wisely select the proper airplane to fill the needs of your company, you will have to define your mission requirements in very definite terms. Any vagueness in this analysis will result in a less-than-optimum fit of the machine to the mission. You will end up with either an airplane that won't do the job or one with excess capability.

The classic error is buying too much airplane. Prodded by very subjective considerations, which are unrelated to mission requirements, companies often purchase an airplane that is too fast, too large, and too expensive. For example, a company might buy a Cessna 340 when all it really needed was a Mooney 201. The Mooney could have functioned on a cost-effective basis, but the company's limited travel needs and utilization rate could never support the twin-engined Cessna. The rationalization is generally based on "safety" considerations or some other reasonable-sounding justification. Unfortunately, airplane selections based on anything but economic realities will ultimately result in serious cash flow problems.

What we are looking for is a better way to do a specific job, and we want to do it at the same cost or less. This means that we must know exactly what the job is, how much it presently costs, and what it will cost if we add an airplane to our inventory of capital assets. "Let's go buy an airplane" is the completely wrong approach and will likely produce results with which the controller of the company will not be happy. The prospective buyer must take a hard look at the needs and future plans of his company and then project both the costs and benefits in a realistic manner before an intelligent decision can be made. This preliminary study should do the following:

1. Establish primary mission goals

2. Establish secondary mission goals

3. Quantify all goals and parameters

4. Establish the budget available

5. Project the costs for ownership and operation

6. Project the tax consequences as they pertain to the acquisition

7. Establish the feasibility of the asset acquisition

Your study of the problem and the potential answers can be as complete and complex as your personality demands or allows. It may be a formal study, or it may be as simple as some notes on the back of a napkin. But the study must be made. And a good deal of thought and consideration must be given to all the variables involved.

Before going out to the local fixed base operator (FBO) to kick tires and fly demonstration rides or even before studying the various aircraft directories and brochures, the prospective aircraft buyer should study the *actual* needs of his company and gather the pertinent facts about the company's operations, tax position, and finances.

Ask lots of questions:

What can this asset do for the company?

How much can we really afford to invest?

How long will it take before the asset will be an effective tool?

Can we afford to do this at all?

What will the impact be on our borrowing power to meet our operating capital needs?

How will an airplane solve the problems that now exist?

If it creates problems of its own, what will they be?

Review your previous travel history. Determine just how far you must usually travel. Examine your travel vouchers to see how often your trips are being made and how much the fares are currently costing. Did you normally travel alone, or were you taking others in the company with you? Will the travel pattern stay the same with a company airplane, or will it change due to the added capability?

Look at the airplane purchase in terms of anticipated benefits. Break these down into three major types: (1) definite benefits that will be readily achievable, (2) probable benefits with their associated assumptions and provisos, and (3) benefits which *might* arise. Attempt to quantify these benefits. This is not always easy to do, but it is important to list your projected benefits in dollar terms. The costs, which are usually more easily identified, will be stated in dollars, so a common denominator is necessary when attempting to weigh the cost-benefit relationship.

The planning for a company airplane should encompass a great deal more than the nuts and bolts of acquiring an airborne piece of hardware. As you move forward in the analysis, you should address the question of what impact a company airplane will have on your total operation. The investment value is usually so great that much thought should be given to every area upon which this decision will have even the remotest effect. It should be realized that this acquisition will affect profit planning and sales strategies, and should be given consideration when planning the future location of the company. It can even have influence upon the method of product distribution. Nothing will ever be the same again. You will be faced with new accounting, tax, and financial problems. The impact will be felt even in the area of employee morale.

The new airplane will be a potential target for a disgruntled employee. He will certainly take the opportunity to complain that you are flitting around the country in your expensive airborne toy, which is being paid for out of his paycheck. It will not matter that you have added a profit-making asset which expands sales, improves utilization of executive time, and ultimately adds jobs. The little airplane has had bad press in both the newspapers and on television. It is highly visible and therefore a prime target for dissension. How you handle the public relations chore within the company will be just as important as how you handle it on the outside.

THE BASIC EQUATION

The number of decisions facing the first-time buyer of a business airplane is staggering. It is difficult to know the best way to go: *new, used, single, twin, four-place, six-place, turboed or not, fixed-gear or retractable?* Each of these considerations will develop additional questions and compromises. In purchasing a company airplane, however, financial considerations will probably be the most influential single-decision element, modifying and coloring all the others.

Given sufficient wealth and a total disregard for prudence in the area of cost-benefit ratios, the entrepreneur could buy or lease a Boeing 747, crew it with professional pilots, and then claim command of a personal airline. This would produce the minimum compromise in mission capability. For all but a handful around the world, such grandiose schemes for business travel are spun from fantasy. The majority of us who fly for business, oil sheiks and wealthy writers excluded, must accept the limitations and compromises imposed by the lack of unlimited funds.

The various compromises involved in business flying are balanced in what might be termed "the basic equation." The interrelated elements are (1) need, (2) money available, (3) equipment capability, (4) pilot proficiency, (5) mission capability, (6) safety, (7) proper utilization planning, (8) tax ramifications, and (9) cost-effectiveness. For any change in one element of this equation, there will be another compensating change elsewhere. For example, if we have a reduction in pilot proficiency, we will have a corresponding reduction in mission capability. There would also be unfavorable changes in both safety and cost-effectiveness.

More often than not, the mission requirements will exceed the equipment capability acquirable due to a lack of available funds. This is the proverbial phenomenon of the champagne taste and beer budget. The problem seems to affect every airplane buyer. It doesn't matter if the airplane in question is a Piper Cub or a Cessna Citation, there will be a long string of trade-offs and compromises made along the way from the buyer's dream machine to the one that he eventually parks in his hangar.

Equipment capability is almost directly related to the amount of money available for the purchase of an airplane. Certainly this is true when it comes to a brand-new aircraft. A buyer can, however, obtain more capability, dollar for dollar, from a used machine than he can from a new one. There are, of course, risks involved when buying an older airplane. For the business pilot, these can be minimized by a very careful selection of the used machine which he might consider buying.

Every year a number of well-to-do pilots are sold the latest model of the very best airplanes available, generally equipped with everything that anyone could want. Unfortunately, for the buyers, they were not as wealthy as they thought, and because they didn't do their homework, they learned too late that the airplane that they had purchased was a lot more expensive than they could afford. This can put some very good equipment on the market with low engine time and a super price. To find and take advantage of such situations, however, requires a willingness to spend a great deal of time contacting dealers for leads, searching the want ads, and talking on the phone. Then, you must have the money ready to buy when an opportunity appears.

New or used, flexibility costs money. Generally, a good performer in the speed area is not the best performer in a short-field situation. That sort of difficulty can usually be corrected by liberal applications of money. Postpurchase modifications can often alter aircraft performance characteristics to more closely suit the buyer's needs than the airplane would as it came from the showroom floor. The primary examples of this would be the Robertson STOL kit or the RayJay Turbochargers.

THE OPTION: ONE OR TWO?

There is something about a beautiful, powerful, new twin which can beat a sympathetic note in the heart of any pilot. If it were yours, then, of course, you would be extremely proud. If you allow this potential pride of ownership, this ego-fulfillment element, to bear on your decision when selecting the company aircraft, this self-gratifying extravagance will make itself unfavorably evident on the financial statements when you and your accountant are looking for the cost-effectiveness of your purchase.

When a prospective airplane buyer decides that a twin is the answer to his need for a company airplane, "twin-engine safety" usually plays a large part in this decision. This particular concept will be looked at in depth later in this book, but the prospective twin buyer should consider that the case for added safety from an additional engine is open to some serious question. What is unquestionable, however, is that a twin will *always* cost more. Lots more!

It is obvious that the original cost for two engines will be more than for one. The same will be true for the cost of maintenance. Hangar rent will invariably be higher, even if the twin is small and takes less space than some larger single. At some airports, there are landing fees for twins and none for singles. At those places where a fee is charged for all aircraft, the fee for the twin will always be higher, usually twice as much. This same approach is generally used to establish transient tiedown fees. For the executive who travels extensively and spends many nights away from his home base, doubling the costs of tiedown will become a significant expense.

Insurance costs for the owner-flown twin will also add to the burden. In 1978, rates for light twins increased in the range of 20 to 35 percent. According to the insurance industry, owner-flown twin-engine aircraft are exceptionally high risks. The rates will reportedly stabilize in several years at about three times the current level if the insurance carriers are going to continue to take on these risks. This attitude on the part of insurance companies does not speak well for the "safety" which can supposedly be found in two engines.

TURBOS

Turbos are a much-discussed item in the aviation press. The arguments pro and con usually center on the question of what it is that you get and if that's worth what it costs. There are claims for high speeds, over-the-weather capability, safety, comfort, and even lower fuel costs. There is no doubt that turbos will improve performance under a wide variety of circumstances for either a single or a twin, but there are the ever-present costs and trade-offs.

These fast-spinning, exhaust-operated superchargers cost money to buy originally, and they continue to cost money for ongoing maintenance. The problem is rarely the turbos themselves but rather the plumbing that goes with them. Nonetheless, there will be added costs for maintenance and oxygen. If you use the high-altitude capability that your blower system gives you, you are going to be spending lots of money on oxygen.

Without pressurization, the flight levels attained in turbocharged airplanes are not physiologically comfortable for extended periods of time. The human body was designed to function under a great deal more atmospheric pressure than will be found at 24,000 feet. Gas build-ups in body cavities can become painful when the external pressure drops to less than half of what it would normally be. Sinus troubles and related problems with the ears can also be troublesome during the long climbs and descents which are involved in using the capabilities of a turbo.

On paper, a case can be built for fuel savings, but as a practical matter, it just won't work out that way. Airplanes simply are not operated within the provisos of "fuel saving through turbocharging" that are used in those calculations. Up at turbo altitudes, the winds blow hard, and as every pilot knows, a headwind hurts more than a tailwind helps. That means, of course, that long climbs to lofty altitudes and the strong winds found there will average out as an addition to the costs.

Are the turbos worth all this added cost?

The answer will depend upon the actual mission requirements of the pilot. For someone operating out of airports where the density altitude is usually 2000 feet higher than the single-engine ceiling of his twin, the turbocharged engine is a must. This is the only way he can really get any benefit out of that second engine. If the pilot does most of his flying east of the Rockies, then a "heavy breather" will be a costly luxury that gives back very little for the added expense.

THE AUTOMATICS

For the pilot who is transitioning from a fixed-gear machine into a retractable, there is the consideration of the automatic gear system. Salespersons for the airplanes that feature this mechanism will often state that insurance companies will give the low-time retractable pilot a better rate based on an airplane with the automatic system. A series of calls to insurance underwriters indicated that this is primarily a sales pitch. From an insurance standpoint, a retractable is a retractable. No discounts were offered by any of the companies interviewed for an automatic gear system.

Having flown several hundred hours with the automatic system in our Piper Lance, I have some very strong opinions about such devices. In some circumstances, the nature of the mechanism creates a situation that is a detriment to safety. At other times, it is simply a nuisance. In total, I find it hard to find any justification for the automatic gear system at all. It is an expense without any offsetting benefit.

In a high density altitude situation, forgetting to set the gear override lever could get a pilot into trouble. The system works on ram air pressure, and the gear will not come up until a specific pressure is attained. Because of this, it is possible to lift off, move the gear handle to the UP position, and then fly off the end of the runway with the gear still hanging down, unable to climb out of ground effect. The drag of the gear prevents attaining sufficient speed to meet the needs of the ram air sensor for retraction, and without retraction, acceleration to the required speed is very slow in coming if it is possible at all. This same kind of problem is confronted in climbs near the service ceiling of the machine where the best rate of climb speed and the automatic gear speed cross, throwing the gear out with the switch still in the UP position.

In an engine-out situation, the automatic gear system again intrudes to complicate the pilot's problems. Speed and altitude are the only things that a pilot has going for him in this situation. If he doesn't get

This is the ram air mast on the Piper automatic gear system. Although highly regarded by many in the aviation press, the automatic landing gear system is a potentially dangerous item for the unwary pilot. If your airplane has such a system, investigate it thoroughly. Understand precisely how it will work in a high density altitude situation or in the event of an engine failure.

that gear override depressed very quickly after his engine fails, the automatic gear extender will go to work to rob him of large measures of these.

Encounters with ice provide another opportunity for the automatic gear system to add to the pilot's problems and cockpit workload. The impact air pressure mast of the gear extender system is particularly susceptible to ice. Although it is protected in the same circuit with the pitot heat, the gear sensor will ice over in circumstances where the pitot tube is totally unaffected. Should the pilot fail to turn on pitot heat when entering conditions where icing might be encountered, he will be rewarded with his landing gear being thrown out at about the same time that his airspeed indicator dies. In my opinion, the automatic gear system is potentially so dangerous that FAA approval of such systems should be withdrawn. To subject a pilot to the dangers of this system for the marginal benefit of *perhaps* preventing a gear-up landing seems absurd.

THE FINAL CHOICE

Once you have determined exactly what it is that your company will need in terms of aircraft performance capability, your search for the proper airplane can begin. The preliminary research can be made in the promotional literature from the manufacturers and the "pilot reports" to be found in the aviation press. Your reading here will be essentially for background. The performance data given in promotional material, although technically true, will often overlook the problems of conflicting limitations and the compromises that this will necessitate.

When you have narrowed your airplane choice down to the two or three models which appear to most closely fit the mission requirements of your company, buy the operator manuals for those machines. At $7 to $10 each, it will prove to be a worthwhile investment. They can provide the material from which a sound decision can be made. All the little compromises overlooked by the brochure writers will make themselves known in the operator's manuals *if you read them carefully.*

Using these manuals, work up a flight plan for each airplane over what would be a typical trip for you. Make a list of the people and cargo that you would generally carry, and then do a complete weight and balance problem for each airplane. Check the range, rate of climb, takeoff run, and the position of the center of gravity (CG) with this typical weight and loading configuration. Consider how each machine will perform under this load at the airports that you will be using under the density altitude conditions which will exist during your travels. This is the only way to really obtain an objective comparison of performance characteristics for the aircraft under consideration.

Don't overlook the effect that a zero-fuel-weight limitation might have on your particular mission needs. That is, of course, if any of the

Once you have narrowed down your potential choices for a new airplane, go out and buy the manuals for the remaining contenders. Read every line of each book. Fly several different paper missions based on the information provided by the manuals. If there is a compromise in the mission capability of a given aircraft, you will want to find it during your analysis, not after you've signed a purchase contract.

machines under consideration have such a limitation. When you start out to "fly your mission on paper," be sure that you have all the facts. Read the manuals in a thorough manner; don't just skim through them. And be sure to get empty weights from the actual weight and balance data of airplanes that are equipped as you would specify. The figures given in the manual sample problems for empty weight are usually hundreds of pounds less than the typical IFR-equipped machine sitting on the flight line. This can be critical, so don't allow yourself to be misled.

After you have flown enough "paper missions" to satisfy yourself that your dream machine is in actuality the Whiz Bang 300, make arrangements to rent the airplane for an actual business trip. A few trips around the pattern or a flight over to a neighboring field for coffee with the salesperson simply doesn't give you enough time or varied experience with an airplane to make a $50,000 or $100,000 decision.

You really have to fly an airplane to get to know it. You must learn how it will actually handle under the conditions created by *your* travel needs. The manuals can show that the machine under consideration will carry your load within the appropriate CG limits, but actually trying to get your passengers, luggage, and samples into the airplane may prove to be both physically difficult and time-consuming. You may also find that the noise level which was acceptable in the pattern will be intolerable for long cross-country flights. You or your passengers may find the seats uncomfortable, the interior dimensions too confining, or the design-induced yaw in turbulence to be literally nauseating. You should become aware of such things *before* you buy, not after you have signed your name to a contract.

Things don't always work out the way they were originally planned. When we bought the Cessna Skylane for our company, for example, we had planned on buying a Mooney. On paper, the Mooney met our needs and provided the most speed and range available for the money. In terms of efficiency, nothing really compared. Unfortunately, when we flew it, we found that it fitted our needs and my body like an overly tight shoe. The same sort of thing happened when we bought the Lance. We had started out to buy a Cessna 210. It was certainly the best choice in its class. It could carry the weight. It had both speed and range. Due to our unique problems connected with the bulk of the sample cases we always take with us, we again selected the more spacious cabin over speed and efficiency. For another company and another pilot, the choices could be very different.

The briefcase salesperson would probably find the speed, size, and economy of the Mooney 201 to be the ultimate answer to his airplane requirements. An engineering firm might see the Cessna T-206 as the best machine for their need to get in and out of construction locations. For many other business executives, the Cessna Skylane RG will most closely fit the mission requirements of their companies. In each instance, the "ultimate airplane" will be the one that can do the job with the least amount of compromise. The problem for the buyer is to define the job well enough *before* the purchase, so his final choice for a company airplane will represent a compromise that he can live with comfortably.

CLOSING THE DEAL

Buying an airplane is not exactly like buying a car, but there are many similarities. The "sticker price" is one thing, the selling price another.

This is a typical load for the Lance and demonstrates why the large cargo doors were so important in the final decision to purchase this Piper aircraft. Although several other aircraft could carry the necessary weight, there were other considerations of range or CG envelope which detracted from their suitability for the requirements of Joyce Jewelry. Every aspect of the mission requirements should be considered in depth before making an aircraft selection. The Lance worked out to be the best compromise for our needs at this time. When we no longer need to carry a plaster giraffe to Dallas, perhaps another machine will be more suitable. Each pilot must work out this problem for himself, but he should be very careful not to overemphasize any facet of his needs and, thereby, end up with more airplane than he can effectively and profitably utilize.

This is certainly as true for airplanes as it is for automobiles. The difference between these two amounts will depend upon a multitude of things. One of these is the amount of equipment that is installed. Margins for accessories are far greater than they are for the airplane itself, so the negotiating room expands with an increase in the amount of equipment that is in the machine.

According to current information, the margin allowed to dealers in new aircraft is about 19 to 21 percent. Beech reportedly works with about a 25 percent margin for the dealer. This is, of course, a gross margin. All the operational costs of the FBO must be covered by this. As any businessperson can easily appreciate, the difference between the dealer's merchandise cost and the selling price of the aircraft is not all profit. Just like you, he has overhead, payrolls, taxes, and innumerable other costs that must be paid.

In percentage terms, 20 percent for a gross margin is not very great. In comparison, the average gross margin in many retail operations runs from 50 to 60 percent of the retail price tag. When applied to the price of an airplane, however, 20 percent does represent a lot of dollars. On an airplane with a list price of $100,000, the dealer cost would be about $80,000. This leaves a dollar margin of about $20,000, not an insignificant amount. How far this amount can be negotiated into savings for the buyer will depend upon many things. On an extremely popular model airplane, it will be a great deal less than it will be on a less popular one. If you are buying an airplane that the dealer has ordered but has not taken delivery of, there may be more elasticity in price than if the machine were in his current inventory. Once he has started making interest payments on the aircraft, he will want to be certain of recovering that cost.

The first-time airplane buyer will probably do much better in a deal than the pilot with a trade-in to dispose of. With a trade, the dealer will want to cover himself on the fact that he will have a certain amount of the money he makes on the sale of a new airplane tied up in the trade-in. Because of this, it may be worth the effort to sell your old airplane and negotiate for the very best price you can get on the new machine. The entire transaction, however, must be viewed as a single deal. The tax ramifications of both the sale and the purchase must be looked at. From your point of view, it is the total amount of money that you must part with which really matters. In many situations, you might be money ahead if you give your trade-in to the dealer at a price less than you could sell it for on the open market and accept the new airplane for a higher price than the dealer would give you if the deal were structured without a trade. It all depends upon the *book value* of the old airplane, what it will sell for, how long you have held it, your marginal tax rate, the price of the new machine, and the rate of the local sales tax.

All the variables in this situation can alter the total outcome. Therefore, you must discuss the specific deal with an accountant who is familiar with your particular circumstances. As a general rule, it is probably best to *sell* your old airplane when the market value is *less* than the book value; this will allow you to take the loss as a deduction from your taxable income. When the market value is *greater* than the book value, it generally will be best to *trade* the old machine in on the new one and thereby alter the depreciable basis of the new asset. The point is that you will always want to look at the entire situation as one transaction rather than as two separate ones. You are looking for the best balance between asset cost and the resulting tax impact created by the way the transaction is structured.

There is a lot of flexibility in the asking price and the trade-in allowance. Almost any deal can be structured in one of several different ways. The primary concern from the buyer's viewpoint, however, is the *cash difference* between what the seller is asking for the new airplane and what he will allow for the trade-in. So long as this value remains the same, the actual dollar values given to the trade-in and the new machine are irrelevant, except for the tax consequences. An inflated trade-in value applied against an equally inflated selling price will add a larger amount of sales tax to the deal. If the trade-in is valued at your book value and the selling price of the new airplane is reduced accordingly, the applicable sales tax will also be reduced. The dealer will still get the same amount for his merchandise, and you will have saved the difference in sales tax.

Should you decide that selling your old machine is the route to go, then remember that any difference between your book value on the machine and the selling price will be taxable gain. If your marginal tax rate is 50 percent, you will be giving up half of any profit realized from the sale to the IRS. In making a comparison between the various approaches to your acquisition of the new company airplane, if the actual dollar costs to you remain the same but in one structure you give up $500 in taxes and in the other that $500 ends up in the dealer's pocket, take the latter option. You will never generate any goodwill by paying taxes, but your local airplane dealer will appreciate the addition to his profit.

Every business transaction should be one in which the value-for-value exchange results in measurable benefits for both parties involved. Although it is your duty to obtain the very best deal that you possibly can when functioning as a buyer for your company, that doesn't require squeezing the transaction of all profit for the seller. Certainly, deal from a strong position, but remember that searching far and wide to save a few dollars on the front end can often cost more in the long run. Your local FBO wants and needs your support. Give it to him.

Long-term profitability for the company airplane cannot be generated by simply getting a "bargain" when you purchase the machine. It takes a great deal more than this. It requires a proficient pilot and an objective, businesslike approach to the entire concept of flying for business. With your proper planning and preparation, leaving the fantasy dreams to others, the company airplane can be made to pay, even for a small company. The key is in the analysis of company needs, planning for sufficient asset utilization, and not buying more airplane than your company can use, regardless of how good the deal may seem.

CHAPTER FOUR

The Bottom Line

WHAT DOES IT REALLY COST?

Nothing in this life is free, and airplanes are perhaps *less free* than anything else. In fact, they are downright expensive.

Figuring out just *how* expensive an airplane might be is an extremely difficult problem of prognostication that goes far beyond the basically simple mathematics involved. It requires being able to predict with some degree of accuracy what the future inflation rate will be; how sales, costs, and pretax earnings will develop in the years to come; and how the government will alter the tax laws in order to manipulate the economy.

In addition to the impact of taxes upon costs, regulatory actions by the government also make themselves felt in the credit markets. For example, in spring 1980, stringent banking regulations were enacted for the purpose of "controlling consumer credit and cooling inflation." Almost immediately, the prime rate went to a historic high of 20 percent. The rate for bank card credit instantly jumped from 18 to 21 percent.

Retail sales slumped and the nation fell into a recession, but there was no relief from the inflationary forces. The economic downturn was so swift and sharp that the regulators quickly lifted the controls and said, "the people overreacted." By July, the prime rate was back hovering at about 12 percent. During the first week of December 1980, the prime again shot back up, reaching 18.5 percent. Economists, quoted in the December 8, 1980, issue of *Business Week,* lay the blame for this most recent surge in interest rates on manipulations of the money supply by government regulators.

Since major assets, such as airplanes, are rarely purchased with cash, the prevailing interest rates have a dramatic impact upon the calculations for determining the costs to own and operate a company plane. Many informed financial experts believe the violent fluctuations of interest rates in 1980 were an anomaly. Therefore, in the calculations, charts, and tables which follow, nominal interest rates will be used. Although these rates will not match the high levels recorded in 1980, they do represent reasonable values for a stable economic environment.

Even if we ignore these particular problems for the moment, we are still faced with some difficulty in determining just what it costs to own and operate an airplane. If we were to present several different accountants with our problem, it is likely that we would come back with several different answers. None of these answers would be particularly right or wrong; they would simply be different because each series of calculations would use a varying set of *assumptions*. These assumptions would probably differ to the greatest degree in the area pertaining to what is known as *opportunity costs*.

This is the money that theoretically you would have made had you put the same dollars into something other than your airplane. In this area, many accountants will make assumptions that are totally lacking in validity when they start off on their very precise calculation of how much money you *didn't make*. At the present time the popular percentage rate is somewhere between 10 and 12 percent. This is usually rationalized as a conservative estimate for the return you could make with an alternate investment. This assumes that an ideal, low-risk investment is available, that this investment will, in fact, return the assumed percentage, and that the return is predicated entirely upon the utilization of capital without any demands being made upon your time and energies. The entire thing can be something like the infamous "shell game," since even if you keep your eye on the pea, it's pretty hard to tell what's happening.

Regardless of the difficulties in determining exactly what they might be in actual dollars, opportunity costs are very real and cannot be ignored by the business pilot. The easiest method, and probably the method which will most closely reflect reality, is to assume that your opportunity costs will equal what would have been earned by a deposit of the investment funds in a savings account. This is a low-risk investment with a known rate of return. Also, it does not require that you spend your weekends and evening hours "managing" your investment.

Opportunity costs exist because of the *time value* of money and the fact that no really successful way has yet been found to spend the *same* dollars for two *different* things. For example, you might take $5000 and buy a new car, albeit a low-priced one in today's market, or you can put the money in the bank to earn interest. You can't do both.

Payment to you of interest by the bank on your deposit is recognition of the time value of money. The specific rate is established by many economic considerations, including loan demand levels, the inflation rate, and the general condition of the economy.

Over a period of time, your deposit will grow into a larger amount. Just how large this will be is dependent upon the interest rate being paid by the bank and how much time is involved. That larger amount which will exist at some time in the future is called the *future value* (FV) of your investment. Conversely, the $5000 you deposited in the bank today is called the *present value* (PV) of your funds. The difference between the PV and the FV is the potential or actual earnings accruing from the time value of money. These earnings, which would be given up if you decided to buy a new car with your $5000, constitute the opportunity costs of that choice. For the following calculations, a nominal rate of 6.5 percent was used. This is representative of the current return on passbook accounts. If you were able to obtain a certificate account paying a 12 percent return, *guaranteed for the entire term of contemplated project,* then your opportunity costs would be calculated on this basis.

These costs are a portion of what is known as the *capital costs* of an investment. Let's look at the purchase of that $5000 automobile in a very simplified manner, which ignores financing and tax ramifications, to determine what the capital costs of such a purchase might be:

Purchase price of automobile: (Paid in cash)	$5000	

Less:
     Selling price
     (At end of 5 years)
	(500)	

Reduction in asset value during period: (Actual market value depreciation)		$4500
FV of investment dollars: (60 months at 6.5%)	6914	
Less: PV	(5000)	
Project opportunity costs:		1914
Total capital cost of acquisition:		$6414

That $6414 is what you must be willing to give up in order to *buy* a $5000 new car. It does not include any of the costs of owning, maintaining, and operating that car, other than the *market value depreciation* for the 5-year period involved. These are simply the capital costs for acquiring and holding this car when the purchase was made with cash. If you finance part of the purchase price, then the calculation to determine the capital costs becomes a bit more complicated, due to the difficulty in establishing realistic opportunity costs for the purchase.

Let's assume that you will make a down payment of $1000, leaving a balance of $4000 to be financed. If you were able to negotiate a 36-month installment loan with a nominal rate of 10 percent interest, your monthly payments would be $129.07. Based on this assumed rate, the time-price differential, or *rental costs,* for the use of the bank's money for this period would be $646.52. Although current rates are higher than the assumed 10 percent and constantly fluctuate with the total economy, the principles presented here remain the same.

Combining the total of your 36 monthly payments with your original down payment of $1000 results in a total cash outlay of $5646.52 for this purchase of the car. However, we must again consider the time value of money. Therefore, we must *discount* the amount that our monthly payments will total at the end of 36 months to its PV. Using our assumed earning rate of 6.5 percent, the PV for our 36 monthly loan payments works out to be $4211.23.

Obviously, the PV for our $1000 down payment is $1000 and does not require any discounting. Combining the PV for the monthly payments and the down payment, we get a total PV for our investment of $5211.23, which is $211.23 greater than the cash amount we paid for the car in the first illustration. At first glance, one might assume that the premium required for the installment payment terms of the loan would be the full $646.52 interest charge, but that does not make any allowance for the fact that each of the payments is made at a more distant time in the future.

Now that we have discounted our cash investment to its PV, we must ascertain the FV of this investment so we can figure out what the opportunity costs for this purchase would be under the terms of an installment loan. This becomes a two-step process of first calculating the FV for the down payment and the monthly payments during the 36-month life of the loan, and then using the sum of these figures to obtain the total FV of the investment at the end of the 60-month useful life of the asset.

Since there will be an additional 24 months after the final payment has been made on the loan before we sell the car, we must calculate the FV of the $6329 at the end of the 5 years we have owned the car.

STEP ONE:

FV of $1000 down payment at end of loan (36 months at 6.5%, compounded monthly):	$1214
FV of 36 monthly payments of $129.07 each (compounded monthly at 6.5%):	5115
	$6329

STEP TWO:

FV of $6329 at end of asset life (24 *additional* months at 6.5%):	$7206

With this figure, we can now go back to our original format to work out the capital costs for our automobile purchase when we are financing it with borrowed funds.

Cash purchase price of automobile: (Paid with $1000 down payment and proceeds from 36-month loan at 10%)	$5000	

Less:
    Selling price
    (At end of 5 years)
	(500)	

Reduction in asset value during period: (Actual market value depreciation)		$4500
FV of investment dollars: (36 monthly payments and the original $1000 down payment)	7206	

Less:
    Discounted PV
    (Investment discounted by
    earning rate)
	(5211)	

Project opportunity costs:		1994
Total capital cost of acquisition:		$6494

Even if this were the end of the story on capital costs, it is easy to see that borrowing to pay for the purchase of the car isn't nearly as expensive as it appeared at first. The capital cost difference between paying cash or borrowing at 10 percent interest to buy the car is merely $80, but that was *before* taxes. Although our figures so far indicate borrowing is just slightly more expensive, when we consider the impact of taxes, borrowing becomes *cheaper* than paying cash.

We must look at our calculated opportunity costs as what they really are, or rather what they would be if we made the alternate choice of investing our money in a savings account instead of the car. Those opportunity costs would then become *taxable earnings*. As such, the tax liability which applies to those earnings has to be considered in our analysis of capital costs. The following schedule shows the effect of taxes on the capital costs of the car acquisition for taxpayers in the 50 percent bracket when one pays cash and the other borrows.

	Cash payer	Borrower
Opportunity cost: (Potential taxable income)	$1914	$1994
Interest expense: (Allowable deduction)	–0–	(646)
Net taxable income: (Potential)	$1914	$1348
Income tax—50%: (Potential)	(957)	(674)
Net aftertax opportunity cost:	957	674
Market value depreciation:	4500	4500
Net aftertax capital cost:	$5457	$5174

Paying cash, in this situation, is clearly $283 more expensive than borrowing to buy this car for the taxpayer in the 50 percent bracket. For the person who is in the 25 percent bracket, the story is even worse. The decision to pay cash will cost him $424.50 more than it would if he borrowed the money.

These figures can be misleading, however, if one fails to remember that although the cash payer *gives up* a greater amount of *potential* aftertax earnings, the borrower must pay a greater amount of *real* cash to obtain a net aftertax return of *smaller* potential. The total cash outflow for the cash payer was $5957, while the cash outflow for the borrower was $6320, which is $363 more. Here is where many non-accountants throw up their hands in total exasperation, opining that the entire thing is an exercise in academic nonsense. Not so. This is a very valid method of examining the comparative merits of two financial alternatives.

The crucial point in any situation which deals with time and money is *when* the cash flows occur. It is also important to be constantly aware that the terms *cost* and *cash* are not synonymous. Regardless of how confusing all of this may seem, it is simply the quantification of the idea that having a dollar today is worth more than having the same dollar a year from now.

Thus far in our examination of opportunity costs and capital costs for an asset acquisition, we have dealt with an automobile purchased for nonbusiness use. The only tax implication has been the deductibility of *interest expense* and its impact upon capital cost recovery. The market value depreciation we have used in our illustrations is not the same as the *asset depreciation expense* allowed by the Internal Revenue Code for business property. Since our automobile was a personal item, neither this depreciation expense nor the *investment tax credit* allowed by the IRS was applicable to our car purchase. When we analyze the purchase of a *business airplane,* however, these additional items must be considered. The depreciation expense deduction and the investment tax credit are so meaningful in the total picture of a business airplane purchase that they become the backbone of the airplane salesperson's sales pitch.

By pushing and pulling on these items and making some assumptions which might be true in some cases, the clever airplane salesperson can build a convincing case that you can buy a $100,000 airplane for just about nothing because "Uncle Sam is going to pick up half the tab." Well, don't you believe it. Always remember that "something for nothing" is the con man's stock in trade. The vulnerability of the "mark" is due to his greed and his acceptance of something-for-nothing concepts.

The basic assumption on tax deductions is false when someone puts forth the argument that "Uncle Sam will pay half." This presumption is based on the irrational belief that your life, your wealth, and your earning power belong to the government, which will gratuitously give you something if you play the game their way. Let's call it as it is. The money is *yours*—not theirs. Governments generally do not generate wealth; they merely confiscate and redistribute it. What they do generate is inflation.

The second fallacy of the "Uncle Sam" syndrome is the assumption that *all* the dollars required to consummate the aircraft purchase will be derived from money falling into the 50 percent tax bracket. This generally will not be the case. It would take, for example, a net taxable income of $88,000 in order to put the potential first-year tax deductions generated by the purchase of a $110,000 airplane into the 50 percent category. What this means is that *after* deductions for your home mortgage interest, allowable medical expenses, state taxes, and all other personal exemptions have been subtracted from your gross earnings, you will *still* have a taxable income of $88,000 or more. Anything less than this and the tax savings of 50 cents on the dollar begins to evaporate. Therefore, the self-employed person who is drawing a gross salary of $75,000 per year and envisions a tax savings of 50 cents on the dollar when he buys a new Bonanza is kidding himself. Certainly, there will be some tax advantages for the business owner with the $75,000 salary, but they won't be anywhere near those pictured for him by the aircraft salesperson.

Several years ago, Beech distributed a neat little gimmick called the *Beechcraft Slide-A-Cost Calculator,* which supposedly allowed you, the potential buyer, to ascertain the net capital cost for putting "the right Beechcraft business airplane to work for your company."

Using this promotional device from Beech, we discover that the monthly net capital cost for a Bonanza A36 is only $235, and for the Baron 58 the magic number is $485, just $250 more than the single. These figures are computed for companies in the 50 percent tax bracket, and they consider the investment tax credit, tax savings from depreciation deductions over a 6-year period, and the aircraft resale value at the end of 6 years. The numbers shown are probably all very *true,* but they are extremely misleading.

The basic problem with the Slide-A-Cost calculator and its 1972 predecessor, the Dial-A-Cost, is that they ignore opportunity costs, the time value of money, and most important, the provisions of the Internal Revenue Code for *depreciation recapture* as *ordinary income.* For the unsuspecting, this last item, *recapture,* can come as a very unpleasant surprise at tax time following the sale of an airplane.

Beech is to be congratulated, however, for their "Capital Recovery Guide." This formatted worksheet allows the prospective buyer to calculate his net capital investment on a bit more realistic basis. Although it doesn't make a big deal about it or call it by name, this guide does mention the possibility of depreciation recapture. It also contains a condensed table showing 1976 tax brackets and percentages. This guide from Beech, however, continues to ignore opportunity costs and the cost of financing, but the "Capital Recovery Guide" is a step in the right direction.

Cessna has a computer program which addresses these same questions, but the prudent business person will conduct his own analysis and consult his personal financial advisor.

The following schedule shows the calculations for obtaining the net capital costs for a Beech Bonanza A36, using the basic format of the "Capital Recovery Guide."

Price of new airplane, equipped:	$94,800
Depreciation over 6 years:	69,800
Trade-in value after 6 years:	$25,000
Investment tax credit—6 years:	$ 6,320
($94,800 × 6.667%)	
Tax savings on depreciation:	33,504
(Assuming 48% corporate rate)	
Trade-in value after 6 years:	25,000
Total costs recovered:	$64,824
Original cost of airplane:	$94,800
Cost recovered:	(64,824)
Net cost—6 years:	$29,976
Net cost per year:	$ 4,996
Net cost per month:	$ 416

The above calculation is extremely sensitive to the trade-in value of the airplane at the end of the 6-year period. Since determining this number requires what is, at best, a guess, the figure used here is very conservative and perhaps a bit on the low side. On the other hand, the figure obtained from the Slide-A-Cost calculator either assumes a lower original price or a trade-in value of approximately $48,000 which seems on the high side. The conclusion, of course, is that the net capital cost for this airplane will be somewhere between $235 and $416, depending upon how much we recover at the sale or trade-in of the machine.

But the airplane salesperson really doesn't want to talk about net capital costs or opportunity costs. They're too nebulous, too hard to tie down, and besides, they don't sell airplanes. *Tax savings*, that's what sells airplanes—so let's look at them. Instead of looking at the total picture as we have just done, let's just look at the first year:

Price of new airplane:		$94,800
Bonus depreciation:	$ 2,000	
(20% of $10,000—max. allowable)		
First-year depreciation:	30,933	
(double declining balance method)		
First-year interest expense:	7,383	
(6-year loan at 11%)		
Total first-year tax deductions:	$40,316	
Investment tax credit:	$ 6,320	
($94,800 × 6.667%)		
Tax savings on first-year deductions:	19,351	
(Assuming 48% corporate rate)		
Total first-year tax savings:	$25,671	

Now we've got something to sell airplanes with—$25,671 in hard facts. Nothing nebulous there, and we don't have to wait until we trade or sell the airplane to find out where we're at. These are the facts about the first year and the tax savings—well, at least part of the facts. In order for the numbers to work out this way, the corporate taxpayer buying this airplane would need a minimum of $90,316 in *net* pretax earnings under the present tax laws. To bring this figure into perspective, the company which is contemplating this purchase would need more than $1.5 million in sales with a net pretax profit margin of 6 percent to obtain the tax benefits depicted here. Even with a net pretax profit margin of 18 percent, more than $500,000 in sales would be required to get the full $25,671 in tax savings.

In addition to needing sufficient sales and profits in order to obtain these tax savings, you must have a bunch of *cash*. That friendly airplane salesperson will be wanting his commission on the sale, his boss will want to get his money out of the machine, and there is always the bank to be paid. Of course, many first-time airplane buyers are so euphoric over all the "free money" they're getting from Uncle Sam that they overlook some of the more mundane aspects of the acquisition. Regardless of their delusion that they can somehow get something for nothing, hard reality starts intruding on those dreams when it becomes difficult to make the payments. Those tax savings require *cash*, and a lot more of it than many pilots realize.

First, there will be a down payment of about 25 percent of the selling price; then it will be the monthly payments against the loan. Using the same assumptions of an installment loan for 6 years at 11 percent with a principal amount of $71,100 as we did for the tax-saving calculation, the first-year cash requirements for this acquisition would be as follows:

Price of airplane:	$94,800
Required down payment—25%: ($71,100 to be obtained from 6-year loan at 11%)	$23,700
First-year loan payments: (12 × $1353.32)	16,239
First-year cash requirements:	$39,939
Less: First-year tax savings	(25,671)
Cash required in excess of tax savings: (first year)	$14,268

Now we are confronted with the other side of those terrific tax savings. It will require $14,268 more in cash than we saved in taxes during the first year. To reshuffle the figures so that the first-year tax savings and the cash requirements would balance each other out would demand that you buy the airplane with about 7.5 percent down, instead of the 25 percent figure used in our calculation. Getting a loan on that basis, however, might prove to be almost impossible.

In our illustration on tax savings, we selected the double declining balance method of depreciation in order to *maximize* the tax savings in the early years of the asset life. This will probably be the method used when an airplane salesperson works up a proposal to show you. This accelerated method of asset depreciation provides the most favorable picture of tax savings in the first 3 years of the proposed project. After that, the figures start running the other way—the tax savings drop dramatically and the cash requirements increase proportionately. The following "Cash Required" table shows the manner in which the cash needed to meet the project payments varies from year to year over the asset life. The amounts shown are *cash* dollars needed *in excess* of the tax savings derived from depreciation and interest expenses calculated at the 48 percent corporate rate.

These figures were developed in a manner consistent with the method used in the previous schedules depicting the first-year tax savings and the first-year cash requirements. A loan amortization schedule was created to obtain the interest expense for each year. Depreciation expense was calculated by the double declining balance method based on a 6-year asset life, without regard for a salvage value. As a result of

Cash Required in Excess of Tax Savings for Project B-A36

Year	
1	$14,268
2	3,288
3	7,136
4	9,949
5	12,098
6	13,833
Total excess cash required:	$60,577

this, the total accumulated depreciation for the period came to $86,667, setting the stage for that previously mentioned unpleasantness called *depreciation recapture*.

When we first began looking at the "costs" for this project, we assumed a trade-in value of $25,000 at the end of the 6-year period. Under that assumption, the difference between the purchase price and the trade-in value would be the allowable depreciation expense during the life of the project. By switching to the accelerated depreciation method in our aggressive effort to maximize tax savings, we have effectively "overdepreciated" our airplane. This will result in a reversal of some of our previous "tax savings" and an increase in the cash requirement for the project.

Purchase price of airplane:	$94,800
Trade-in value after 6 years:	(25,000)
Actual depreciation of asset:	69,800
Depreciation per tax returns:	(86,667)
Depreciation subject to recapture:	(16,867)
Additional tax liability:	$ 8,096
(48% of $16,867)	

The result of this situation, of course, is an increase to $21,934 for the excess cash required in year 6, and the project total will be bumped up to $68,673. Remember that this is cash required in excess of all the tax savings realized over the life of this project. The real problem inherent in this situation, however, is not the recapture of $8,096 in taxes, but the fact that the business pilot is usually not expecting it. Not only will this unanticipated event be emotionally shocking but it may also find the taxpayer financially unprepared to handle this significant increase in his tax bill.

On the brighter side of the recapture picture is the fact that year 6 now has the largest excess cash requirement of aftertax savings. If this was part of the overall project plan, instead of a nasty unexpected surprise, then we have done something that may be desirable. After all, if a dollar today is worth more than a dollar a year from now, then paying out $8096 in year 6 is a lot better than paying out that same $8096 in year 1!

In our discussion so far, we have looked at most of the important considerations involved in analyzing the acquisition of an expensive business asset. Although a complete analysis would require exploring the cost-benefit relationship of a purchase such as an airplane, we have restricted ourselves to the *cost* side of that relationship. Specifically, we have been looking at the various aspects and workings of that group of costs pertaining to capital. For the sake of clarity, we have done this on a piecemeal basis. Now let's bring the whole thing together, using all the assumptions and figures that we have previously generated pertaining to the B-A36 Project.

The Beech "Capital Recovery Guide," mentioned earlier and used as a basic format for our calculations which resulted in a net capital cost of $416 per month, completely ignores the cost of financing. This difference between the amount that we borrow to buy the airplane and how much we pay back to the bank seems more appropriately categorized as a "money" cost instead of an "airplane" cost. Therefore, it should be included in the calculations used to obtain the net capital cost for the project. Recasting the figures to recognize this cost of financing results in a net capital cost of $606.57 per month for Project B-A36, as shown in Exhibit A.

Exhibit A Net Capital Costs for Project B-A36

Price of new airplane, equipped:	$ 94,800
Depreciation over 6-year project life:	69,800
Trade-in value after 6 years:	25,000
Time-price differential:	$ 26,339
($71,100 at 11% for 72 months)	
Investment tax credit—6 years:	$ 6,320
($94,800 × 6.6667%)	
Tax savings on depreciation:	33,504
(Assuming 48% corporate rate)	

Exhibit A   Net Capital Costs for Project B-A36 (continued)

Tax savings on interest expense:	12,642
Trade-in value:	25,000
Total costs recovered:	$ 77,466
Original price of airplane:	$ 94,800
Cost of financing:	26,339
Total capital cost:	$121,139
Total costs recovered:	(77,466)
Net capital cost for project:	$ 43,673
(6-year project life)	
Net capital cost per month:	$ 606
($43,673 ÷ 72 months)	

As it was previously pointed out, this calculation is very sensitive to the trade-in value of the asset at the end of the 6-year period. You will find that as the trade-in value goes up and the net capital cost comes down, the *tax savings* will also come down and the monthly *cash* requirement will increase. There is a direct relationship between the trade-in value and the monthly cash requirement. The difference between the net capital cost for the project and the net cash required is the amount of the trade-in value, which explains the reciprocal manner in which they function.

Looking at Exhibit B, we find that the net cash required per month is $953.79 (rounded to $954). This is the amount of cash you will need each month to meet the loan payments during the project life *in addition* to the money you *will not* pay out in taxes. In some ways this might be looked upon as an "accounting" number, since it is the figure that *would* result if you were able to convert your tax savings into cash money on a monthly basis. In actual practice, however, things just don't happen that way. The down payment is made at the beginning of the project, the loan payments are made each month, the tax savings are realized at tax time each year, and the final recovery of the trade-in value is obtained at the end of the project life. Therefore, when you sit down to write a check to the bank each month, you will need the full $1353.32.

In very realistic terms, Project B-A36 will have a net capital cost per month of $606.57, a net cash requirement of $953.79 above and beyond all realizable tax savings, and the demand for a gross cash pay out of $1353.32 for each of the 72 months of the project life. All this is, of course, after making a down payment of $23,700 and *without flying the airplane for 1 minute.* Remember that these calculations are based on the assumption that your company will have sufficient earnings to ensure that all tax deductible expense connected with the airplane, including depreciation, interest, and the operating costs, will be applied against pretax profit dollars which fall into the 48 percent bracket. If sales slip or the operation of the airplane reduces corporate net taxable earnings to a point below the sum of $50,000 plus the total of all aircraft expenses, the net capital cost will increase dramatically.

Assuming that we fly the new B-A36 250 hours and our cost for operation comes to $28 per hour, or $7000 for the year, our net taxable earnings will have to be $97,316, or we will lose our tax savings at the rate of 26 cents for every dollar that it falls below that number. Surprisingly, many first-time airplane buyers overlook this aspect of the tax savings and cost analysis. Also be aware that this figure of $28 per hour was based on 1978 prices. Since that time, fuel prices, which are the main constituent of direct operating costs, have just about doubled. Therefore, you must factor in such increases when analyzing your anticipated tax saving.

Exhibit B   Net Cash Requirements for Project B-A36*

Down payment required:	$ 23,700
(25% of $94,800)	
72 monthly payments of $1353.32 each:	97,439
($71,100 at 11% for 72 months)	
Gross cash amount paid out:	$121,139
Investment tax credit:	$ 6,320
(94,800 × 6.667%)	
Tax savings on depreciation:	33,504
(Assuming 48% corporate rate)	
Tax savings on interest expense:	12,642
(Assuming 48% corporate rate)	
Total tax savings on project:	$ 52,466
Gross cash amount paid out:	$121,139
Total tax savings:	(52,466)
Net cash required:	$ 68,673
Net cash required per month:	$ 954
($68,673 ÷ 72 months)	

*The cash requirements shown here are after allowance has been made for all tax savings but do not include any cash demands resulting from operations or the ownership of the asset, such as taxes, insurance, etc.

Exhibit C   Opportunity Cost Analysis for Project B-A36

FV of project down payment:	$ 34,967
(72 months at 6.5% compounded monthly)	
FV of 72 monthly payments:	118,782
($1353.32 per month at 6.5%)	
Total FV of cash flows:	$153,749
PV of down payment:	$ 23,700
PV of 72 monthly payments:	80,507
($1353.32 per month discounted at 6.5%)	
Total PV of investment:	$103,207
Total FV of investment:	$153,749
Total PV of investment:	(103,207)
Project opportunity costs:	$ 50,542
(Potential taxable earnings)	
Federal income tax on potential earnings:	(24,260)
(Assuming 48% corporate rate)	
Net aftertax opportunity cost:	$ 26,281
Net opportunity cost per month:	$ 365
($26,281 ÷ 72 months)	

In Exhibit C, we return to the concept of opportunity costs and ex-amine them for Project B-A36. Following the same basic method we used for the automobile, we develop a net aftertax opportunity cost of $365 per month. Adding this to our previously established net capital cost of $606 per month, we now have a total of $971 as the amount we must be willing to give up for the privilege of *having* this airplane. Maintaining it, insuring it, and flying it will cost even more. If you are able to obtain an investment which will give a greater return than the 6.5 percent used for the calculations here and it will provide that greater rate over the entire life of the project, then this higher rate should be used in computing the opportunity costs for the project. This, of course, will increase the total cost of owning the airplane.

Many people object to the idea of "opportunity costs," since they would be involved in every purchase decision in life, including the everyday ones pertaining to food and shelter. But there are no options to evaluate in those questions. We would probably never find ourselves trying to decide if it would be better to eat and have a home or buy the latest model Cadillac.

Although there is solid logic in computing opportunity costs and adding them to the net capital costs to quantify exactly what we must give up when we make a certain purchase decision, this is not the primary value of the concept. Where opportunity cost calculations become most meaningful is in evaluating the relative merits on a long-term basis of two *viable* financial alternatives. It is a mathematical tool with which you can compare and decide if it would be better to buy, rent, or lease an airplane or any other major asset. Additionally, when you set out to establish the cost-benefit relationship of a specific project, the calculated opportunity costs provide a convenient target goal for the anticipated benefits to be derived from the acquisition.

Because of the large dollar amounts involved in the purchase of an airplane and the fact that the relative values of the tax savings, the total cost, and the total cash required are extremely sensitive to the manner in which the deal is structured, it is imperative that the business pilot understand the distinction between *cost* and *cash* and that he be comfortable with the concepts pertaining to the *time value* of money. Money is power, and it should be used wisely. Without understanding its nature, making wise decisions about its use becomes impossible.

As entrepreneurs, many of us tend to do our financial planning in a seat-of-the-pants manner at times and to leave things such as planning cash flow and tax strategy to the "accountant." But airplanes are major assets and represent "big money," and they deserve close and careful attention from the person who will ultimately pay for them.

The actual calculations for figuring compound interest, PV, FV, and loan amortization schedules are extremely complex, but they can be learned quickly and done with ease by any business executive on one of the preprogrammed financial calculators available today. At a cost of about $125, a pocket-sized financial calculator, such as the Hewlett-Packard HP-22, will more than pay for itself during the financial analysis involved in the purchase of a company airplane. With the aid of this powerful tool and a little common sense, the business pilot will be able to look at his own needs, resources, and the options available and then make realistic decisions about how much the purchase of an airplane will really cost.

NEGOTIATE HARD AND SHOP FOR YOUR MONEY

The business pilot who goes out to buy an airplane with a list price of $94,800 will usually possess sufficient business acumen to perceive that this is an *asking* price. He knows this price can be negotiated for some

If you don't already own a preprogrammed financial calculator, a good time to buy one would be *before* the purchase of a new airplane. This is a powerful tool for any business executive, and it will return its cost many times over during the first few months of ownership.

meaningful savings. What he may not be aware of, however, is just what those savings really mean. He probably assumes that when he gets the salesperson to knock a thousand dollars off the asking price of the airplane, he has just saved a thousand dollars. Not so. He saved $1452.68!

Using the basic assumptions from the B-A36 Project and assuming that the purchase was made in California, the plane buyer saved an additional $452.68 when he persuaded the salesperson to cut the price back $1000. In California, where the sales tax is 6 percent, that $1000 reduction in price sliced the sales tax obligation on the transaction by $60. The other $392.68 in savings results from the 11 percent finance charges which would have accrued had the $1060 been added to the balance of the 6-year loan. If the loan rate is 13 or 15 percent, then the resulting savings will be proportionately greater. Don't forget, however, that these higher interest rates will also demand greater amounts of cash to meet the monthly payment.

With a $6000 discount from the asking price, the actual savings would be $8716.09, with $360 coming from sales tax savings and $2356.09 being derived from averted interest charges. The money saved in this manner amounts to 45.3 percent of the actual dollar reduction in the selling price of the airplane. Therefore, those dollars are really worth fighting for.

Compound interest is what makes these savings so large. If you were buying a really expensive airplane and the loan terms ran for 120 months, as they often do, every dollar of discount obtained would result in a total cost savings (pretax) of $1.65!

In order to effectively negotiate when you are buying an airplane, you must know the facts, understand their implications, and deal from a strong position. And nothing makes for a stronger position in the marketplace than money. If you can barely qualify for the necessary loan to close the deal, chances are good that you will not only pay the top rate for interest on the loan but also pay top dollar for the airplane itself. You are dealing from a weak position and the salesperson will know it.

The best way to combat this is preparation. Go shopping for the loan money *before* you try to close the deal with the salesperson on a particular machine. Do your homework. Establish a budget for the machine you want. Figure out what the down payment and the principal amount of the loan will be. Then get on the phone and find out from the local lending institutions just how much they will charge to *rent* you the money that you need. As a business executive, you will probably find your own bank the very best source of money available to you, so *call them last.* After you've found out the best rate you can get elsewhere, you can negotiate with your own banker and probably end up with a deal for the money that's a half of a percentage point lower than any previous offer.

Is this really worth it? Well, look at Exhibit D and decide for yourself. If we had been able to get the loan for Project B-A36 at 10.5 percent instead of the 11 percent rate that we used, our savings on the monthly payment would have been only $18.14, but the total over the life of the loan would have amounted to $1305.96, enough to buy and install an encoding altimeter. So it would seem that a little shopping is well worth the effort. The most important thing, of course, is to have a solid loan commitment when you negotiate with the airplane salesperson.

The rates on airplane loans are generally higher than they are for real estate, so it is possible that the equity in your home could be used to obtain the money to finance your airplane at a lower rate than you could get for an airplane loan. There are a lot of things to be considered

Exhibit D Dollar-Cost Comparison of Interest Rates
($71,100 Loan for 72 Months)

Interest rate percentage	Monthly payment amount	Time-price differential	Total cash paid out
9.0	$1,281.62	$21,176.33	$ 92,276.33
9.5	1,299.33	22,451.80	93,551.80
10.0	1,317.19	23,737.47	94,837.47
10.5	1,335.18	25,033.30	96,133.30
11.0*	1,353.32	26,339.26	97,439.26
11.5	1,371.60	27,655.29	98,755.29
12.0	1,390.02	28,981.35	100,081.35
12.5	1,408.57	30,317.39	101,417.39
14.0	1,465.07	34,384.91	105,484.91
15.0	1,503.41	37,145.52	108,245.52
18.0	1,621.63	45,657.64	116,757.64

*Rate used in calculations for Project B-A36.

before taking this route. Primary among these considerations would be the presence of a pay-off penalty clause in your mortgage and whether or not the mortgage market was offering a rate that would make refinancing your home a profitable move irrespective of your antici-pated airplane purchase. If refinancing does not make economic sense on the basis of a more favorable rate being available than the existing one, it is doubtful that this would be a prudent method to finance the airplane.

One other consideration tied to the concept of compound interest would be the establishment of a "sinking fund" to cover the expense of engine overhaul when it comes due. This idea, of course, is based on the thought that you will be keeping the airplane of your choice until an overhaul is needed rather than "trading up" at midlife on the engine.

If the airplane of your choice has an engine with a time before over-haul (TBO) of 2000 hours and your anticipated use will be 400 hours a year, then it will be 5 years until overhaul time. You decide that you will want a factory-remanufactured engine at that time and the cost for it will be $9000, including installation. To cover this expense, you es-tablish a sinking fund (a savings account) to accumulate the required money by the time it will be needed. You are able to get 5.75 percent interest on your savings, compounded quarterly. If you deposit $391.61 in the bank each quarter, the full $9000 will be available when it is needed even though you have only placed $7832.20 into the account. The remaining $1167.80 will be generated by the effects of compound interest. Since this sinking fund will be a long-term proposition, you will probably be able to avail yourself of a series of 12-month certificates which will provide 8.5 to perhaps as high as 14 percent interest, depending upon the condition of the money market.

THE COST OF FLYING

In the February 1972 issue of *AOPA Pilot*, Bryant Andrews, a technical writer for Pratt & Whitney, explained a beautifully simple but effective way to estimate the cost of operation for piston-powered airplanes. The entire process is based on the number 6 and multiplying various items by this figure and moving the decimal point back and forth until "the answer looks reasonable."

Andrews points out that aviation gasoline weighs 6 pounds per gallon, that 0.1 hour on the tach equals 6 minutes, and that the average fuel consumption for a light aircraft will be 0.06 times the rated horsepower of the engine. He goes on to relate that at the end of 6 years an airplane will depreciate to 60 percent of its original value and that a pilot can get a relatively good estimate of the variable operating costs for an airplane by multiplying the engine horsepower by 0.06 to get an answer stated in dollars. He has developed a six-step procedure for calculating the costs of aircraft ownership and operation which even includes *opportunity costs* at the rate of 6 percent on lost investment income.

Had it not been for the oil sheiks of OPEC and the general inflation wrought by our own leaders, the "Andrews factor" might have been the final word on the subject of figuring airplane costs. The bureaucrats and Mideastern potentates were unable to repeal the laws of physics, so 0.06 times the horsepower still gives the fuel consumption, but their heavy hands have so distorted the price of fuel that the factor 0.06 for cost calculations is no longer valid. These miscreants have managed to foul the simplicity and symmetry of the method, but the concept remains intact. All that is needed is a new factor.

In search of that magic number, requests were made of all the general aviation manufacturers for current data on the cost of operating an airplane. Beech sent back the Slide-A-Cost calculator, Cessna supplied their annual report, and Piper sent several brochures containing color

Exhibit E Operating Costs (1976)
Mooney Executive M20F

	250	500	750
Flight hours per year:	250	500	750
Flight miles per year:	43,000	86,000	129,000
Gasoline (10.2 gph at $.75):	$ 7.65	$ 7.65	$ 7.65
Oil (0.3 p/h & 50-h oil change):	.64	.64	.64
Airplane maintenance & inspections:*	3.48	3.48	3.48
Reserve for overhaul (1600-h engine):	3.13	3.13	3.13
Total direct cost:	$14.90	$14.90	$14.90
Storage at $50/month $600/year:	2.40	1.20	.80
Insurance:† Hull—$200 deductible $760/year:	3.04	1.52	1.01
Liability—$178 $50,000/person, $700,000 total $300,000 property:	.71	.36	.24
Total indirect cost:	$ 6.15	$ 3.08	$ 2.05
Total hourly cost:	21.05	17.98	16.95
Operating cost per mile:	.122	.105	.099
Cost per seat mile:	.03	.026	.025

*$13/hour shop labor used for computations.

†Insurance rates based on 500 hours total time, 100 hours retractable time and zero time in type.

pictures of their line of twins—only Mooney responded with operating cost data. Unfortunately, even this data from Kerrville, shown as Exhibit E, is woefully outdated with its assumptions based on gasoline at 75 cents per gallon and shop labor costs of $13 per hour. The manufacturers can be faulted neither for their hesitancy to publish operating costs nor for the fact that much of what is available is outdated. Since figures for operating costs are extremely sensitive to fuel costs, the volatility of the oil market, along with the additional inflationary bias written into the economy by Congress and governmental regulators, would make any publication obsolete before the ink was dry. It would probably take a weekly update to keep current any form of cost data.

A tour of several of the larger Cessna operations in the Los Angeles area, turned up a salesperson who had some photocopies of estimating sheets that he had worked up. Although he had made some basic math errors in his calculations, they are for the most part insignificant. This data is reproduced in Exhibit F, with the math errors (marked ‡) still intact. Like the data from Mooney, no consideration had been given in these cost estimates to the federal use tax or local property taxes, which can add significantly to the hourly operating costs, dependent upon the annual hours of use.

The impact of the number of hours flown per year upon the *indirect* and hence the *total* hourly costs of operation is clearly shown in both Exhibit E and Exhibit G. The influence of annual hours flown on the figure for total hourly costs for the Mooney is less than it is for the B-A36 simply because the Mooney figures do not include any capital costs in the category of fixed costs. Just because they are not included in this cost estimate, however, does not mean that they do not exist. Capital costs are a reality; and when they are properly represented in cost estimates for a specific airplane, they will generally function in the same

Exhibit F   Estimated Operating Costs*

Aircraft model:	Skylane	Turbo-Centurion	Turbo-Skymaster
Flight hours per year:	400	480	360†
Flight miles per year:	64,800	94,560	66,600
(Speed basis—mph)	(162)	(197)	(185)
Gasoline at $.83/gal:	$11.62	$13.61	$16.87†
(Consumption basis—gph)	(14.0)	(16.4)	(20.9)
Oil—includes 50-hour change:	.90	.95	1.15
(Labor & oil at $.90/qt)			
Maintenance:	3.50	6.00	10.00
Reserve for overhead:	3.23	4.25	6.13
Direct cost per hour:	$19.25	$24.81	$34.15‡
Storage costs:	$ 1.50	$ .95‡	$ 2.00‡
(Basis—monthly $)	(50.00)	(50.00)	(65.00)
Insurance:	2.94	5.40‡	8.80‡
(Basis—annual $)	(1,175)	(2,600)	(3,200)
Indirect cost per hour:	$ 4.44	$ 6.35‡	$10.80‡
Total hourly operating costs:	$23.69	$31.16‡	$44.95‡
Operating cost per mile:	.1462	.1582	.2340

*Operating costs estimated by a Cessna sales representative at a large West Coast dealership. Calculations are based on mid-1977 prices.
†Due to these varying hours of annual use, the total costs per hour and per mile for the three models are not comparable.
‡Erroneous data due to math errors made by individual preparing the estimates.

Exhibit G   Estimated Operating Costs for Project B-A36 (1978)

	250	500	750
Flight hours per year:	250	500	750
Flight miles per year: (Basis—190 mph)	47,500	95,000	142,500
Gasoline at $.87/gal: (14 gph)	$12.18	$12.18	$12.18
Oil—includes 50-hour change: (Labor & oil at $1.00/qt)	.92	.92	.92
Maintenance & inspections:	4.50	4.50	4.50
Reserve for overhead:	5.50	5.50	5.50
Direct cost per hour:	$23.10	$23.10	$23.10
Storage: ($75 per month)	$ 3.60	$ 1.80	$ 1.20
Local property & federal use taxes:*	2.43	1.21	.81
Insurance: ($1800 per year)	7.20	3.60	2.40
Indirect cost per hour:	$13.23	$ 6.61	$ 4.41
Total operating cost per hour:	$36.33	$29.71	$27.51
Operating cost per mile:	.1912	.1564	.1448
Capital cost per hour: (Includes net opportunity cost)	$46.61	$23.30	$15.54
Total cost per hour:	$82.94	$53.01	$43.05
Total cost per mile:	.4365	.2790	.2266
Cost per seat-mile:	.0728	.0465	.0378

*During the latter part of 1980, the law expired under which the federal use tax was authorized. Industry observers are split about the future of this item. Some believe it will be renewed by Congress, and others fear that it will be replaced with an increased general aviation fuel tax. The IRS, however, is continuing to collect taxes for the partial year (1980) for which the law was effective.

manner as the total costs shown for the B-A36 Project when the annual hours of use increase.

Analysis of the data presented in Exhibits E, F, G, and H, along with that from similar charts published in various aviation magazines, was conducted to see if a factor could be obtained that would work to provide a "quick-and-dirty" estimate for operating costs of an airplane. The data was adjusted to reflect 1980 fuel prices and labor costs, and it was arranged in the format shown in Exhibit H. Using the assumption that there is a direct and valid correlation between engine horsepower and *both* direct and indirect operating costs, it was found that calculations produced factors which fell in a relatively narrow range. For

direct operating costs per hour, this data produced a *mean* factor of
0.1333. The amount of data was more limited for the total operating
costs per hour, but the resulting mean factor was 0.2175. The factor for
total operating costs was developed *without* any consideration for capital costs and was based on 250 hours of use per year.

If the raw data were reasonably accurate and the assumption of
correlation between horsepower and cost is correct, we can obtain a
rough estimate of what the direct operating costs for a specific piston-
powered airplane will be by simply multiplying 0.1333 by the rated
engine horsepower. This figure would include fuel consumed at 75%
power, annual inspections and routine maintenance, reserve for engine

Exhibit H   Estimated Operating Costs for Project B-A36 (1980)

	250	500	750
Flight hours per year:	250	500	750
Flight miles per year:	47,500	95,000	142,500
(Basis—190 mph)			
Gasoline at $1.55/gal:	$21.70	$21.70	$21.70
(14 gph)			
Oil—includes 50-hour change:	1.38	1.38	1.38
(Labor & oil at $1.50/qt)			
Maintenance & inspections:	5.85	5.85	5.85
Reserve for overhead:	7.15	7.15	7.15
Direct cost per hour:	$36.08	$36.08	$36.08
Storage:	$ 4.08	$ 2.04	$ 1.36
($85 per month)			
Local property & federal use taxes:*	2.43	1.21	.81
Insurance:	8.00	4.00	2.67
($2000 per year)			
Indirect cost per hour:	$14.51	$ 7.25	$ 4.84
Total operating cost per hour:	$50.59	$43.33	$40.92
Operating cost per mile:	.2663	.2281	.2154
Capital cost per hour:	$46.61	$23.30	$15.54
(Includes net opportunity cost)			
Total cost per hour:	$97.20	$66.63	$56.46
Total cost per mile:	.5116	.3507	.2972
Cost per seat-mile:	.0853	.0584	.0495

*During the latter part of 1980, the law expired under which the federal use tax was
authorized. Industry observers are split about the future of this item. Some believe it
will be renewed by Congress, and others fear that it will be replaced with an increased
general aviation fuel tax. The IRS, however, is continuing to collect taxes for the
partial year (1980) for which the law was effective.

overhaul, and 50-hour oil changes. The resulting dollar cost per hour is based on fuel prices which average about $1.65 per gallon and shop rates ranging between $28 and $35 per hour. The bias in this figure will probably be toward the high side, so any surprises which result should be pleasant ones. The figures produced by this formula will be more correct for inefficient airplanes and will tend to overstate the costs for efficient machines, such as the Mooney 201 and the Aerostar.

The factor 0.2175 for computing total operating costs includes consideration of the federal use tax and an average of the property taxes which would be assessed over a 6-year period in California. It also includes storage costs ranging between $75 to $90 per month and insurance costs for an instrument-rated pilot with more than 500 hours in his logbook. It does not include any allowance for depreciation, interest expense, opportunity costs, or any other aspect of capital cost. The results from the use of this factor will probably be less accurate than those obtained from the factor for direct operating costs, but it will give you a "ball park" number to work with. Remember, however, that this factor is based on 250 hours of use per year.

Recognize also that the various calculations and tables presented in this chapter are only rough approximations of what actual costs will be. Prices for fuel and services vary widely on a regional basis, and the manner in which a machine is operated will influence both the direct and indirect costs. This material is here primarily to illustrate the various considerations involved in determining aircraft costs and to demonstrate the techniques used so that you may develop meaningful figures of your own.

CAN YOU AFFORD IT?

The primary reason behind all these mathematical gyrations we have examined is determination of an answer to the question: "Can I afford it?" The purpose of obtaining complete and accurate cost information for the airplane is to find out how it will affect the *total* financial picture of your business. In order to know if you can make the loan payments, you must know precisely what those payments will be and when they will be due. You must also know how much cash will be available in the company's bank account at the required times to determine if sufficient funds will be there to cover not only the airplane payment but also the operating costs as well as the normal company cash demands for payroll, rent, and supplies.

What is required is some sort of *cash budget* which looks at the anticipated future cash demands to be made by the airplane acquisition, the historical cash requirements for your business operation, and the reasonably anticipated levels of cash availability which will result from sales and the collection of accounts receivable. Comparing these figures on a monthly basis will reveal if and when the acquisition of the airplane will create a cash problem and to what extent.

If your business is literally booming and your bank account is bulging with cash, the acquisition of an airplane will probably have a very small impact upon the figures of your company's balance sheet and operating statement. On the other hand, if you are really stretching your resources to buy the airplane, it is imperative that a very carefully constructed cash budget be created and the effects of the acquisition on the financial statements of your business be discussed with a knowledgeable accountant. You should be particularly concerned over the alterations which will occur in your company's debt/equity and current ratios.

Perhaps the very best thing that you could do would be to have your accountant generate a set of *pro forma* financial statements for your company. *Pro forma* statements are the "What if" exercise of the accounting trade. These do not have to be in great detail, nor do they have to conform to all of the generally accepted accounting practices. There isn't even any need for them to be typed up. They will suit your purpose just as well if they are simply pencil figures on a worksheet. You are looking for information, and you want it at the lowest cost possible. If you have decided that you will use one of the methods of accelerated depreciation, then these *pro forma* statements should at least cover the first 3 years of the project life.

In this way, you will be able to see very accurately what the effects will be on all the major areas of your operation from the airplane acquisition. You will be able to verify the value of those anticipated tax savings, and you will find out if there will be sufficient cash to cover your needs. This service may cost you $100 to $150, but it will be well worth the price in the long run, for you will know when you sign your name to the contract for a $90,000 airplane that you can really afford it. And, *that* is a comforting thought.

OWN, RENT, OR LEASE?

As it is with so many other things pertaining to airplanes, the question of owning, renting, or leasing has many facets. Owning, of course, offers the greatest amount of asset availability and usually is the most convenient approach for the business pilot. Leasing on a long-term basis provides the same sort of availability and convenience as ownership. The lease, however, will generally prove to be more expensive than ownership, in gross dollars, since the lessor recovers the entire purchase price, the costs of financing, and his profit during the period of the lease. In addition, the lessor retains all residual value of the asset at the end of the lease, and the lessee usually still assumes all the risks and responsibilities of ownership.

At one time the equipment lease was touted as a means of presenting a "better balance sheet," since a long-term lease was not considered a liability. Today, generally accepted accounting practices demand full disclosure of any long-term leases in the financial statements. The real value of the lease is in its ability to conserve capital. It can allow the lessee to have the equipment in question without the need for large down payments which are required on conditional sales contracts. The other advantages are closely tied to the manner in which the tax laws work pertaining to lease payment deductions, depreciation, and interest expense.

Evaluation of the decision to lease, buy, or rent requires that the specific cash flows for each method of acquisition be analyzed in terms of its respective *net* present value and the earning capacity of cash in your own business. This is not a simple procedure, but it will be generally found that for a closely held corporation or individual entrepreneur the so-called advantages of a lease rarely outweigh the added costs. Bonus and accelerated depreciation plus the interest expense deduction will usually equal the 100 percent write-off of the lease payments after every aspect of the project has been considered. With the purchase, however, the residual value remains with the purchaser.

In those instances where a lease is structured with "an option to buy," the residual value is still available to the lessee, but during an IRS audit, that lease will be viewed as a purchase arrangement and the lessee will lose the lease payments deductions and end up with a *very* expensive purchase instead of a moderately expensive lease. For any business pilot who wants to enter into a lease arrangement on his airplane, it would be wise to investigate the content of Internal Revenue Ruling 55-540 with a competent tax advisor before consummating the deal.

Generally, a lease of an airplane is of interest to the business pilot when the user of the airplane will be a corporation controlled by the investor-lessor himself. The basic scheme is for the business pilot to purchase the machine personally and then lease it to his own corporation. The reason behind this would be to avail himself of the depreciation and interest tax deductions on the airplane, while the corporation makes the payments. In effect, the business pilot has constructed himself a one-person tax shelter. The problem with this sort of deal is a thing called Section 482 of the Internal Revenue Code dealing with "arm's length transactions."

Basically, Section 482 allows the IRS to reallocate income between related parties, and the result to the business pilot who has structured such a deal could be disastrous. The appeal of this type of arrangement can be great, but the pilot who would venture into this water had best not try it as a do-it-yourself project. This kind of deal requires a *tax attorney* who is very familiar with this aspect of the tax law.

The popular aviation press has given a good bit of coverage to the "lease-back" arrangement. In this situation the idea is to buy the aircraft and then lease it back to the FBO from which you bought it. He makes out very well because he now has a captive customer and a new airplane in his flying inventory which required absolutely no capital investment on his part. As a lessor, you get essentially two things: (1) the tax deductions on the airplane and (2) a broader hour base over which to spread the fixed costs of ownership.

Reviewing the savings accorded to an owner by increasing the annual hours of use from 250 to 750, represented in Exhibit H, it is easy to see that the savings will be significant. The problem is that in a lease-back deal, the costs represented in the usual cost estimates are no longer valid. Your insurance costs will skyrocket the moment your airplane begins being used as a rental or training machine. The same thing also applies to your routine maintenance and inspection costs.

For the average entrepreneur/pilot, the lease-back arrangement really isn't a viable consideration. First, the airplane that is a good machine for the serious business traveler will be too well equipped and too expensive to generate any significant amount of rental income. Second, the business pilot who has sufficient use for an airplane to justify owning one will be unable to compromise his travel schedule to accommodate previous arrangements made by rental customers. The exception to this general judgment against lease-backs for the business pilot might be the individual who is going into a cabin-class twin and can make a lease-back arrangement with a Part 135 operator who has a need for that particular type of airplane for charter work.

A complete and definitive discussion of the myriad aspects and complexities of tax law, as it applies to aircraft ownership, lease-backs, and "arm's-length transactions," is beyond the scope of this book. The variables of each individual case make generalizations extremely risky and ill-advised. Once aware of the pitfalls presented here, the business pilot should discuss his particular circumstances with a trusted tax advisor and follow his recommendations.

Up to a certain point, renting is the least expensive way to fly. Precisely where that point will be is dependent upon many things, but the industrious business pilot can determine that spot for himself by making a thorough analysis of the rent/buy alternative with his preprogrammed financial calculator. Usually, the break-even point, in an economic sense, comes between 250 and 300 hours per year. There are, however, things other than just dollars to consider when contemplating the use of a general aviation airplane for business travel.

For me, the greatest consideration in favor of owning is that I fly the same airplane every time, and I know all the peculiarities of the machine and how it has been flown and maintained. Of course, the use of our company airplane far exceeds the point at which owning becomes more economical than renting.

Once the decision is made to use your airplane for business, accurate and very detailed records become mandatory. Depending upon your personal logbook to support your claims for business deductions on your tax return is probably not the best approach. Shown here is the Record-A-Flight log, which provides a small but detailed record of your business flying and expense. Such a record will be extremely valuable to you and your accountant in the event of an IRS audit.

Regardless of how you obtain the use of your flying machine, be it owned, leased, or rented, the one thing that remains constant is the need for documentation. When you are deducting the business use of an airplane from your taxes, you must be an excellent record keeper. You must document everything: Record the flight time, the date, the *business purpose,* where you flew, why, and with whom. In an audit, it won't make a bit of difference how expert your CPA or attorney happens to be; if you don't have the appropriate records, you are likely to lose your deductions.

There are several prepared logs for keeping track of all this information for the IRS, and using one of them makes the paperwork a bit easier and more organized. The best of these are the Taxlog and the Record-A-Flight. The former combines a tax record with a personal logbook. In addition, it has tips and pertinent information pertaining to many aspects of the business use of general aviation aircraft and the tax ramifications involved. The Record-A-Flight is much smaller and provides strictly an expense record. It has no provision for keeping a record of your flight time in the normal format of a pilot logbook. Each of these items has its own advantages and disadvantages, dependent upon your particular likes and needs. This type of record to support the business use of your airplane is probably better than depending upon the aircraft logs and your own logbook to substantiate deductions on your tax returns. If your use is partially business and partially pleasure, then good records will be even more important.

AIRPLANES AND THE IRS

Within the provisions of the Internal Revenue Code, your general aviation airplane is just another capital asset, but that message somehow hasn't been received by all the agents in the field. At least, this is the opinion held by many aircraft owners. The news media, of course, has done its part in "educating" both the public and the IRS agents that airplanes are the playthings of "fat cat" millionaires who use them to "fly" through loopholes in the tax laws at the expense of the average taxpayer. With this kind of stigma attached to our machines, it is a miracle we fare as well as we do.

Part of the problem, perhaps, is the airplane enthusiast who has been told that he can "take it off the old tax bill" if there is even the remotest connection between his airplane and his business. This leads to the concoction of the most inane and convoluted stories imaginable.

Having listened to a few of these, it is no wonder that a jaded IRS agent becomes very negative when he sees an airplane on a tax return during a field audit.

As a general rule, airplanes make very poor tax shelters. If this is the underlying reason for buying a company airplane, you would most probably be better off making some other type of investment. The tax incentives pertaining to capital assets only make economic sense when those assets contribute to overall profitability of the company.

To qualify an airplane as a legitimate business tax deduction, this asset must be, in the words of the IRS, "*ordinary* in your trade, business or profession and *necessary* for its operation" (italics added). What does this mean? Well, in the opinion of the Supreme Court, *ordinary* means that it is a common and accepted occurrence in the particular field of business and *necessary* means appropriate and helpful in maintaining a trade or business *but not indispensible.*

Business use of an airplane and hence tax deductions require that there is a business involved which is attempting to generate taxable income. For the pilot with incidental business use of his airplane or use connected with a secondary avocation or trade, it will be wise to explore the provisions of the "hobby rules" with a competent tax advisor. There can be some surprises here for the uninformed, so check it out.

If you have been a business executive for any length of time, you will already have an understanding of just how capricious the tax laws can seem to be. It will likewise come as no surprise to you that enforcement of those laws is seemingly almost arbitrary. To know precisely the meaning and intent of a certain law usually requires a decision of a court, and the determination which results will be dependent upon which district the decision was made in.

Tax law is a fluid thing that is constantly being defined and redefined in the courts. Therefore, when it comes to tax matters, the business pilot should not accept something from a friend, an airplane salesperson, a magazine article, or a book as being valid and applicable to *his* situation. Tax strategy and planning should always be done with the aid of a *knowledgeable professional* in the field.

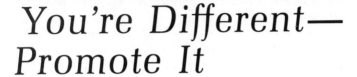

CHAPTER FIVE

You're Different— Promote It

THE HIDDEN BENEFIT

When the decision was made to purchase a company airplane and become involved in business flying, you set yourself apart from the majority of others in your particular business. You took a major step in expanding your own personal time and the effective area of your sales territory. Because of its capability to do these things, the general aviation airplane has been called a "time machine." But, if transportation and time savings are all that you are getting from the company airplane, you're not really getting full value from your investment.

Very few corporate assets possess the extraordinary capability of the company airplane for exploitation, in terms of publicity and promotional purposes. Even in our sophisticated society, airplanes continue to possess a mystique which makes them interesting and newsworthy. This fact is often overlooked by business executives who are not publicity oriented.

It is a very difficult thing to quantify the monetary value of the company airplane. Comparisons of cost per mile can be made against alternate forms of transportation, but the value of intangible benefits, such as promotional potential, is almost impossible to assess in hard-dollar terms. Yet, this hidden benefit, if properly used, can add significantly to the total profitability of your company.

Unfortunately, the publicity benefits of a company airplane do not accrue automatically. You must set the whole thing into motion. You must learn to capitalize upon that competitive edge you acquired when you purchased the company "time machine." Just owning the airplane is not enough; you must tell someone about it.

The *someone* you want to tell your story to is your customer. You want to be sure your message is presented in a manner which will stress to your customer the benefits *he* will derive, even if indirectly, from your use of a general aviation aircraft.

FREE ADVERTISING

Any business person who has launched even a modest advertising program will confirm that advertising is an expensive proposition. Paper and printing costs are horrendous. A competent photographer gets paid at least $500 a day, and dependent upon the publication, space costs run anywhere from expensive to astronomical. In addition to this already weighty sum, there will be an agency commission of 17 percent, so any "freebies" that can be had in this area can add to the bottom line.

Publicity is not precisely the same as advertising, but in many ways the results are the same or even better. The prime purpose of any promotional endeavor is to communicate information pertaining to you, your company, and your product to your potential customers. Both advertising and publicity attempt to do this in various ways, but in publicity—there are no space costs. This is money that can stay in your bank account.

The essential difference between publicity and advertising is a matter of packaging. Advertising is a straightforward commercial communication promoting your company, your services, or your product; and it is presented as such. Publicity, on the other hand, is presented as *news*. The commercial message remains, however, subtly interwoven into the news story. This provides the second advantage of publicity over advertising: There is no indication that anyone is advertising anything, allowing a more receptive attitude toward the material by the reader.

Creating effective publicity is an art. It requires an understanding of the needs of editors and what constitutes "news" to a given publication. It also demands a thorough knowledge of whatever it is that you wish to publicize. None of this, however, is beyond the capabilities of the average, successful business person.

The first question pertaining to use of the company airplane to obtain publicity would be, What publications would be most interested in *your* story? The obvious answer, of course, is the publication in which your company advertises your primary product. The fact that you buy advertising space can be a very good lever with which to pry loose some editorial space for your story.

Every industry from worm farming to fashion has at least several trade journals serving it. If you have been in your particular business for any length of time, you are probably receiving more "controlled circulation publications" than you have time to read. These magazines and newspapers are the fields into which you will attempt to plant your publicity pieces, so a few hours of really analytical reading is in order.

You will be searching for any common thread which links the various articles, trying to ascertain what constitutes news to the publication under study. Does the format make use of lots of photographs or is it heavy with text? What is the tone of the writing? Is it highly technical or more informal? Is there a high order of coincidence between the companies who buy space advertising and those who are the subjects of the various articles?

By asking enough questions as you read, you will be able to develop a fair idea of how the editor thinks and what he feels are the needs of his audience. From this picture you can structure your story to fit the editorial format of the publication you are focusing on.

After you have an idea of the editor's viewpoint, look at your potential story from that perspective. Start asking questions again, looking for some sort of "editorial hook" from which to hang the story of your company's use of an airplane. The story angle might be concerned with how you have solved a problem similar to those faced by this publication's readership, or it might hinge on how your airplane allows you to better serve the needs of a specific member of that readership. The approach used will depend upon the publication and the story you have to tell.

Even if you feel that you can't write an acceptable story yourself, there is no reason to shut the door on the opportunity for free advertising. There are many advanced journalism students at the local colleges who would be delighted to create such a piece in return for a nominal payment and the chance of getting into print. If you have a strong story with an angle which ties together with the general interest areas of the publication in question, the editor might even assign a staff writer to do the actual writing. In most of the "trades," however, your chances of seeing your story in print are better if you can provide a complete package of text and photographs.

Another channel for publicity based on the company airplane would be the aviation magazines. Here the news value of your story would be an entirely different thing. The aviation publications are in the business of informing and entertaining airplane enthusiasts—and selling airplanes. The focus in this type of publication would, therefore, be directly on the hardware or some flying technique. Still, in building background for such an article, it will be possible to mention the company name and perhaps even work in a sentence or two about your operation. It would probably be very limited, but in today's competitive market, every little bit of free advertising helps.

THE PRESS RELEASE

In attempting to place a feature article in a trade publication, we discussed a technique that might be compared to using a rifle. We selected a specific target, took careful aim at that target, and then fired our best shot with the hope of getting some meaningful publicity for the company. It was a matter of trying to hit one target at a time. You would *never* send your feature story out to two or three editors simultaneously. That is not the case with the press release.

The press release is the shotgun of the publicity effort. It is short and to the point. It usually is based on a specific event, and it is used to convey information about that event to as many potential users as possible.

Generally, the press release is a single, typewritten page, giving the *who, what, where, when,* and *why* of the event. If it is appropriate to the event, a single photograph may be sent out with the release. Because there is always the chance that some editor may want some additional details, always include your name, address, and phone number on the release. Traditionally, this information is typed in the upper left-hand corner of the page.

Among the events which could provide suitable materials for a press release might be the purchase of a new airplane by your company or when a member of your firm solos or gets a private license. Even something as simple as taking an important customer for his first ride in a small airplane can be worked into a successful press release. The customer selected for this release should be important in *his* field. In this way, you will have a broader market for your release, and you and your company can possibly benefit from *his* importance. To get the maximum exposure from this type of press release, a photograph would, of course, be mandatory.

Many business executives will feel that such mundane subjects could not possibly warrant space in an important trade journal or a major metropolitan newspaper, but they are wrong.

Never accept defeat before giving it a try.

The wisdom of this thought was demonstrated to me several years ago when my company, Joyce Jewelry, moved into new and larger quarters. I decided that I would write a press release pertaining to our move. There were about a dozen small trade papers that I intended to hit with this release. Not wanting to type the information a dozen times, I took the original to the local instant printer.

They wouldn't print less than one hundred pieces, and I only needed twelve. So not wanting those extra copies to go to waste, I expanded my mailing list. In total, fifty-two copies were mailed, but I really didn't expect that more than five or six of the smaller trades would pick it up. I was wrong.

Not only did *Women's Wear Daily* print my three-paragraph news release verbatim, but so did the *Los Angeles Times!* Right in the middle of the second page of the "Business and Finance" section, right there next to a story about IBM, was *my* press release, detailing that momentous event when Joyce Jewelry moved from one building to another in Westlake Village. Our change of address did not logically seem of sufficient news value to warrant space in such prestigious publications, but there it was.

Including the *Los Angeles Times* and *Women's Wear Daily,* I found that there were at least seven newspapers which saw fit to publish the release. There may have been others, but without a clipping service, an exact count of the publications using the release was impossible. It really didn't matter. Those seven publications alone represented a readership of several *million* people, so I felt that the release was very successful and worth the effort.

Certainly, any event concerning an airplane can be made into a more exciting and newsworthy press release than a move from one industrial building to another. Don't scrap an idea just because you think no one will be interested. Think about it. Work with it. Look for an angle which will make the event newsworthy and interesting. Study both the trades and the general interest publications for the best potential outlets for your press release. Build a mailing list of editors, and provide them with a release whenever your company is involved in an event which would be of interest to their readership.

Editors are generally very busy people, and they are constantly bombarded with requests to publish things which, for one reason or another, are totally unusable. Because of this, most of them won't even bother to read anything which isn't typewritten and professional in appearance. There is a standard format for the news release, and you should use it.

The following press release shows this format and gives an example of how the purchase of a new airplane might be handled. For your company, the details, of course, would be different. The format, however, would be the same.

FROM: Paul E. Hansen
           P. O. Box 86
           Agoura, CA 91301
           (213) 889-0112

FOR IMMEDIATE RELEASE
JOYCE JEWELRY ACCEPTS NEW AIRPLANE

Joyce Jewelry, a progressive, West Coast manufacturer of contemporary costume jewelry, has recently accepted delivery of a new company airplane. The keys to the six-place, air conditioned Piper Lance were presented to Joyce Hansen by a customer service representative at Piper's Vero Beach facility.

Mrs. Hansen, who designs the entire Joyce Jewelry line and still finds time to be a student pilot, stated that cost-effectiveness and the current energy problem led to selection of this single-engine machine. She added that the use of general aviation aircraft plays an important role in her company's overall marketing plan.

"Our segment of the women's wear market is extremely volatile," she said. "It is, therefore, imperative that we present our sample line to our customers as quickly as possible after the onset of a new season. The speed and load-carrying capability of the Lance will enable us to visit more of our customers with a *full* sample line in a shorter time span," Mrs. Hansen concluded.

Following a brief preflight inspection of the new airplane, Mrs. Hansen, accompanied by her flight-instructor husband, departed Vero Beach for an extended sales trip through the Midwest before returning to California.

–end–

Perhaps the most important thing to notice about this sample news release is the fact that it may be terminated after the first, second, or third pargraph without destroying the *sense* of the story. Paragraphs two and three could be eliminated entirely and the remaining material would still work well. This allows an editor a great deal of flexibility to cut the release down to fit his available space, should he need to. *This* increases its chance of publication.

Remember, your goal is to have your release read and printed; therefore, you want your material as flexible and readable as possible. Always double-space your copy and use a black ribbon on the typewriter, preferably a carbon ribbon. It is really beyond the scope of this book to delve into all the mechanics of creating and distributing press releases. There is, however, abundant material available on this subject at the public library; and it would probably be worthwhile for every business pilot to look into this aspect of publicity.

A LASTING VALUE

If you work hard, use a good bit of imagination, and persist, the day will come when a story about you, your airplane, and your company will show up in print. It will provide a lot of ego-boosting fun to show your clippings to neighbors and other pilots; but if you let it end there, you've stopped too short again.

The right kind of story, once it has been published, can be a very valuable promotional tool on a continuing basis. Like all other tools, however, your press clippings will produce absolutely zero for you if they are left unused in a drawer.

Dependent upon your product and the nature of the industry in which you work, "the right kind of story" will vary. For example, Joyce Jewelry is involved in designing and manufacturing extremely trendy items of costume jewelry. Each season, we introduce more than one hundred new products into our line, and by the end of each year our selection of almost three hundred styles will have completely changed several times. Therefore, a story which is based on this season's "hot sellers" from the Joyce Jewelry line will have little value as a promotional tool beyond the current season. Yesterday's fashion, like yesterday's news, is a pretty stale commodity.

Due to the ephemeral nature of our product, we have found the most useful press exposure to be that which is based upon our use of the company airplane. These stories are invariably people-oriented, and our experience has been that they provide more lasting promotional value than a product-oriented story. People, it seems, are really interested in other people and what they do.

One of the most successful pieces of publicity our company has had, both in terms of original interest and continuing usefulness, is a full-page story which appeared more than a year ago in the California *Apparel News*. The article titled "Joyce Jewelry: Doing Business from a

Accent on Accessories

Joyce Jewelry: doing business from a cockpit

By THERESA VILLA-McDOWELL
For the Apparel News

The man with the two suitcases walks into the airport restaurant — is this Bakersfield, Riverside or Marion, Illinois?

That they-all-look-the-same look quickly vanishes when his customer approaches, exchanges warm civilities with him, then the two set down to work the line — the Joyce Jewelry line.

For Paul Hansen, co-principal at Joyce Jewelry, the airport rendezvous has become a way of doing business. Hansen and his wife, Joyce, decided to join their 20-year affair with all type of aircraft and their burgeoning business.

"We were finding that, when I was in Los Angeles, Joyce was in Rhode Island, and when I was in Texas, Joyce was in California," says Hansen. "We were constantly traveling, primarily separately." The couple decided they needed a balance, and began to question that grow-at-any-cost syndrome.

"I think it's far more important to be doing what you want to do than it is to accumulate money," says Hansen.

Then too, Hansen (who came into the business six years ago "when he discovered I only knew design and didn't know management systems," as Joyce puts it) was hankering to get back into planes.

Hansen had flown antique planes and had worked as a free lance photographer and writer for aviation magazines for nearly 20 years.

"So all this experience, all this valuable education and background was being wasted," he says. "I've always, since the introduction of the business, had to handle the economic and financial end. I ran a cost analysis and figured a light aircraft, its cost compared on a cost per mile basis, was about the same as a medium-sized Chevrolet."

The Joyce Jewelry line, which was being carried throughout the country at this point, was doing less volume in California — which once accounted for up to 45 per cent of its business — than any other part of the country.

"We thought we ought to work the Los Angeles area," says Hansen. Too, "our decision was to work for a closer, more personal relation between ourselves and our customer. It kind of comes down to that's where the fun of the business is at. It enables us to travel together and we are meeting the principals of specialty stores and family department stores as we travel the country.

As the Joyce Jewelry line grew, the Hansens found they needed storage space to accommodate two large sample suitcases, plus other assorted luggage when attending shows. And, like many manufacturers, they had had the experience of losing sample lines on commercial airlines.

"Traveling as we did, we found it was more practical, in terms of flying from there to San Francisco, to fly our own plane," says Hansen. "Almost any distance under 1,000 miles is favorable — we'll beat the airline's time hands down with less trouble. Plus we know we'll have the samples." Small towns also frequently have airports near a customer's retail store which aren't served by commercial airlines.

"It's definitely an interest arouser with customers," says Hansen. "We'll sit in restaurants at airports and work the line."

Customers are also just as likely to receive a lecture on general aviation.

Paul Hansen is as dedicated to general aviation as he is to his business. But after 20 years of writing for aviation press, he is convinced "we wind up talking to ourselves."

"A lot of people are Sunday flyers, which is valid," says Hansen, "but you have to be professional in background and attitudes, otherwise you're a danger to yourself and others."

Weather, which might be a problem to businesses in other

Apparel News photo by Timothy Jacob

Joyce and Paul Hansen of Joyce Jewelry

parts of the country, rarely comes into the picture in California

"Here in California, we can fly 98 per cent of the time, at least," says Hansen.

A large part of their success is due as well to Joyce herself. She coordinates her styles with current clothes fashions, offering original designs at popular prices.

"We structure pricing on our styles on a rigid formula created by my husband, which means when we get into something unique, our customers are not paying for a designer name," she says. The formula takes in material, labor and overhead costs.

Ms. Hansen also tries to cover several looks in several price ranges "for different pocketbooks." All her styles can be put together for a layered effect as well.

"The consumer wants to make choices," she says. "So as a designer I don't try to force anything on her. Certain styles might be my preference but I would like to offer many ways to wear my things so she can build a look best suited for her."

Cockpit" featured a photograph of my wife and me in our company Skylane. This photo, showing an airplane interior, together with the boldface headline, created a "stopper." Surrounded by articles concerned with the latest fashion trivia and which manufacturers were currently wallowing in Chapter XI, our story was an interesting and refreshing oasis for the reader. As a result, the article enjoyed a very large readership and the response was terrific.

"That's all very nice for the ego," quips the cynic, "but does it sell goods?"

In our experience, the answer to that question is an unqualified "Yes!" Even without consulting our accounting records, I can easily think of almost $5000 in sales which resulted either directly or indirectly from the original publication of this particular piece. At an average price of about $24 per dozen, that's a *lot* of costume jewelry.

The residual value of this article, however, is perhaps even more meaningful. Ever since its publication, we have been using reprints and photocopies of this story as a follow-up item in our "prospecting" program. Since the *Apparel News* reporter managed to stuff a great deal of general information concerning the background of our company, our method of operation, our personal philosophy, and our fashion position into this 1000-word package, it has proved to be an excellent tool.

Whenever one of our company sales representatives has made an initial customer contact, attempting to obtain an appointment to show our sample line, we currently follow up by mailing a photocopy of the *Apparel News* article. A brief note, appropriate to the situation, is handwritten on the face of the photocopy in the white space bordering the article. The exact wording varies according to the circumstances involved, but the following example demonstrates the basic idea:

Hi Linda,

Thanks for your time and courtesy on the phone today. I'm looking forward to meeting you in Detroit next Tuesday.

Thought you might be interested in this article which gives some background on our company.

Best regards,
Carolyn

The copy of the article is then mailed to the potential customer in a plain, unprinted envelope. It is always addressed by hand, and we use a postage stamp instead of the normal routine of running our outgoing mail through the postage meter. We do this purposely to increase the appearance of this being a piece of personal correspondence.

The next time our representative contacts this buyer, either by phone or face to face, the news clipping provides a convenient and interesting topic of conversation. We have often found that the buyer will have a friend or relative who flies, and she is genuinely interested in learning more about "little airplanes." Such is the material from which rapport is built.

Our company has been in business over ten years; and during that time, we have enjoyed what is probably a better-than-average amount of "free advertising" from the trade press. The most effective publicity, however, has consistently been that based on our use of the company airplane. It works for us; with a little bit of effort and a lot of persistence, it can work for you, too.

SHOWMANSHIP

Up until very recently, advertising by attorneys just wasn't done. It was frowned upon. It simply wasn't dignified. It was forbidden. But, in 1977 the U.S. Supreme Court gave its approval to advertising by members of the bar. Even before this momentous decision, however, the name of F. Lee Bailey was a familiar one in many households. Through newspaper stories detailing his work, TV interviews, and several hardcover books, this business pilot became one of the most famous attorneys in the United States.

Early in his legal career, Bailey learned about both the practical and promotional values of an airplane—and he made it work for him. Combining his abundant legal talents with an apparent flair for publicity, this ex-military pilot climbed to the top of his profession and along the way stepped up from a Luscombe to a Lear Jet.

Among his other skills, Bailey seems to possess a keen sense of showmanship. In his 1977 book, *Cleared for the Approach,* he relates an incident which demonstrates his affection for the dramatic.

He had recently obtained his Lear Jet. This was back in 1968 when the Lear was still a relatively rare bird. The locale for the incident was Otis Air Force Base. The catalyst for the minidrama was a mild put-down of the Lear by a military tower operator.

Bailey, annoyed by the implied slur directed at his Lear, requested and received permission to make a short-field takeoff. Being light on fuel, the Lear broke ground after about 800 feet. Bailey then pulled the nose up to "about forty degrees above the horizon, lifted the landing gear, and left the flaps down."

When the Lear crossed the field boundary at *nine thousand* feet, the impressed controller asked, "What do you boys do for an encore?"

Bailey, the consummate showman, casually replied, "Why, son, we light the other engine."

The subtitle of Bailey's book reads *In Defense of Flying.* This is appropriate since an excellent defense of both commercial and general aviation is presented in the text. The book, however, does more than just build a case for airplanes and the folks who fly them; it *promotes* F. Lee Bailey.

Within the covers of this book, F. Lee Bailey has conveyed to me (and to untold thousands of others) a great deal of pertinent information pertaining to F. Lee Bailey. He has told us that he is an experienced pilot, a successful attorney, a curious, intelligent, and dedicated man, and that he possesses expertise in the complex area of aviation law. He has also related that he is rational, determined, self-confident, and completely capable of remaining relaxed in the tense atmosphere of a courtroom.

Aren't these the attributes you would want in an attorney who was representing you in a difficult lawsuit?

Isn't this the precise information that any aware attorney would want to present in his advertising efforts directed toward his potential clients?

If your answer to those two questions is "Yes," you will probably agree that Mr. Bailey has done an excellent job of "advertising." It does not matter if this "advertising" is the result of conscious thought or simply occurred by chance as the book took form. The effect is the same, and Bailey benefits from it.

Most of us will never defend a doctor accused of murder or share cocktails with high-ranking politicians and labor leaders, but we can still be alert to the publicity and promotional opportunities which occur in our own lives. Remember, good things happen more often to those people who work to make them happen.

FALL OUT

As a business executive you are probably a member of the Optimists or Rotary or some other civic group. In this position, you are looked upon as a community leader, and you have the opportunity to influence both thinking and action on the part of others.

Yours is a strong position from which you can inform other non-flying business executives and local politicians of the facts pertaining to general aviation in terms of jobs and other economic benefits brought to the community by the flying segment of society. It might even be beneficial to introduce these men, on an individual basis, to flying.

Arrange to take some of your associates for a flight. Have a business meeting somewhere away from your usual location. Select a site which will be visually pleasing and allows a meaningful meeting to be conducted. Brief them first. Tell them what they can expect to see and feel. Be sure to provide your passengers with disposable earplugs, such as the E-A-R. They are not that expensive, and you will add immeasurably to the comfort of your guests.

Think like an airline captain. Remember that you want these passengers to return with positive feelings about "your airline." Fly like a professional—no steep turns, abrupt pull-ups, or letdowns. You are trying to convince nonbelievers that they can be comfortable and safe in a small airplane and that general aviation is a rational means of transportation.

If it is at all possible, you should equip yourself with a boom mike for this type of flight and one of those voice-activated intercom systems. In this way you will be able to keep your passengers informed of what is happening during the entire flight. Cheap headsets will suffice for your passengers, and they won't need a mike at all. You will want this to be a one-way conversation.

Whatever you do, don't repeat any horror stories from the last hangar session. If you decide to give them the bit about "Jonathan Seagull and the freedom of flight," do it with restraint. To most people, general aviation is still very much a helmet-and-goggles affair, and you really don't wish to reinforce that concept.

It is up to each of us as business pilots to be informed and work as public relations representatives for general aviation. We must become better informed and then educate those around us to recognize the value to *them* of both little airplanes and local airports. We must help erase their fears. The average person sincerely believes that the non-professional pilot is a threat to life and property on the ground. Mr. Average American looks at your 210 as it flies overhead and remembers the oil crisis of 1973.

He doesn't know that most general aviation singles are more fuel-efficient than his station wagon or the average piece of airline equipment. He just remembers sitting for hours in long lines to get gas for his station wagon while the idle rich "wasted" fuel flitting around the skies in their expensive, dangerous, airborne toys. He may be wrong and stupid and uninformed, but it is his "truth and understanding" of the problem which will influence legislation. He will vote what he believes. It is of little consequence that he learned the "truth" from the local newscaster who puts an MU-2 and a J-3 Cub into the same category.

If we wish to ensure our future as pilots, if we wish to continue to fly at all, we had best be very active using our clout as business executives to obtain as much good press for our airplanes as we can. If we leave our publicity to the TV newscaster with the $35 haircut and the $10 head—we're in big trouble!

Everybody knows that the manufacturers of general aviation airframes and their trade association are powerful and will lobby in Washington to preserve their own hides. They will protect us as pilots because pilots and airplanes and airframe manufacturers are all in the same boat. But while you are being complacent about the very real threat to the aviation world as we know it, because someone else is going to protect your rights, give some thought to the dinosaur. He too was big and powerful. He too had a lot of clout, but you will notice that today he is very much extinct.

Is the dinosaur too far back in history for you? Well, let's remember the story about the Corvair, that nice little car from Chevrolet. That's an extinction story of more recent vintage. It *was* a super design. I had one and drove it for more than 50,000 miles. I really liked it. I wasn't alone; lots of people liked it. Then this fellow, a well-intentioned crusader, began to say bad things about the little Corvair. He said it was dangerous, and people believed him. Soon sales were terrible. General Motors (GM) was big and powerful and rich, and they tried to save the Corvair; but GM failed. Why? Simply because people function in accordance with what they *believe,* and the crusader had convinced them that the Corvair was bad. All of GM's power and money couldn't convince them otherwise.

Whether the Corvair was good or bad, safe or unsafe, is really irrelevant. It was killed by bad publicity and what people believed about it. This same thing can happen to general aviation for the very same reason.

We have more enemies than we have friends. Therefore, we should all work to gather as many new friends for general aviation as we can. We must guard against adding any new names to the list of enemies and try diligently to convert as many as possible to our side. We must fly with courtesy. We must fly with thoughtfulness for those on the ground. We must improve our accident rate; and most of all, we've got to stop talking to ourselves!

Our message has to be brought to the general public, to the people outside our own ranks. Volunteer to speak to your local business group, your homeowner's association, or a local trade group. Become a goodwill ambassador for general aviation in your local area. Sell your customers, vendors, and business associates on the value of airplanes and airports.

If you think that you can't speak in front of a group, then do something about it. Join the local section of Toastmasters International. Every business person should be able to stand before a group and express himself. If you can't now do so, you owe it to yourself as a business person to learn how, and Toastmasters will help you.

Both GAMA and the National Business Aircraft Association (NBAA) have films and slide presentations which tell the general aviation story. These are available to you for your use on either a loan basis or at a very nominal cost for purchase. These two organizations have tremendous amounts of facts and figures pertaining to general aviation from which you can build your own public relations presentation.

If you are beginning to think that I am suggesting that you spend time and money in some sort of altruistic crusade which will primarily benefit the likes of Cessna, Piper, and Beech—you are wrong. I do not hold with philosophies which advocate individual sacrifice for the betterment of some "greater cause." All such crusades are, to my mind, rubbish.

On the contrary, I am proposing that you become involved in an effort which will not only help preserve your freedom to fly but also provide tremendous opportunities for personal recognition and solid business benefits.

The business opportunities and potential benefits which arise from increased public exposure and publicity are rarely direct, however. They will generally come via a circuitous route and from unexpected sources. In order to make the most of this "fallout of fortunate coincidences," you must be very alert, recognizing opportunity when it presents itself, no matter how well disguised it may be.

THE COMMON INTEREST

Hangar flying is an activity enjoyed by almost every pilot from the newest student to the most seasoned professional. It is part of the flyer's mystique which creates an informal bond between all pilots. It is also a useful tool for the business pilot in a sales situation if it is used with restraint and discretion.

The common interest in flying can be a very strong door opener. For example, my wife had been trying to get an appointment with the jewelry buyer of a small chain of department stores in southern California for more than a year. She was convinced that our line would do well in these stores, but the buyer had used every excuse and delaying tactic imaginable to avoid looking at the line.

While shopping at the main store of this chain, Joyce learned that the jewelry buyer was a private pilot and had an interest in the Navion. This information became one of those "fortunate coincidences" as I had at one time written a pilot report for an aviation magazine on the North American Navion. A photocopy of this article with a brief note was sent to the buyer. This was followed up by a phone call during which a solid appointment was made. After more than a year of rebuffs and rejections, the buyer had finally relented simply because of a mutual interest in flying.

Another time, in Michigan, while I was working with one of our independent sales representatives, the buyer for a group of specialty shops was "all bought up," and far too busy to look at the line. As we were being dismissed, I noticed a copy of *Flying* under a stack of papers and other magazines on the buyer's desk. A casual question about his interest in flying brought out that he was "working on the instrument rating," and was part owner of a Cessna 172. It also led to an invitation to show the line and a new account for the company.

These are not isolated incidents. Again and again, a common interest in flying has successfully opened doors for us where other methods had failed. Although once the door is open, you must be able to present a product or service which will benefit your potential customer.

At Joyce Jewelry, we are very careful in qualifying our prospects before contacting them. We shop their stores to see whether our merchandise is suitable for them in terms of both fashion image and price range. We also check the prospect's credit rating and payment history *before* we even try to open the door on a selling situation. Therefore, in those instances where the common interest in flying had led to the opportunity to show our line, we have *never* failed to open the account and write a substantial order.

In order to benefit from the common interest in flying shared by you and your potential customer, a certain amount of mutual awareness is required. Since it would probably be ineffective to query all of your prospective customers about their interest in aviation, you must bring your story to them. Include your airplane in your regular advertising scheme. Bring your company name, your product or service, and your airplane together in your space advertising. Have your copywriter tie your airplane use to a progressive company philosophy of giving fast and special services to your customers. Stress how your use of a general aviation airplane creates benefits for your customers. If you do this job well, your prospects who fly will be aware of you and your interest in flying when you call.

If your budget doesn't allow for continuing space advertising, then you might have some color postcards printed showing your airplane in flight. A brief caption under the photo could give some information about your company and your airplane. On the message side of the card, you can print an announcement of the next tradeshow where your products will be displayed or perhaps just leave it blank so that the card can be used for brief notes. In this way, it can serve your needs for any kind of written communication from a thank-you note to an appointment confirmation.

The purpose of your efforts in this project is to create a vehicle which says, "Look at me; I'm different—I fly." Perhaps this will strike you as being corny and undignified. If it does, remember that any idea can be executed to any degree of refinement. Your promotional piece can run the gamut from crude and corny to a dignified work of art dependent entirely upon your taste, your sense of propriety, and the limits of your pocketbook. Regardless of how expensively, tastefully, directly, or obliquely stated, the message should remain the same: "Look at me."

GOING BIG TIME

After reading an article about one of the top Cadillac salespersons in the country who would park in front of a prospect's home and then call on his car telephone to invite that prospect for a demonstration drive, I was convinced that the airborne phone was the ultimate promotional tool. What could be more impressive to a buyer than getting a call from 8000 feet over Indianapolis confirming his appointment with a jewelry salesperson? Absolutely nothing could be more impressive than that!

We had to have one! It would pay for itself in a month. That is, of course, if an airborne phone could be had for less than the price of a three-axis autopilot.

A little research indicated that not only could we get an airborne phone for less than the cost of a Cadillac, but the economy model from King was tagged an amazingly low $995 and weighed a mere 3.5 pounds. The *Buyer's Guide* showed that even the most expensive unit was less than $3600, so compared to other avionics equipment, the airborne telephone might be considered a bargain. It was almost too good to be true.

The promotional literature I gathered told a story of simple systems and operations. Merely push a button marked with a number corresponding to the zone over which you are flying; then give the operator your billing number and the number to be dialed. From that point on, it is standard telephone procedure except for the need to operate a push-to-talk switch on all but the most expensive units. All of the brochures promised "astonishing clarity of reception"; however, information pertaining to the costs for using the equipment was not to be found.

After several frustrating calls to the local telephone bureaucracy, I felt the reason the flight phone manufacturers had omitted any information about the cost to use their equipment was simply because it was impossible to get. In the April 1977 issue of *Business and Commercial Aviation,* however, I was told that effective April 8, 1977, the cost for an air-to-ground connection would be a flat $6; and current station-to-station or operator-assisted rates would apply to the land-line portion of the call. According to this article, a typical 3-minute call from Atlanta to Kansas City would result in a $7.14 charge. That works out to be $2.38 per minute and is several times the total operating costs of our airplane. And that is based on station-to-station rates. The cost for person-to-person or credit card calls would be even higher! I already knew that talk was *not* cheap, but anything that works out to $2.38 per minute is downright expensive. Based on the fact that phone rates in general have increased in the years since 1977, it seems safe to assume the costs for air-to-ground calls will have done the same.

My curiosity was aroused about the costs of telephone service in general, and I decided to review this expense item on our operating statements. Much to my surprise, I found that our company *consistently* spends more for telephone expenses than it does for the direct operating costs of our airplane. This was an astonishing revelation and the deciding factor pertaining to our acquisition of an airborne phone. Impressive or not, we certainly weren't going to buy a promotional gimmick which costs more to use than an airplane.

My decision, of course, was more emotional than rational. The tendency to react that way when I am faced with a situation in which the value-for-value equation seems abnormally skewed in the favor of those who hold a captive market is almost irrepressible.

On a rational level, however, the airborne phone does have a moderate amount of promotional potential, but it seems a bit too costly for that limited purpose. If your particular operation could benefit from a more practical application of this specialized transceiver, then the cost-benefit relationship might become a favorable one for you.

WHAT IF IT BACKFIRES?

If you are really active in promoting your company and its use of a general aviation airplane, the day will arrive when you will come face to face with some in-depth hostility. The source may be an ardent environmentalist or an angry customer who is offended by your "high-priced toy." Perhaps your antagonist will be the fellow who enjoys a three-martini lunch and loudly shouts from the back of the room what he believes are witty disclaimers to your proaviation presentation. In any case, you will be open to a most difficult and painful experience unless you are prepared.

In almost every instance this hostility will be the product of emotionalism and ignorance, spawned by the fulminations of pandering politicians and uninformed media representatives. To respond on the same level would be counterproductive. You must answer your attacker with a rational presentation of substantiated facts pertaining to the specific situation in question. To be taken by surprise will lend credibility to the irrational position of the opponent who attempts to supplant logic with intimidation, so do your homework and *know* your facts.

PROMOTING AT HOME

One of the most difficult promotional jobs facing many business pilots is convincing a frightened spouse that flying is not only safe but enjoyable. Having successfully accomplished this, he may still find difficulty convincing his nonflying mate that purchasing a new weather radar has a higher priority on the company budget than paying himself a bonus so that the house can be redecorated. Such conflicting priority problems rarely respond favorably to logical, well-reasoned, and valid arguments. In fact, arguing with one's spouse, regardless of how logical the presentation, is about the same as arguing with a customer. It is a no-win situation and ultimately you are the loser.

The first goal must be to increase positive affirmations pertaining to flying and reduce or eliminate any negative reinforcement. This can be an extremely difficult task if it is known that you fly and your spouse is somewhat less than enthusiastic about the activity. At every social gathering, there will be those who will pounce upon her fears, delighting in the opportunity to recount the grisly details of the most recent plane crash as it was depicted on TV or in the newspapers. This seems as inevitable as day following night. These party-circuit ghouls can create more insecurities in 10 minutes than you will be able to counteract with years of patient assurances.

The solution, if there is one, lies in education and reorientation. Neither of these is possible, however, if at the onset "logical arguments" create an emotional barrier in her mind. It is not important that the "facts" demonstrate flying is safe or that owning an airplane is profitable for the company. These are *your* facts. What you know is irrelevant; it is what *she* believes that is important. What she believes will not significantly change until she becomes more actively involved in flying.

For many, the first step in getting a disinterested or frightened spouse to actively participate in flying is the AOPA Pinch-Hitter Course. Designed primarily to teach a nonpilot how to get an airplane safely back on the ground should the pilot be disabled in flight, this course has often been instrumental in motivating a nonflying spouse into becoming a licensed pilot.

Although the Pinch-Hitter Course has proved to be an interesting and exciting experience for those who have participated, it can still be a long and frustrating problem to convince a reluctant spouse to actually enjoy flying. In my own case, it took 15 years of coaxing (and a certain amount of subterfuge) to get my wife, Joyce, to consent to taking the Pinch-Hitter Course. After completing the first 3 of the required 6 hours of flight time, she announced that she was going to become a licensed pilot! Only two times during all our years together had I seen her demonstrate greater outward signs of happiness and enthusiasm. The first was the day our daughter was born, and the second was the day she soloed.

The Pinch-Hitter Course had provided an extremely positive experience for Joyce. Although she had always been comfortable in small airplanes with me, being able to actually fly and land the airplane herself added immeasurably to her security, understanding, and appreciation of flight. Now the facts were becoming *her* facts. She had become an active participant in flying instead of being merely a passenger. Now she would see the old familiar world of flight from a slightly different perspective.

During the final hours of that Pinch-Hitter Course in San Diego, one of those "fortunate coincidences" was in the making. The news director for one of the local TV stations had decided the activities at the airport might make an interesting item for the evening news. When the crew arrived, they conferred with the AOPA officials, and then selected Joyce to be the subject of their interview. An attractive woman executive who was learning to fly was precisely what they were looking for.

They worked with Joyce for almost 2 hours, filming her in the cockpit as she flew them around the city of San Diego. Then the cinematographer deplaned and shot more footage while Joyce executed several touch-and-go landings in our Skylane. The crew was doing a very thorough job.

Cut and edited, the interview was screened twice that night. It went very smoothly; Joyce was confident and professional as if appearing on television were a daily occurrence for her. I was very proud of my wife and extremely pleased with the way the TV station had handled the interview. Since they were most interested in the woman-executive angle of the story, this naturally focused attention on our company and its products. It could not have gone better had we hired an expensive Hollywood publicist.

My wife's television debut seemed a fitting climax to what had been a thoroughly memorable weekend. Things were going right! Joyce had decided to obtain her license. Our company had received an enormous amount of favorable publicity as a by-product of the multiple screening of her televised interview, and the company airplane had proved once again its value as a promotional tool.

Protect Your Investment

PHYSICAL SECURITY

Keeping your airplane in a hangar is one of the more important aspects of protecting your investment. It not only provides the best in terms of physical security but it also extends the life of the paint, upholstery, and avionics.

If an individual hangar is available, this will be the most convenient and, of course, the most expensive way to go. We have kept both our company Skylane and our Lance in a large, common hangar; and for the most part, over a 3-year period, there have been only a few times when it has been problematic. In many ways, due to the convenience of the radio and mechanical repair facilities located in the same hangar, this arrangement has proved to be even better than a single unit.

Another consideration is the relatively new Port-A-Port, which allows you to buy your own personal hangar and place it on the airport property. Essentially, the Port-A-Port is a mobile home for airplanes. It is generally treated and taxed in the same manner as a mobile home. Many county airports, however, not only charge you rent on the land space for your hangar but will also assess you for a thing called "possessory interest tax." Since they own the land and can't tax themselves, they had to come up with some way to get the property back on the tax rolls. This tax is in addition to whatever personal property taxes are levied on your mobile hangar.

In large, metropolitan areas, hangar rents are extremely high and the available space is limited. You should still try to obtain a hangar for your airplane. Part of this cost will be absorbed by lower insurance rates, and you will probably be able to get a premium when you sell or trade your machine. Of course, the biggest benefit derived from keeping your airplane in a locked hangar is the protection provided from the aircraft thief.

According to a report by the International Aviation Theft Bureau, airplane and avionics theft losses in 1976, although down from previous years, amounted to $3,311,500. Eighty-three U.S. registered aircraft and an estimated $410,664 of avionics were stolen. Only nineteen of the eighty-three stolen aircraft were recovered and returned to the owners.

California and Arizona led the nation with the greatest number of aircraft thefts. The proximity of the Mexican border and the great demand for aircraft to carry illicit drugs out of Mexico into the United States probably account for the higher theft incidence in these two states. These same circumstances also contribute to the popularity of the turbo 210 and the turbo 206 as the aircraft types usually stolen.

During a recent AOPA Safety Clinic being conducted at Phoenix, the problem of light-plane theft was dramatically demonstrated to a small group of pilots who were taking the Instrument Refresher Course.

Arriving at the airport in predawn darkness, our group straggled out to the remote tiedown area which had been temporarily established to handle the large number of visiting AOPA aircraft. My instructor was helpfully removing the ropes from the Skylane as I stood, dumbfounded, looking at the aircraft door. It was standing slightly ajar. I had carefully locked that door the previous evening. The latch was still locked, but the door was definitely open.

The implications of the open door had not fully penetrated my mind when it became apparent the sounds coming from the direction of the next tiedown space were not the usual student-instructor preflight banter. People were shouting. There were sounds of a scuffle. Someone yelled, "Catch that bastard!"

My instructor and I ran around the 182 to see what was happening. We were greeted by a turbo 210 with two open doors and the sound of shouts and running footsteps from the distant darkness.

We had just about pieced together a sequence of events that seemed plausible when the out-of-breath owner of the Cessna 210 returned and confirmed our speculation.

The thief had opened the Skylane door by the simple means of violently rocking the wing. We tested this theory and it worked; several good tugs on the left wing and the *locked* door on the pilot's side popped open. Getting into the Skylane, however, merely presented the thief with a new problem which he apparently was not ready to solve. Due to the window covers on the 182, he did not know that the radios and complete instrument panel were covered by a metal plate secured with *two* padlocks. Once he saw this, he took the easy route and went on to the next airplane on the line, the Cessna Centurion.

When the owner of the Cessna 210 arrived that morning, the thief was seated in the airplane. Confronted by the owner, he tried to brazen through the situation with the lie that he thought he was in his own airplane. Failing with this ploy, he bolted from the right door and ran. Unfortunately, he managed to escape.

The device covering the panel in the Skylane, which in this instance probably prevented the loss of our radios, was made by Robertson Aircraft Corporation. At one time the Robertson Panel Guard was widely promoted in the product news columns of all the aviation magazines. Recognizing the value of this item, I bought one for the company Skylane immediately.

Frustrating to me and much to the surprise of Robertson, their standard Panel Guard would not fit on a 1975 model Cessna Skylane.

After lots of phone calls and a lapse of several months, a new Panel Guard was delivered to Joyce Jewelry. It was much larger, required two locks instead of one, and it was obviously a handmade prototype. Robertson reported that the problem developed out of changes made in the Cessna production line when they substituted some collars on the control column. The new Panel Guard design, however, would overcome this, and it would be adaptable to both Piper and Cessna models. Although obviously more expensive than the original and also a bit more cumbersome to handle, it certainly would do the job for which it was created. This fact was demonstrated by the experience at Phoenix.

There are smaller and simpler items available to prevent theft of your aircraft. One of these is the $64.95 Wheel Lock. This device is a cast aluminum chock with a double-tumbler, tamper-proof, keyed lock. Once the Wheel Lock is secured to the aircraft brake disc, the airplane cannot be moved, at least not by rolling on its own wheels. This fact is simultaneously the Wheel Lock's greatest virtue and its major shortcoming.

Use of the Wheel Lock all but prohibits storage of your airplane in a large, common hangar, due to the almost constant need to shift airplanes around. The Wheel Lock also becomes inconvenient to use at many major airports where the normal procedure after fueling is for a lineman with a tug to pull your airplane away to some distant transient area and tie it down. Struggling with this device under a low-wing aircraft is even less convenient. Obviously, it can do nothing to prevent theft of your avionics, which very often are worth one-third to one-half of the total aircraft value.

Less expensive and still an effective deterrent to theft of the *entire* airplane is the installation of a small engine control lock which is being marketed by a company called *Skylock* for a modest $19.95. The device is made of aluminum alloy with a hardened steel shackle. In use, this control lock prevents starting the engine by securing the mixture control in the idle cutoff position. Again, there is no protection for those expensive avionics.

Advances in electronics have created a variety of burglar alarm systems to help you protect your aircraft investment. These systems run from the simple to the very sophisticated, offering a complete selection of toots, whistles, sirens, flashing lights, and even beeps on a belt-worn paging device. An alarm might be of some benefit when combined with a good, physical security device, but you must be prepared for a lot of midnight trips out to the airport due to false alarms. My experiences with similar systems on automobiles have left me with the feeling that such items can be more trouble than they are worth.

Short of locking your airplane in a vault, the Robertson Panel Guard gives about the most protection and convenience for the money spent. At $49.95 it was an excellent bargain. The absence of any promotional material in recent months, however, makes me wonder if perhaps Robertson has given up on this project. If they have scrapped the Panel Guard, and we are unable to obtain one for our new Piper Lance, we will just have to have our mechanic custom make one. It will be expensive, but worth it, as I have not forgotten what happened at Phoenix.

For the business executive that really uses his airplane for travel, his expensive machine will spend a great deal of time in the transient tiedown area of various airports. Perhaps just as much time will be spent this way as in the home-base hangar. To prevent damage to interiors and avionics that inevitably result from an airplane sitting unprotected in the sun, the wise pilot will invest in window covers and *religiously use them.*

Heat is the enemy of those tiny little electronic components that allow those black boxes in the radio stack to do their magic. Research has found that the component failure rate is fifty times greater when the device is operated at 65°C than when the operational environment is only 25°C. At 85°C, the failure rate soars to a multiple of more than 500 times. It is easy to see that *cooler is better.*

Typically, avionics designed to technical standard order (TSO) criteria will withstand maximum temperatures of 55°C. For short periods, such equipment will function at temperatures as high as 71°C. Non-

The Robertson Panel Guard will not only protect your aircraft from being stolen but will also frustrate the efforts of the avionics thief. Secured by two padlocks, it offers a maximum amount of protection for your aircraft investment when it is away from your home base.

TSOed equipment, however, has a more limited operational temperature maximum.

During field investigations by one of the leading manufacturers of avionics for general aviation aircraft, it was found that cabin temperatures of airplanes sitting on the ramp went as high as 185°F (85°C). You will notice that this is higher than the "short-period" limit for TSOed equipment. The avionics are being subjected to an environment beyond design limits even before being turned on. No one has figures detailing the number of radio failures attributable to heat soaking on the ground, but every leading manufacturer of avionics will quickly agree that the effects are detrimental to the service life and reliability of your aircraft radio equipment.

For about $65 you can buy yourself a lot of really valuable protection for those expensive avionics—a set of reflective window covers. There are several manufacturers making window covers for airplanes; some make external covers and others, like Morgan Standford Aviation, make internal covers. There are arguments for both approaches, but we have found the Thermacon heat screens, which are internal covers, to be about the most effective, lightest, and most convenient to use.

It may be nothing more than chance; but during the 500 hours since we first installed the heat screens on our company Skylane, we have only had two avionics problems. Our radio maintenance costs for the period were less than 25 cents per hour. Another airplane, equipped with more expensive gear than our standard Cessna radios, came into service about the same time, accumulated hours at the same rate, and has experienced failure rates and maintenance costs that exceed ours by a factor of six. The only real difference, at least superficially, was the use of window covers.

Certainly this instance would not satisfy the demands of any meaningful scientific study. It may be simple coincidence, just a matter of luck; but our avionics repair costs have been far below average during the time we've been using the screens.

If the price seems a bit high for the covers, you can make them yourself. The materials and procedures are fairly simple. All you need is a roll of masking tape, last Sunday's newspaper, a couple of the better quality "space blankets" from the sporting goods store, a pair of scissors, a marking pen, and some binding tape and Velcro from the notions department of the dime store.

Tape the newspaper pages together to make them large enough to cover the window areas of your airplane. After careful placement of the newspaper over the windows and taping it in place, mark the outline of the window and the future position of the Velcro fasteners on the template. When all the templates have been measured and marked, you are set to cut the space blankets to your patterns. The binding tape is simply sewn around the edges of the space blanket material, and the Velcro sewn in place. Installation requires that the mating Velcro part be glued to the airplane in the proper position to match the Velcro sewn on your window covers. After the first time, installation and removal will require only a matter of seconds, due to the amazing qualities of Velcro.

An additional benefit provided by the Thermacon heat screens is pilot comfort. On those days when the outside air temperature (OAT) is near 100°F and the cockpit of the average airplane is like an oven, the cockpit of a protected aircraft is within a couple of degrees of the outside air. Since the internally mounted screens can stay in place right up to the moment before engine start, there is no need for the occupants to swelter while preliminary checklists are completed.

MAINTENANCE

In an old issue of the FAA Aviation News, there is a story concerning an air-taxi pilot in a brand new Seneca, who lost both engines on a short flight from Jacksonville to Tallahassee. The pilot did an excellent job with the forced landing, and no one was hurt. But what if this had been at night or IFR?

The resulting accident investigation revealed that the engines had failed due to overheating. The spark plugs were checked and found to be the wrong type for the engine. Taking the situation back to the 100-hour inspection and the mechanic who performed it, it was discovered that a supply clerk had misread his specification chart and that the mechanic didn't notice the error and installed the improper plugs.

Accidents due to mechanical failures in general aviation are rare; however, when they do occur, the official determination often states the cause as "inadequate or improper maintenance." Such accidents don't just happen; they are created. They are engineered through complacency and manufactured by carelessness.

In a fatal crash of a Navajo, it was found that a small screwdriver left by a mechanic during routine maintenance became lodged in the control linkage as the ATP-rated pilot was making a VOR/DME approach. In another fatal twin accident, it was found that the Cessna 310 crashed on takeoff due to the fact that a mechanic had reversed the aileron control cables during the 100-hour inspection. The pilot might have been able to have figured this one out had the situation not been complicated by an engine failure. In a single-engine Mooney, another ATP-rated pilot and his passenger perished when they experienced an engine fire while IFR. The Mooney had just been worked on. It was found that during recent maintenance a nut which secures the fuel line had been loosened but not retightened.

With monotonous regularity, accident reports detail similar stories. Far too often, the occurrence is immediately after an annual or 100-hour inspection. These FAA-mandated procedures are to ensure the mechanical safety of aircraft, but there are times when these inspections result in just the opposite. From my own experiences, I have concluded that the highest risk for mechanical failure in modern aircraft will be experienced in either a factory-new machine or one that has just been certified "airworthy" as a result of an annual or 100-hour inspection.

In factory-new equipment, I have had a complete electrical failure, flap failure due to an intermittent battery contactor, reversed inputs from the couplers to the autopilot, failure of each of the gyros, encoding altimeter failure, a glideslope hooked to the DME antenna, failure of each of the nav and comm radios, transponder failure, ADF failure, failure of a main gear actuator, and other assorted failures too numerous to list. But, on a factory-new airplane, I've never had an engine failure. So, compared to some new-aircraft owners, I've just been very lucky.

It is an unfortunate fact of life that the consumer has become the quality control inspector for most products manufactured in the United States. It is even more unfortunate that the buying public has accepted this role. The condition is so widespread that the customer has come to expect a certain "debugging" period for every complex item he buys, and he accepts this condition. There is no need for this situation. It is certainly not endorsed nor knowingly encouraged by *upper-level* management, if for no other reason than it is counterproductive to the profit motive. Clearly, the culprit is the deluded American worker who believes he can produce a poor product in the factory and then buy quality in the marketplace. Somehow, he is unable to connect his own lack of caring with the unending list of squawks on his new car, refrigerator, or airplane.

Years ago, when I bought my first airplane, Richard Bach, a close friend and antique airplane enthusiast, suggested that I buy a book and learn how to tend to the mechanical needs of my machine. After watching him scrape his knuckles and bleed through the layer of rocker-box grease which usually covered his hands during the long hours he spent "maintaining" his Detroit Parks Speedster, I decided to leave this aspect of flying to the professionals. My Luscombe would be maintained in accordance with all the FAA rules, and it would be done by a knowledgeable professional.

I was convinced that this was the proper approach until shortly after my first annual inspection, when I experienced a mechanic-induced engine failure. Again, I was very lucky. The engine stopped within gliding distance of Santa Monica Airport. The cause was such a simple thing. The FAA-certified mechanic had taken the airplane apart. He had peeked into all the inspection holes and dutifully checked off all the items on his list. When he put the Luscombe back together, however, he overlooked tightening one clamp. The result was that the carburetor heat hose fell off at some time between my run-up and the moment when the engine failed due to carb ice. Had I been lower or further away or over a different part of the city, the story might have ended in injury and death rather than momentary anger and embarrassment.

Why did this happen? Perhaps it was a phone call or some other mechanic walking into the shop with a question. It certainly wasn't lack of knowledge or caring; it was merely some form of distraction. Probably, it was a series of multiple distractions. But, whatever the reasons, it did happen.

Since that occurrence, similar things have continued to happen. Some of the items were caught during the very thorough preflight inspection I conduct whenever my airplane has been in a shop; others, unfortunately, were not. Most of the items were little, annoying, nuisance-type things. The others had the power to kill.

After one annual inspection, for example, I discovered that the tapered roller bearing for the left main wheel had been installed backward. This seemingly impossible task was accomplished by forcing it in place by tightening the wheel retainer nut. In so doing, the tremendous physical forces which developed crushed the bearing race, allowing the roller bearings to dislodge. Twice I have found screwdrivers rolling around awaiting the opportunity to lodge in the control mechanism as one did in the previously mentioned Navajo crash.

Once, after having wingtip strobes installed on a new Cessna, I found that the mechanic had left his bucking bar in the wing. His error was not discovered until several months after the strobe installation. I was washing the underside of the wing when I noticed the skin had developed a rash of minute eruptions. They were extremely difficult to see, but they certainly could be felt. It was as if a message had been written there in braille. It was meaningless to me, but the responsible mechanic instantly recognized the telltale tracks of the bucking bar in the wing. It is conceivable that in time this heavy, sharp-edged piece of steel could have pierced a fuel cell in the wing or lodged itself in the control cables. The result in either case would have been disastrous.

The only reason this lethal situation was discovered is a rigid rule I follow pertaining to the washing and waxing of my airplane: I *always* do it myself. Even if my wife and daughter help with this chore, I make a point of covering every square inch myself. If one of them applies the wax, I will follow behind and buff. Through experience, I have found this method to be an effective means of detecting potential problems.

The syndrome of "doing everything yourself" can be a real trap for the entrepreneur. Even if you are the best time manager in the world, physically doing every job there is to do is impossible. It sometimes seems that it might be easier to undertake the chore of doing everything than to face the endless frustration of missed deadlines and poor workmanship—but forget that idea. Eventually, you would be forced into an overload situation, and *you* would then be responsible for the missed deadlines and the poor workmanship.

The answer, of course, is not *doing;* it is *controlling.* The key to success in this endeavor, particularly as it applies to airplane maintenance, is planning. You should plan all your maintenance to occur when *you* want it to be done. With proper planning, almost all maintenance work can be done at your home-base shop. In the long run this will be cheaper, and it will avoid those costly, frustrating, inconvenient situations which inevitably follow a mechanical breakdown at some distant airport.

Critical inspection on a periodic basis is imperative. This is the real reason behind my rule about washing and waxing the airplane. As any homemaker knows, thorough cleaning of an item brings the intimate details of that item to the attention of the cleaner. Washing down the belly of your machine will probably tell you more about the health of your airplane than twenty preflight inspections. It gives you an opportunity to really look at those brake lines and gear actuators. During your usual preflight, you are normally dressed for a client interview, not crawling under an airplane. Certainly, you will perform the necessary functions, but not with the thoroughness you can achieve from the deck of an automotive creeper when you are dressed in an old pair of jeans.

A small, spiral-bound notebook should be permanently kept in the airplane to record irregularities, observations, and definite squawks found during your wash-and-wax inspections. These notes will be the basis of your maintenance planning. They will also provide clues for the resolution of those infuriating problems which are intermittent. Should you ever have a confrontation with a manufacturer over a warranty item, such as the one we had with Cessna over oil consumption, detailed records can make a real difference in how your claim is treated.

Changing the oil in your aircraft engine is an extremely important item. It should be done on a scheduled basis in accordance with the manufacturer's recommendation. Theoretically, spectographic analysis of oil samples should be a tremendous aid to an informed maintenance program. However, recent information presented by *Aviation Consumer* opens some questions about the value of such a practice due to the inconsistencies and control problems involved.

Like most other business executives, I have neither the time nor the inclination to actually do my own aircraft maintenance. The idea of changing the oil on Saturday and then greeting a customer on Monday with dirt under my fingernails leaves me cold. Still, I do manage to be involved with this important aspect of aircraft ownership.

My wife, Joyce, schedules all our sales calls and trips, making certain that any out-of-town appointments which would involve airplane travel are made at least a week in advance. This allows me to coordinate with our shop and establish specific maintenance appointments. Working with the service manager in this manner, I am generally able to be at the shop just before the mechanic replaces the cowling on the engine. With the engine sitting bare, I can inspect all those hoses, belts, and clamps that are hidden during a normal preflight.

Making a point of looking inside whenever the cowling comes off is part of being a safe pilot. This practice enables you to have a better understanding of the machinery that keeps you aloft. After all, when you fly nights and IFR, you're betting your life on that engine, so you really ought to be interested in its health. Whenever the spark plugs are due to be cleaned on our machine, I request that the actual cleaning be postponed until I have had a chance to look at the color of the plugs. A great deal can be learned about the health of your engine and the effectiveness of your cleaning procedures by simply looking at the color and condition of your spark plugs. Being there before the mechanic buttons it back up also allows you to make on-the-spot decisions pertaining to replacements of minor items that could cost lots of money and time if they failed away from home.

The Federal Aviation Regulations stipulate that we must have an annual inspection of our airplanes every 12 calendar months. FAR 91.169 goes on to say that if the aircraft is to be used for hire, 100-hour inspections must also be performed. Some owner-pilots feel that if 100-hour inspections are required by government regulation to protect the public when airplanes are operated for hire, then following such a practice on their company airplanes will make them supersafe.

I do not agree. One-hundred hour inspections for the average owner-flown business airplane that accumulates a couple of hundred hours a year is a waste of money. It may even be an unsafe practice due to the added opportunity for maintenance-related problems; plus, the airplane is being subjected to the additional wear and tear of being taken apart more often.

The final date for the annual inspection is one that is known well in advance, which simplifies the planning problem. I inform the service manager a month before the date, then remind him again when there is only a week to go. I plan my own appointments so that I can devote 2 *days* to the annual inspection of our company airplane. It is generally complete in 1 day; but if it should run over into a second day, I will not have conflicting appointments.

In the final month before relicensing, I review all the service letters, open squawks, and airworthiness directive (AD) notes, if there are any, with the service manager. If any parts are needed, they can be ordered

Many shops are strongly opposed to having customers in the shop area. The reasons are usually sound, but I will not allow a mechanic to work on my machine if "company policy" prohibits my being present when the work is being done.

in time so that the airplane will not be grounded while waiting for the distributor to ship something. This approach has been very successful for me. Whether it has been due to just uncommonly good luck or to the maintenance method, I do not know; however, we have never had to cancel a flight due to a mechanical problem, nor have we ever had to obtain any maintenance work away from home.

During the early days of my relationship with our FBO, the service manager looked upon me as being somewhat eccentric. Now the relationship has mellowed; I even think that he grudgingly respects the keen interest I have in our flying machine. He knows that I am there neither to hamper his operation nor to save money by doing part of the work myself. I will lend a hand if it seems appropriate, but mostly, I just observe.

Some shops have a policy that strictly prohibits customers from being in the shop area. The reasons for this, in many instances, are extremely sound. Certainly I would not presume to argue about management's right to conduct their business in this manner, nor will I give my consent to such a shop to work on my airplane. The comparison may seem strange to some, but my life is as important to me as their shop policy is to them.

Perhaps, I am eccentric.

THE INSURANCE GAME

Some years ago, in a Midwestern meadow, Richard Bach and I unfurled a sign which read, "Fly—$3.00."

We were involved in an adventure, flying from dusty fields, flitting through the corridors of a bygone era, and seeking to learn if our old airplanes could still bring a moment of magic to a few people whose senses were not completely sated by TV violence, multiple wars, and the associated maladies of modern times.

In our innocence, on a single day that summer, we flew 130 people with nary a thought of anything but the smiles, the happy eyes, and the knowledge that we had shared something very special with these folks. The people were eager to share in our adventure and experience the joy of flight as we carried them aloft to view the rooftops and Main Street of their town. They traded their dollars for a safe experience and a lifelong memory; it was a fair bargain and everyone was happy. Everyone, that is, except one suspicious man.

"Your airplanes are insured, of course." His eyes flashed with knowing smugness.

"The insurance on these airplanes is what we know about flying," Richard responded defensively. "There is not 1 cent of any other kind of insurance; no property damage, no liability."

Confirmed in his suspicion, the unhappy man shook his head from side to side; as he stalked away, he lectured his young son about the irresponsibility of certain individuals. Richard grumbled some very profound insights related to reality and blindness; and I stood contemplating the chasm between these two divergent minds and the vulnerability of our enterprise.

Richard and I were both commercial pilots, certified by the FAA as capable and qualified to fly passengers for hire. Our aircraft were airworthy, and they were being operated safely and legally; yet, our position was most precarious. *We were not insured.*

Most probably we were uninsurable, at least at a premium cost which would have allowed us to continue selling airplane rides at a $3 rate. An underwriter would have looked at our operation, surveyed his charts and tables, and then he would have quoted a premium cost that would have exceeded the combined values of our airplanes.

But, we were younger then. We were dealing in dreams, not a *real* business enterprise. That was a time before either of us understood much about balance sheets and net worth and the incredible vulnerability that comes with even moderate success and earning potential.

One of the major burdens of success and wealth in the extremely complex legal environment in which we live today is the constant threat of litigation. It is generally accepted in legal circles that one can follow both the letter and the spirit of the law and still end up in the middle of a lawsuit, and the potential of such an occurrence increases geometrically with the value of the individual's net worth.

An interesting insight into the problem of insurance and tort law is gained as one considers the frightening fact that in California the filing rate for civil lawsuits is rising seven times faster than the population. Certainly, this situation is not limited to California alone.

This single fact and its associated implications provide ample reason for some serious thinking and thorough research pertaining to insurance coverage for your airplane and planned operations. The amount of insurance coverage secured should be directly related to your total net asset value and earning potential. The richer you are, the greater will be the amount of liability coverage needed to protect your money. If you're dead broke and intend to stay that way, then it really doesn't matter if you have little or no insurance.

The perceptive reader will quickly recognize how he might be able to avoid the high costs of insurance premiums—*don't own anything.* Since aircraft liability insurance is required by only a few states, this is an entirely workable plan for most individuals who have enough money to buy their aircraft outright, never need credit to obtain supplies and operate their companies, and can pay for a gear-up landing out of this week's pocket money.

If you can meet all the above requirements, you can also afford the high-priced legal fees entailed in structuring your financial affairs in such a way that you may continue to enjoy your wealth and at the same time become "judgment proof." For the average business person, however, this cure is far worse than the disease; and he must reconcile himself to the continuing high cost of insurance premiums.

Figuring out just how high those premiums are going to be for a given pilot and machine combination seems to be an art which is totally incomprehensible to anyone not involved in the insurance industry. It is a mysterious computation generated by churning together statistics and intuition, market competitiveness, and the facts pertaining to the pilot's age, ratings, total flight time, retractable time, time in type, and previous loss experience. Based upon my own experience of being quoted premiums which varied as much as 35 percent for what were supposedly the same limits of coverage on the same airplane, it pays to shop around. Even with varying rates from different companies, there is at least one item of constancy: when a low-time private pilot gets into an expensive, high-performance retractable or a multiengine machine, the premiums will be astronomical. If that private pilot then flies his newly acquired twin 100 hours per year or less and is inclined to calculate his insurance costs on an hourly basis, the resulting figure would be chilling to all but a few millionaires.

Insurance costs today are extremely high and are going higher al-

most daily. The reasons for this are varied, most complex, and range
through the areas of philosophy, politics, and law. That a crisis is developing in the insurance industry is unquestionable; the recent medical malpractice situation was only the leading edge of this storm. The
next and perhaps most formidable problem is that of product liability.
It is currently estimated that the anticipated insurance costs of product
liability have added about $7000 to the price of a new top-of-the-line,
single-engine airplane.

Deciding who should wear the villain's hat for this situation depends upon whether you wish to align yourself with the lawyers, who
claim to be "defending the rights of the people," or with the insurance
companies, who attack unscrupulous claimants and the lawyer's fat
contingency fees. One thing remains certain, however, you and I as
consumers will ultimately pick up the tab.

Reluctantly accepting that we currently live in a society suffering
from an advanced form of "sue" syndrome and that insurance is a
necessary and expensive evil, we are now faced with a long string of
questions:

What kind of insurance do we need?

What dollar-value limits will be appropriate for our particular circumstances?

What level of unprotected risk are we willing to assume?

What sort of exposure will be presented by our operation?

Are there circumstances in the financing of our airplane or
in our operations which will require special consideration in
a policy?

How will we know that we have adequate coverage?

Unfortunately, the adequacy of liability coverage can only be determined *after* an incident when the resulting litigation is underway. Reviewing some of the recent aviation accidents, it seems the major deter-
minants in the denominations of the lawsuits filed are the avarice level
of the plaintiff's attorney and the net asset value of the defendant.
Within the irrational atmosphere where juries have awarded $100,000
for the loss of a fingertip and $22,000,000 in a wrongful death suit, any
attempt to quantify *adequacy* of liability coverage would be absurd.

Hull insurance, on the other hand, can be evaluated in a more logical
manner. If the aircraft concerned is new, you will probably want insur-

ance coverage for the original purchase price. Unless you paid cash for the entire purchase amount, a lender will be involved; and he will require hull coverage for at least the amount of the loan. The lender will also demand that your coverage include a "breach of warranty" clause. This is an endorsement to your policy which provides payment of the lien amount to the lienholder in case of a loss, even if you have broken some of the fine-print stipulations of the basic policy. This is an extra cost item to you, and it generally adds about $25 to the premium.

With a used airplane the story is basically the same. The only exception is that the basis would be the current market value.

The rates on hull insurance generally run from 1 to 2.5 percent of the insured value for a "good-risk" pilot in most light twins and high-value singles. This rate can be lower, or it can be a great deal higher, dependent upon any number of factors included in the underwriter's establishment of a particular risk profile.

The best thing that any pilot can do to improve his risk profile is to become an instrument pilot. Maintaining currency is also important, and of course, he must meet the requirements of the regulations pertaining to the Biennial Flight Review. A pilot's risk profile makes itself felt in the premium rates for both liability and hull coverage.

This statistical picture of a pilot is not static, however. A 500-hour pilot, for instance, who has built most of his time in a Cessna 172 will be regarded as a good risk by his underwriter so long as he continues to fly a fixed-gear, low-performance, single-engine airplane. The day this pilot wants to trade up to a high-performance retractable or to a twin, his risk profile takes on an entirely different complexion in the eyes of the insurance company and his insurance rates will increase correspondingly.

If gambling is your game, a few premium dollars can be saved through the device of "risk retention." What this means is that you are essentially "going bare" for a certain portion of the risk.

Let's consider a situation where a pilot has purchased a new aircraft for $90,000, of which he financed a $55,000 balance after making his down payment. The lender would then require hull insurance for the amount of the loan, but there is no requirement beyond that. If the hull rate were fixed at $1\frac{3}{4}$ percent and the purchase value used as the basis, hull coverage premiums would be $1575 per year. Electing to cover *only* the value of the loan would result in a premium of $962.50, a direct cash savings of $612.50 per year!

That is a terrific saving, but don't forget what happens if there's an accident and that $90,000 machine is a total loss. The bank gets their money, and the pilot is out both $35,000 and his airplane. Doing the math on these figures results in the break-even point being just a bit more than 57 years. Even considering compound interest of 6 percent on the annual premium saving of $612.50, it would still take over 25 years to offset a single $35,000 loss. The mathematics of this situation only make sense if there is an ironclad guarantee that the pilot will never experience a total loss of his aircraft. For most of us, such guarantees are hard to get, so the alternative is obtaining the best coverage we can and paying the premiums.

Aircraft insurance, due to its interrelationship with tort law, is a complex, confusing, and frustrating quagmire. The underwriters who structure their policies in incomprehensible legal terms just add to the problem. The best bet for the buyer trying to wade through this mess, however, is to learn to read a policy himself and then find a knowledgeable broker specializing in the aviation field. Learning the basics of policy argot will enable you to ask meaningful questions when evaluating the potential broker. It seems customary in many specialized fields for practitioners to attempt elevation of their importance by spewing forth volumes of esoteric jargon. Taking the time to learn the language is an investment which will provide benefits in the long run.

Aviation insurance policies are not really that standardized; they can be tailored to the needs of the insured with greater flexibility than most other types of insurance. Certain aspects, however, are common to all policies.

To understand what is being insured, read the *insuring agreements,* which will generally be right up at the beginning; the *exclusions,* which list those items which are not covered, will be found further back in the policy; and the *limits of liability, definitions,* and *conditions,* which are the legal text that defines, modifies, and qualifies the insuring agreements and exclusions. It is here, in these modifiers, that all those unpleasant surprises, which usually appear *after* the accident, are to be found. The time to find them, of course, is before paying your first premium.

The major problem is usually one of misinterpretation of either the coverage itself, definitions of what constitutes improper use, and just precisely who and what is or is not covered and to what extent. The policy language is generally vague in certain areas, and I suspect that it is intentionally so. This allows the lawyers a lot of room for legal "interpretation" and sidestepping when the specifics of an accident are known.

The following incident, involving Fred Franklin and his claims adjuster, is a fiction. Still, some disgruntled aircraft owners, who have suffered losses and made claims against their carriers, may find this fiction comes closer to the spirit of truth than does the information they received from the insurance agent when they first bought their policies.

"Mr. Franklin, you sure are one lucky fellow," the insurance company representative said with a smile.

"It isn't every day that one of our insured pilots can manage to have an accident that is covered by our EXCLUSIVE PERVERSE PROTECTION PLAN POLICY."

Fred Franklin nodded silently, forcing a weak smile of agreement as his mind flashed a vivid picture of his beautifully restored, IFR-equipped airplane, lying torn and crumpled at the side of the runway.

It had been a strange day, Fred mused . . . a very strange day.

"You know, Fred, if it hadn't been for that albino elephant getting loose and then stepping through your left wing panel after your gear-up landing, things would have been very different," the adjuster said solemnly, shaking his head in wonderment over the strange events.

"The gear-up landing, of course, was due to a faulty component," the adjuster said quickly. "And your PERVERSE PROTECTION POLICY specifically excludes coverage of damage due to a faulty component."

"But you sure are lucky, Fred—now, if you will just sign this claim release form, I have a check here for $123.54 as *payment in full* for your loss."

"One hundred and twenty three dollars and fifty-four cents—are you crazy?" Fred shouted, glaring at the man.

"Well, you do understand, Mr. Franklin, that your policy *only* covers the elephant damage to the wing, and your aircraft was an old one, coming under the *Components Parts Provision*.

"After figuring depreciation, the company settled on $123.54 as an appropriate and equitable amount.

"If you hadn't violated the FAR pertaining to endangering paranoiac pachyderms, we may have added a few more dollars for damage to the undercarriage, but . . . " the adjuster shrugged; his final word just hung in the air.

Fred Franklin responded. He was last seen chasing the insurance adjuster down the road from the airport. Fred was screaming incoherent profanities about insurance adjusters, their employers, and modern high-rise buildings in the financial district.

Fantasy? Certainly. The story of Fred Franklin is a gross exaggeration. Yet, it does highlight some of the problems involved in dealing with insurance companies.

For a look at reality, let's turn to the January 1977 issue of *Aviation Consumer,* which relates the problems of a real person who had a very real accident. The story concerns a man who had a takeoff engine failure in a Piper Arrow due to some defective metal studs. The insurance company reportedly agreed to pay for the hull damage but refused to pay for any engine work, citing that "the entire engine, rather than just the studs, constituted 'the defective part.' Therefore, by definition, it was excluded from coverage."

As stated previously, those unpleasant surprises often lie hidden in the exclusions section of the policy. One such exclusion which will be of concern to the business pilot is that of employees. Most standard policies *do not* cover them; it is assumed by the aviation underwriters that they will be covered by workers' compensation insurance.

Checking into the workers' compensation policy carried by our own corporation, we learned that there was no exclusion for flying in a company aircraft, but the coverage extended only to the borders of California, making it practically meaningless. The insurance company wanted to know if any employees, other than corporate officers, used the company airplane. They were given a negative reply on that question; but, unknown to us at the time, the mention of the word *airplane* was the beginning of an insurance problem for Joyce Jewelry.

As a result of this inquiry into the specifics of our company's workers' compensation policy, we later received a letter from the insurance company's agent. This letter stated that the underwriter requested that my wife and I sign an endorsement to exclude ourselves from the workers' compensation coverage. The implication made was that if we refused, the company would terminate the entire policy. Effectively, this would put our company out of business, as it is illegal to employ people in California without providing workers' compensation insurance.

Reflecting upon the situation as it existed 3 years earlier, this demand seemed like a grotesque joke. When Joyce Jewelry had been incorporated in 1973, this same insurance company insisted that it was mandatory for *all* employees of the new corporation to be insured under their workers' compensation policy, including me and my wife. But, mention of an airplane changed all that. Now, the rules were different. And they were being spelled out for us with subtle intimidation. We had been made an offer we couldn't refuse.

The message for the business pilot is to check the exclusions of *all* his insurance coverage. Find out how the use of a company aircraft affects every area of the company's entire insurance program. You might find some catchall in your group medical program which excludes injuries sustained in a small aircraft. Look into the provisions of your life insurance policy. Take nothing for granted. Commonsense assumptions are meaningless; they will simply lead to unpleasant surprises in the event of an accident.

Telephone interviews with several aviation underwriters indicate that it is almost universal in the field to exclude the employees of a corporation under the workers' compensation assumption. In a small, closely held corporation where some of the employees are also members of the same family, many policies provide for additional exclusions to cover this. The variations on the exclusions theme are almost endless.

It is entirely possible for a closely held corporation which owns and operates an airplane, but limits its use to carriage of employees and family members, to pay thousands of dollars in premiums for coverage which effectively is nonexistent due to policy exclusions. The problem is not that such coverage cannot be had; it can be obtained—for a price. Application of sufficient premium dollars can get coverage for almost anything, but the average policyholder sincerely believes he is covered for any situation that may conceivably occur. Secure in this generally false belief, the insured rarely questions his broker about policy specifics. Since there are no incentives for brokers and agents to educate their customers, the accepted industry practice seems based on a philosophy of what the insured doesn't know can't possibly hurt the insurance companies. Today, this attitude is straining the fragile relationship between the insured and the insurers. Since integrity and mutual faith are necessary for any workable insurance scheme, a major change in direction is sorely needed.

Perhaps one of the most potentially dangerous exclusions is that which pertains to those persons who are known in the insurance vernacular as *aviation pros*. Almost every aircraft owner runs the risk of being touched by this one. Here again, the owner is usually confident that he has nothing to worry about; he is completely covered.

Wrong!

Let's assume that you have just purchased a new airplane from a dealership which *is not* located on your home field. You have put 50 hours on the machine, and it is now time for the preliminary warranty inspection. Flying over to the dealer's airport, you pick up the fellow who sold you the airplane and return to your own airport where you left your car. You have to get back to work, and the salesperson will fly your airplane back to the dealership, as a service to you.

Enroute back to the dealership, the salesperson and your airplane crash, killing two people on the ground, along with the salesperson pilot. Three people are dead; your airplane is destroyed; and a mountain of litigation will soon be heaped upon you and your company. Making matters even worse, there is the strong possibility that you will be totally unprotected by your aviation policy due to the "aviation pro" exclusion.

Certainly, *you* are not responsible. The dealer's employee was flying the airplane. If the problem were due to mechanical failure, then responsibility probably belongs to the manufacturer; if it were pilot error, then the dealership should be responsible. And you can argue the rightness of this assertion until the end of time, but under the circumstances presented, your company *will* be drawn into the complex and expensive lawsuits which will develop. Right and wrong and common sense are seemingly irrelevant in such situations. If you have sufficient wealth to make suit a viable consideration and you can even remotely be connected to the case, some plaintiff's attorney will see to it that you are involved. Such legal action is usually based on the important legal concept known as the theory of "throw lots of mud on the wall."

The subject of insurance policy exclusions is almost endless. Insurance companies have developed a multitude of clever ways to avoid payment of a claim or diminish the value of that claim when they do pay. In addition to those that have already been covered, there are the blanket FAR exclusions and the "improper use" exclusion. These two cover all those little technical items:

Was your medical current at the time of the accident?

Did your gear-up landing happen the day after your Biennial Flight Review was due?

Have you *logged* the required number of night landings within the appropriate period?

Did your passenger give you $5 to help you pay for the gas at your last fuel stop?

Yes, my friend, acceptance of that $5 can constitute "improper use." It all depends upon how far the insurance company wants to press the point. Some companies are more lenient on these things than others, and most good policies no longer contain a single blanket FAR exclusion, but to gamble your future financial security on the *beneficience* of an insurance company is foolishness.

Know the FARs applicable to you, your airplane, and your operation. See to it that *all* the requirements are met and the appropriate log entries are made in a timely manner. Stay current for all your ratings and operations, and be sure to *log* your time. Don't allow any vulnerability in your position, due to noncompliance with the FARs, even if your policy doesn't have a blanket FAR exclusion. Should a claim arise, any technical item open to question may be used as a negotiating tool by your "lenient" insurance carrier to diminish the value of your claim. Don't let it happen.

Understand that there are policies which provide for "current replacement value," and that the replacement airplane will not necessarily be one of your choosing nor equipped like the one you lost. The answer to this, of course, is the "stated value" policy which supposedly pays the dollar amount of the policy. Unfortunately, there are companies that avoid paying the stated value by using so-called *depreciation exclusions*. Insurance people offer glib justifications for this practice by saying that the reduction in claim value correctly reflects a corresponding reduction in actual aircraft value due to use. If there is a logical basis for this position, it would seem equally logical to apply this reduction to the premiums, but it never happens.

Occasionally, your aircraft will be down and you will have to rent. Certainly, there will be times when you will want to take some instruction; and perhaps the corporation owns the airplane and you want to use it for a vacation. Due to a desire to avoid problems with the IRS, your accountant advises you to repay the corporation for that personal aircraft use. Each of these situations is just a little out of the ordinary in terms of your regular aircraft use, but each poses a danger of not being covered should an accident occur.

You *can* get endorsements to cover all these things. The problem is that the average business pilot doesn't have a law degree and would never anticipate all the complications which can arise.

If there is the slightest doubt in your mind about just exactly what you are buying, spend the money required to have your attorney read the policy and explain it to you. The danger here is that he will find a million things for which you will have exposure and no coverage. Should you then suggest to the underwriter that you must have coverage for all the contingencies listed by your lawyer, you might find your premium to be greater than your aircraft payment.

The entire insurance thing can be looked upon as a game. The challenge is to find the pitfalls and the traps. The object is for the insured to ask *all* the right questions he needs the answers for in order to have some peace of mind about the coverage he actually gets for the money he spends. Will he fail to ask that one special question about exclusions which will be the case when his accident happens? This allows the company not to pay his claim because he broke a rule he didn't know existed and couldn't understand even if he had. Will the selected company find some perfectly legal maneuver to sidestep a settlement or reduce the amount of the payment? Perhaps they will only postpone the outflow of cash by means of an incessant chain of trifles designed to weaken the claimant's demand for justice. This will force him into resignation and acceptance of a smaller settlement just to end the turmoil.

Certainly, over the years, the insurance companies have been abused. Perhaps this abuse is responsible, at least partially, for the way things are. But, recognize the facts; it is now the insurance company's game. They write the rules, and like them or not, we have to live with them or find another game.

Short of becoming "judgment proof," theirs is the only game in town. Therefore, we must as pilots and consumers educate ourselves to the rules. We must learn to ask the right questions and be sure that we are indeed getting the protection we need and are led to believe we are getting. Grumbling about the inequalities and cursing the system is a waste of energy. Besides, this usually doesn't come until after an accident. We need to do something *before* a loss occurs.

In the final analysis, Richard Bach was right. The best insurance is knowledge, experience, proficiency, and the wisdom to turn around or stay on the ground when the circumstances dictate. There is no real protection—no real security—to be obtained from a bunch of vague promises and provisions on a scrap of paper. A *good* insurance policy may afford us a limited amount of protection for our financial assets, but little more. Our own personal safety and that of our passengers is always derived from what we know about flying and ourselves.

LEGALITIES

In the complex world of today's air traffic control system where the rules were written to the delight of lawyers and the eternal confusion of pilots, it is hard to get an airplane off the ground and around the pattern without tripping over some technical aspect of the FARs. For the business pilot, especially the individual who has just recently acquired that appellation, there are several FARs of specific interest.

The student still working on his private license will be tempted to combine a business engagement with one of the required solo cross-country flights. To a business person this seems both logical and efficient, but the Feds frown on this practice. In fact, FAR 61.89(a)(4) forbids such a flight. Along with several other prohibitions, it states: "A student pilot may not act as pilot in command of an aircraft in furtherance of a business."

The private pilot, on the other hand, is given more privileges in this area. FAR 61.118(a) states: "A private pilot may, for compensation or hire, act as pilot in command of an aircraft in connection with any business or employment if the flight is only incidental to that business or employment and the aircraft does not carry passengers or property for compensation or hire."

Paragraph (b) of that same FAR allows the private pilot to share operating expenses of a flight with his passengers, but does not define the specific limits of what would constitute expense sharing. Your insurance policy, however, may be very specific in this matter; and you may learn that what is allowed by the Federal Aviation Regulations may be contrary to the provisions of your insurance.

Generally, questions pertaining to expense sharing and reimbursement are of interest to the business pilot in connection with lease-back arrangements involving the pilot's own corporation. Another area in which these questions may arise is where the aircraft is corporately owned. The pilot uses it for personal reasons, and he wants to reimburse the corporation for that use to avoid problems with the IRS. These various ownership structures are usually selected on considerations of financial and tax implications, not on anything pertaining to actual operations. It is not, however, the reality of the circumstances that matters; it is how these circumstances are viewed by the IRS, the FAA, and the pilot's insurance company which is important.

To the IRS, personal use of expensive corporate equipment might be construed as "disguised dividends"; and they will demand additional taxes. The insurance company will question the point at which *reimbursement* ends and *rental* begins, as their rates are much higher for commercial operators who "rent" airplanes. The FAA probably doesn't want to be involved at all, but their position will be used by the others to define the circumstances to *their* own advantage at the particular time.

In order to obtain some precise answers regarding expense sharing and reimbursement, a call was placed directly to the underwriter of the policy carried by Joyce Jewelry. This particular insurance company is generally accepted as one of the better ones in the industry. The gentleman on the other end of the phone stated that he was "reluctant to discuss *anything* with a policyholder without the agent or broker being present." No reason was given for this, although he finally agreed to answer some general questions pertaining to his company's position.

Concerning the definition of expense sharing and reimbursement, he said:

> Our company is perhaps more liberal about this than many others. We try to align our thinking with the FAA. Acceptable reimbursement can include all direct operating costs, such as fuel, oil, tie-down, cost of insurance on a daily basis, landing fees, and an additional charge of 100 percent of the fuel for the flight that day, but excluding all profit.
>
> Of course, if you were to use your company airplane for personal business, planning to reimburse costs to the corporation, you would need an endorsement to your policy setting the parameters of that use and the reimbursement. For us, this will be a no-cost endorsement, but you should have it before doing anything of the nature you described.

Basically, the opinion expressed by this underwriter was that the allowability of any reimbursement hinged primarily on the exclusion of *any* profit. He consistently avoided any direct answer as to what constituted "profit." He also declined to express any opinion about the treatment of fixed costs.

On the matter of insurance for a corporate airplane being used personally or the individually owned machine being leased to the owner's closely held corporation, the underwriter stated that his company's standard business and pleasure policy would cover both situations. There were certain provisions and the policy would require the appropriate endorsements; but his company would not look upon either structure as a commercial one. He did stress, however, that this position could not be used as a guide for the other companies in the industry. He warned that some companies might look upon *any* expense sharing or reimbursement as "improper use."

To get a feeling for the FAA's position on these matters, I called the Los Angeles office of their legal department. When the question was posed to the FAA lawyer about the personal use of a corporate airplane and reimbursement to the corporation of expenses to satisfy the IRS requirements, the FAA man laughed and replied:

> I think your problem is not with the FAA but with the IRS.
>
> Reimbursement of expenses in dealing with business flying comes up more in the area of Part 91, Subpart D, in dealing with certain

> forms of larger aircraft and turboprop aircraft being used under some types of 'share-the-expense' arrangements that have been approved in the last few years with the adoption of the new Subpart D.
>
> There's no all-encompassing definition of the term *reimbursement* or, for that matter, what constitutes *for compensation or hire* that forms a nice, handy tool. There are so many factual variations on arrangements that are made that I doubt if you ever will see one.

Since the insurance man was so definite about this situation and had said that his company was using the FARs as a guide, I questioned further, repeating the items as they had been given by the underwriter.

"That phraseology comes from Subpart D," the lawyer replied. "That 'plus 100 percent' is the magic phrase. The itemization that they are talking about is in 91.181(d) and can apply to a couple of different types of flights, but we don't have anything comparable, as such, applicable to small aircraft in Part 91 operations."

As they pertain to business pilots, the Federal Aviation Regulations split along a line between flying for business and the business of flying. The former is the situation which concerns the average business pilot and is covered in FAR Part 91; the latter describes operations which derive their primary income from flying and are generally covered in Parts 121 and 135. There are some commercial operations conducted under Part 91, but they do not include the type of operation being conducted by the average business pilot. Some large corporate flight departments, however, might inadvertently slip across the line due to structuring suggested by an accountant or lawyer who failed to do his homework in the FARs.

For the majority of us in business flying, our concern with the FARs will be the same as any other private pilot who flies for his own pleasure. We must observe the applicable operational requirements of Part 91 and the appropriate certification requirements of Part 61. We must stay current and log night and instrument experience, along with fulfilling the requirements of the Biennial Flight Review. We must maintain our equipment in accordance with applicable FARs, but 100-hour inspections are not mandatory.

If the occasion should ever arise that you are charged with some violation of an FAR, the best advice that I have ever seen was presented by Bob Buck in *Flying Know-How*. The rule, in dealing with the FAA according to Buck, is "Don't say anything unless requested, and then say as little as possible."

THE POLITICAL PROBLEM

If the proverbial three blind men were set the task of researching and describing an elephant and each was respectively given the tail, the trunk, and a leg, it is easy to see that the resulting descriptions might not draw an accurate picture of the animal. So it is with almost everything: Varying points of view generate varying perceptions of reality. These perceptions will not alter the objective realities of the item under examination, but the differing perspectives will have a marked effect upon the behavior of the perceivers toward the entity in question.

The current energy flap is a typical case of blind men and elephants. The CIA claims that fuel demands will totally outstrip availability by 1985; this is in complete conflict with a United Nations study done by seventy geologists who forecast at least another 100 years of plentiful fossil fuel. The president of Arco predicts rationing and advocates a gasoline tax of 50 cents per gallon to discourage consumption, which seems naive since gasoline prices have already increased more than 30 cents per gallon following the original Arab oil embargo and the motorists have continued to drive and consume as much as ever. Although the "facts" pertaining to our energy problems are contradictory and muddled, you may be assured that the people of the United States will be subjected to the elephantine weight of yet another wasteful, inefficient, and burdensome bureaucracy.

Politicians are the consumate opportunists. Mention a problem, and they cannot resist elevating it into a crisis. That the facts are missing or not clear will be irrelevant; something must be done. The political solution proposed, of course, is always one which increases the power of government and reduces individual freedom. Politically inspired answers will invariably be expensive, coercive, and ineffective. This seems an immutable rule, as if it were chiseled on tablets of stone.

Your freedom to fly, unfortunately, is totally enmeshed in the political decisions which will be made pertaining to the automobile. Although general aviation is generally more fuel-efficient than most other forms of transportation and consumes a miniscule portion of the fossil fuel used, when the politicians begin searching for a scapegoat in the energy situation, general aviation will be a prime target. Little airplanes are not very popular with the uninformed general public, so they will be an ideal victim for the pandering politicians who wish to appear to be doing something about the energy problem.

When the suburbanite is faced with gasoline prices of $2 per gallon, rationing books, or both, he will rail against the waste of his precious fuel by a bunch of "fat cats" flitting around in "Piper Cubs." He will find a lot of support for that position. As demonstrated in 1973, the politicians are eager to cut back on this "outrageous waste of energy." Our elected officials know that there are more votes to be garnered from nonpilots than from pilots, and they will act accordingly.

If you wish to protect not only your investment in your airplane but also your business and your home, you should make time to become involved in your government, while you still have a choice. When *Flying* or *AOPA Pilot* takes an editorial stand about a political issue, make a point of supporting them. Write a letter to your member of Congress.

Become a goodwill ambassador for general aviation; spread the word about the important role your aircraft plays in your business. Educate your neighbors, customers, and suppliers to the facts of general aviation. Tell them how efficient our airplanes are. And always fly carefully and courteously. Safety, noise, pollution, and energy will be the issues upon which we can expect to be attacked. We should be ready to answer any attack with facts, information, and favorable statistics.

If we are to continue to have adequate fuel and access to our airports and if we are serious about protecting our freedom to fly and our investment in flying hardware, we can no longer afford to sit back while AOPA, NBAA, GAMA, and the other interested organizations carry our fight to Washington. We must *all* become involved as individuals. We must help our elected officials, on the national, state, and local levels, to learn the facts and the importance of business flying. If we are apathetic about this task, then we need not be concerned over hangars, airports, insurance, and aviation thieves. These problems will become academic. Business flying will simply succumb to the political problem. We will be priced, taxed, and regulated right out of existence.

CHAPTER SEVEN

Planning—Here and There

THE COMPANY LOCATION

Right at this moment, the location of your company is a fixed item. It is where it is. Either you own a building which houses your business or you are committed to a lease which ties you to a specific location for a certain amount of time. You may not be planning a move at any time in the near future, but should relocation become an item for evaluation, be certain to consider your company airplane in your plans and decisions.

Give lots of consideration to the position of local politicians toward general aviation. Do they encourage the development of airport industrial parks, or have they been active in trying to close down the only airport in miles? It is a safe bet that a political body which is antiaviation will also be very antibusiness. The two seem to be invariably linked.

Follow the lead set by the Dow Chemical Company which withdrew from plans to open a $500 million facility in northern California that would have employed 1000 workers with an annual payroll of $15 million. The decision was made *after* Dow had already spent more than 2 years and $4 million trying to cope with the red tape and antibusiness attitude of the Brown administration in California.

The cities bemoan their spiraling deficits and constantly cry about the loss of tax revenues, yet the bureaucrats continue to create an increasingly hostile environment for the productive entities in society. Ignoring their own responsibility for the situation, these same political opportunists announce amazement when beleaguered businesses relocate to more agreeable areas. At the inevitable news conference which follows, these Machiavellian manipulators will denounce the "immoral corporations" who have added to the disastrous unemployment rate, "thinking only of their scandalous profits and not of the social problems left behind."

As business executives, we cannot waste our lives and resources trying to change those things which are beyond our personal control. Instead, we must seek that which fulfills the needs and goals of our own respective enterprises. We are stuck with the imperative of "no other choice," which constantly forces us to monitor the bottom line of the profit and loss statement and adjust costs, goals, and operations in accordance with the realities displayed there.

If there is an antiaviation bias in the city council or the state legislature, then find another place to locate your company. Withdraw your consent. Remove yourself and your company from the tax base of the community which is antiaviation and antibusiness. Take your jobs and your money to a place where you, your company, and your airplane will be welcomed and appreciated.

Urban ills, constantly higher taxes, and unending labor strife have set the stage for the current trend for corporate moves away from the cities. The smaller, suburban industrial complexes are spreading into areas which only 10 years ago were considered "too remote" to function effectively as a location for corporate headquarters. Much of this "suburbanization" of industry is due to the effectiveness of business aircraft and the fact that more and more communities are supporting the idea of airport industrial parks.

When considering a future move of your own corporate headquarters, remember that government which is responsive to the needs of aviation will most probably be equally responsive in other areas of concern for business executives.

Should you decide that an airport industrial park would fit into your future plans, make the specific location selected the subject of thorough and continuing research. Check into city, state, and county tax structures. Attend meetings of the city council and airport boards to get the flavor of the local political stew. Examine the zoning "master plan" if such a thing exists. Find out, if possible, where the community intends to go in the future.

Talk with local pilots and get a picture of the airport situation from their viewpoint. Look into what type of instrument approaches are available at that airport and if there are any changes planned in the immediate future. This type of information can sometimes be obtained over a cup of coffee with a local employee of the FAA.

Look at the surrounding terrain. Investigate the local weather patterns. Check your charts for alternates. What sort of approaches are available at those alternates, and what kind of terrain lies between?

When you move to your new home, you want to be happy there. The best way to ensure this is by avoiding unpleasant surprises. Look into *everything* before making any long-term and expensive commitments.

AT THE OTHER END

The prime reason that entrepreneurs become involved in business flying is to utilize an alternate form of transportation which is convenient, economical, and adaptable to their specific travel needs. To obtain the maximum return on what is usually a large capital investment, however, requires a good deal of planning, preparation, and attention to the logistics of every trip. The success or failure of any business trip will, in large measure, be determined by the preparations made weeks before your actual departure. This planning is even more important when you travel in a small airplane.

Create a complete itinerary before you leave. In your appointment book, establish target dates for each of the cities you plan to visit. At first, these will only be tentative and will progress from one place to the next according to the most efficient flight route. This original sketch of the trip will be modified as you call your customers and establish solid appointments.

Once an overview of the entire trip is relatively well formed, you can begin working out the details of which airports you'll be flying into and where you will be needing a rental car and a room. Then, the bulk of the reservations can be made. If your itinerary lists a city which is not included in your regular *Jeppesen Airway Manual* Service, you will want to order a "trip kit" sufficiently in advance of your departure date.

Always allow plenty of time to put your trip together. If you wait until the last few days before departure, things will be forgotten and the efficiency of the entire trip will suffer. Develop a checklist which calls out the necessary equipment, materials, and actions needed to make your trip a success.

Recognize that when you launch a 2- or 3-week sales trip across the United States, this is tantamount to moving an entire sales office around the country. To be successful requires that you have the appropriate records pertaining to your customers and prospects. You will need names, addresses, phone numbers, purchase history, and perhaps the status of their current orders. All this information wants to be reduced down to its smallest possible size and weight, since you will be traveling in a small airplane and not in a truck.

We have found the most convenient arrangement of organizing this material is by creation of a "city folder." This is an 8½-by-11-inch, double-pocket folder that can be obtained at any stationer or school supply store. Photocopies are made of the customer accounts receivable ledger, which gives the name, address, and complete purchasing history on the account. A carbon copy of current invoices and sales orders provides information on current order status, and 3-by-5-inch index cards are used to keep track of prospects.

Local street maps, which can be obtained from real estate offices, stationers, or from a coin-operated vending machine, are also kept in this city folder. Notes pertaining to local motels, car-rental agencies, restaurants, and other strictly local data are made and then kept in the city folder. We find that recording the names of the people who work at the places you stay, eat, and rent cars is a very helpful thing. Being able to greet these people with their own names, when you get into town on your next trip, impresses them; and you will get much better service. Because they have become important to you, you will become important to them.

Our company has divided the United States into separate sales territories which encompass varying amounts of geographic area. For each sales territory, we have a legal-sized envelope, one of those heavy-duty types with the elastic band, into which we place the proper city folders. Then, the territory envelopes, containing their respective city folders, are placed in a large catalog case.

This approach enables us to plan a sales trip, place the appropriate territory envelopes in a single case, and leave Los Angeles confident that we will have everything we need to conduct our business knowledgeably at the other end. This reduces the need for long-distance telephone calls back to the factory to obtain information just prior to an appointment with a customer. Reorders are an important part of our business, and the territory files are extremely helpful in generating reorders.

Usually our territory files for an extended sales trip will weigh about 31 pounds, including the case. In addition to this, our sample line weighs about 90 to 120 pounds depending upon the season. The sample line is contained in three cases and requires approximately 10 cubic feet of space. Often we travel with two *complete* sample lines, but this is normally done only on shorter trips.

In total, we are almost always lifting from the runway with a 1385-pound combination of people, fuel, samples, and assorted business paraphernalia. Subtracting the people and fuel, we end up with more than 500 pounds remaining in the business paraphernalia category, which is distributed into more than a dozen separate cases. Imagine hassling

Carolyn Dosick and Joyce Hansen each stand behind one of the bulky sample lines carried in the company's Piper Lance. Each line is comprised of three cases, weighs approximately 100 pounds, and measures about 10 cubic feet. The special, handmade dollies are used to secure the cases in the aircraft, and they allow these petite women to negotiate curbs and other urban terrain with ease. The business pilot should be alert to the potential benefits to be derived from the use of custom-made cases or racks to adapt his particular cargo to the space and shape of his aircraft.

that on a six-city tour via your favorite airline. Anyone with good sense would recognize the difficulties involved and simply would not make the trip.

In your preparation for a trip, use all the planning tools which are available to you. Consult the *Mobile Travel Guide,* for example, for suggestions on places to stay and eat. Large motel chains publish directories listing all their locations and their rates. Your trip-planning library should include several of these. For aeronautical information, you can go to the *AOPA Airport Directory,* the *Airman's Information Manual (AIM),* and your *Jeppesen Airway Manual.* Personally, I have never found a need to subscribe to the *AIM,* since all my information needs in this area seem better fulfilled by the various Jeppesen publications.

If your product and your relationship with your customers are such that you can conduct your business at the airport, you should attempt to do so. Although many buyers will be "too busy" to come out to the airport to work with you, there will be others who will enjoy the break from the normal routine. There are advantages to this approach for both you and your customer, not the least of which will be the lack of interruptions. In addition to added convenience for you, there will also be some significant savings in both money and time.

Were you able to arrange *all* your appointments with your out-of-town customers at the airport, not only would you save the expense of car rentals but you'd probably be able to see *twice* as many customers in the same number of days. This would instantly drop your cost per sales call by 50 percent. Unfortunately, expecting a high rate of customer acceptance for a proposition in which he must leave his business and drive to the airport is probably unrealistic. Still, it can be accomplished often enough to make it a meaningful consideration.

Assuming you are to meet a customer at the airport and it is your intent to sell that customer something, then you must have a place to meet, and that location should be a pleasant one. Your sales graph would probably bust the bottom border if your invitation were for a business meeting to be conducted on an old army blanket beneath the wing of your airplane. Generally, arrangements can be made to meet with customers in the airport restaurant or one of the FBOs might have a "conference room" available for your use. Just remember to call ahead to make such arrangements.

Many business pilots, who have come up from a humble start in a Cessna 150 or a Luscombe and have not yet graduated to a Lear, are intimidated by those opulent FBOs who provide such services as a conference room and cater to the "jet trade." Generally, the fear is that an operation which sports epoxy-painted floors in the hangars and color TV in the pilot's lounge will be the private pilot's equivalent of a Bangkok tourist trap. Well, that isn't necessarily so. You may occasionally find one of these operations that will "gouge" the little guy, but for the most part, their fuel prices are competitive and they want your business.

Preparation for an extended trip across our country would be incomplete without a look into the pilot's flight case. Here is the repository of those small but important items needed to plan and execute the aeronautical aspects of the journey. The contents of a pilot's "brain bag," like the contents of his head, will affect the quality of the anticipated flight. If it is filled with lots of irrelevant junk, it will be heavy, cumbersome to carry, and provide endless distractions from the primary job. If it contains too little, there is a danger that the flight will wander into an area of unknowns—a place from which some have never returned.

Charts are the first item on the list of required equipment. The extent of your territory will determine the charts you will need, which in turn will establish the size of your flight bag. For instrument charts and approach plates, you may choose between those printed by the government or those from Jeppesen. In my opinion, there is no choice—the Jeppesen charts are superior and their service is excellent. In addition to your instrument charts, your flight case should *always* contain VFR charts for the areas over which you will be flying. If your territory is large, carry World Aeronautical Charts (WACs); it only takes eleven of them to cover the entire United States.

Next on the list will be flashlights. Plural! Two—at least. My flight bag has one D-cell flashlight and one penlight. These are in addition to the *two* D-cell flashlights which are *always* in my airplane. One of the airplane flashlights has been modified by stuffing crumpled paper behind the lens to reduce its intensity until it is barely perceptible except in a dark cockpit at night. This allows me to use this light to read my charts by white light without creating the inevitable adaptation blindness that follows exposure to an unshielded flashlight in a darkened cockpit. An alternative to this would be to rig one flashlight with a red lens; this might even be better, but the crumpled paper works very well for me.

As I was leaving the AOPA Plantation Party last year, someone handed me a little blue and white box and shortly thereafter my flight bag gained another *must-have* item—earplugs. In the past, I had tried several different types of earplugs with only limited success and definite discomfort by the halfway point on most of my flights. That blue and white box contained two pairs of the E-A-R foam-type earplugs which I have found to be excellent. They are comfortable on long flights and significantly reduce the fatigue usually produced by the high noise level of the cockpit environment. I not only recommend that you use them as a pilot but also that you carry several fresh pairs to give to occasional passengers.

Rounding out the flight case will be the usual assortment of such things as a flight computer, kneeboard or folding flight desk, plotter, and an electronic calculator. My preference for the latter runs to those with a liquid crystal display (LCD) rather than those with light-emitting diodes (LEDs) which have a red-glowing display. The LCDs are usually larger than the LED displays and use less energy, resulting in longer battery life. For in-flight computations of ground speeds and fuel consumption, I still prefer the computer side of the E6B, restricting my use of the calculator to adding leg distances and straight multiplication and division problems.

A note of warning is probably in order here. The digital circuitry used in calculators can generate radio frequency (RF) noise signals and transmit these signals to the avionics equipment in your panel. This tendency is generally more pronounced with those calculators which use LEDs as opposed to LCDs.

If you fly rented airplanes or share the use of an airplane with several other pilots, then you should add a spare microphone and a headset to your flight bag. With your own airplane, you can store these very important items in the airplane itself rather than toting them back and forth with your personal gear. In any case, these items are absolutely mandatory.

One final suggestion for inclusion in your flight bag would be a dozen sandwich-size Ziploc bags. If you carry them on a regular basis, you will be amazed at the number of uses you will find for these inexpensive plastic containers. Of course, the primary purpose will be to function as a convenient receptacle and disposal unit for liquid human waste. There are commercial units designed to accommodate in-flight relief of a distended bladder for either men or women. The Ziploc bag will provide an adequate and handy substitute for the male pilot, but females will probably prefer one of the commercial devices.

Resisting a compelling need to urinate until arrival at your destination is more than just contending with a minor biological discomfort. It is an unwise practice which, due to the physiological factors involved, will lead to increased tension and fatigue, resulting in headache and a lowering of the pilot's ability to perform his duties. The problem can often be avoided entirely if the pilot will simply curb the desire for a second cup of coffee before departure.

Most pilots, when they first become involved in business flying, will believe that flight planning and the aeronautical problems of the trip will be the most demanding and time-consuming. This is rarely the case. It might be true for the corporate pilot whose responsibility is simply one of getting the boss to a specific place on time; but for the business pilot, who is the boss, flight planning is only the tip of the iceberg. Fortunately, this aspect of trip planning is one of the easiest to standardize.

A safe, comfortable, and efficient trip involves thousands of small decisions and attention to innumerable details. With experience, it becomes evident that the decisions and arrangements for car rentals, motel reservations, and the other mundane trivia of business travel are easier to handle from the home office than they are at the other end.

THE PROBLEM OF CLOTHES

In a sales situation, it behooves the sales representative to always present a clean, neat, well-dressed, and successful appearance. This is an easy task for the person who travels with a steamer trunk filled with clothes and a personal valet, but it requires a good bit of planning when your useful load will only allow 10 pounds per person for a 3-week trip.

Extensive travel is common for most business executives. If it has always been part of your job, and the only thing which has changed is the vehicle, you should already be wise to clothing selections which are lightweight and easy to care for. Almost all the new "miracle" fabrics will survive packing and travel and still come up looking fresh, but some are a great deal more comfortable to wear than others. In fact, some of the fabrics are downright *uncomfortable* to wear and are prone to developing objectionable odors in an extremely short period of time. This phenomena is well known in the apparel industry, so a knowledgeable clothing salesperson will be able to steer you away from such fabrics when you go out to renew your wardrobe. Generally, the offending garments are those of 100 percent synthetic fabrics.

If you travel for business with two women, as I often do, the problem of wardrobe selection and weight can be an onerous one. Fortunately, women's clothing is usually lighter than men's, but the women always need more variety and matching accessories, so the result is that it takes as many or more pounds to dress the lady as it does the gentleman. Often this problem of wardrobe versus weight is a prime objection that women have against travel in small airplanes. If we are to enjoy their company when we travel, then we must arrange to satisfy their fashion needs. Fortunately, this can be accomplished without compromising either the woman's fashion sense or the airplane's gross weight limitations. All it requires is discipline and planning.

The first consideration should probably be your selection of luggage itself. Many times the suitcases that most people use will weigh more than the items they contain. This is particularly true of the more expensive pieces of leather or formed synthetic materials. They may be expensive, beautiful, and sturdy, but they are too heavy to use in a light aircraft. By switching to lightweight nylon garment bags and duffles, you may easily be able to carry an extra week of clothing for three within the same weight limitations.

Cosmetics and toiletries are extremely heavy. Again, it is the container, rather than the contents, which contributes the most to total weight. By transferring the needed items from their heavy glass jars to smaller, lightweight, plastic containers, you will have gained another small weight advantage. Also, it is a good practice to pack your toiletries in plastic Ziploc bags to prevent any messy surprises should a cap on a bottle of liquid manage to vibrate loose during flight.

Color coordination of each person's wardrobe is essential in order to get the most variety and number of days' wear from a specific amount of clothing in pounds. By following a single, basic color theme, you will be able to eliminate the need for duplication of many accessory items. You will also avoid the problem of having a *clean this* and a *clean that* but still not having anything to wear because the colors clash.

A man should not, for example, pack one blue suit and one brown one. This would necessitate carrying shoes of differing colors. It would also increase the number of ties that he would have to bring along. There would be a need for more pairs of socks and certainly more shirts would be required. On an extended trip where he would need to use the services of a laundry and cleaning establishment, this planning error would increase his out-of-pocket costs and add complications to his daily dress decisions. For a woman, proper consideration of color coordination is even more important.

Rather than carrying one of those popular zipper-topped shaving kits, use one of the new "Get-A-Way" bags with a shoulder strap which will carry not only the necessary shaving gear but also a change or two of underwear and socks. There will even be room for a properly folded, fresh shirt. Here again, the use of a large Ziploc bag will help maintain the freshness of your shirt and provide a convenient, odor-proof container for your laundry.

If you wish to push on the following day in the same traveling clothes, your Get-A-Way bag will provide everything you need for your overnight stay at the motel. We use a small, multipocketed leather bag from Samsonite which weighs about 7 pounds when it is stuffed full. It has ample room to fulfill the remaining overnight (RON) needs of our family of three; and when I am traveling alone, it provides me with fresh socks, shirts, and shorts for several days.

This "one-bag-RON" concept is very important to me since it requires more than 30 minutes to completely unload our luggage from the airplane and then an additional 30 minutes to load it back again. I have calculated that on one of our average sales trips, this savings amounts to more than 16 hours! Aside from this significant time savings, who wants to spend 30 minutes unloading an airplane after having flown a 4-hour leg? I certainly don't wish to.

Packing strategy is what really separates the amateurs from the professionals. Here is where the line is drawn which decides if the trip will run smoothly or be a series of frustrating minor annoyances. A decision error in packing can leave you standing in your Chicago motel room in socks, shorts, ruffled shirt, and black bow tie while your tuxedo trousers are still in Los Angeles. This sort of thing does happen. For example, I once arrived in Dallas with three suits, six coordinated ties, gold cuff links, and *not a single shirt!*

The most successful approach we have discovered to the packing problem has been to "unitize" each garment bag. The procedure is simply to collect all the clothing items to be taken on the trip and then assemble them into complete outfits, including all the necessary accessories. If both my wife and daughter will be accompanying me on the trip, then three complete outfits, one for each of us, will be placed in a single garment bag. Each garment bag then becomes a complete "clothing unit" for the family.

For the business pilot who travels alone, usually within a short 200- or 300-mile radius, and is essentially a "briefcase salesperson," this discussion may seem laborious and trivial. If this lucky individual ever decides to take an aerial vacation and his family wants to bring everything including the kitchen sink along for the ride, he will find the suggestions made here are very practical and worthy of consideration.

A PLACE TO STAY

As pointed out in the following section dealing with car rentals, there are special arrangements between certain motels and car rental companies which create a savings for the business pilot who needs both a room and ground transportation. In addition to those who offer a discount on combination deals, there are many hostelries which will grant reduced room rates for a night's lodging to general aviation pilots simply on the basis of the individual's possessing an FAA certificate. In order to obtain this special consideration, however, you must ask for it.

For example, when I went to pick up our Lance, I stayed at a hotel in Vero Beach, Florida, which offered a reduced room rate for pilots coming to the Piper facility. Unfortunately, I was unaware of this policy. As I checked in, I noted the rate card showed $40 per night for a single. I was tired, without transportation, and I really didn't feel like running around Vero Beach looking for another room. I certainly felt the price was rather high for a place to lay one's head for 5 or 6 hours, however.

On the next morning, there were problems with the avionics of the new machine. First it was one thing and then another. Ultimately, it was obvious that I would have to remain in Florida another day. Complaining of the high hotel rate to the Piper public relations man, I asked him to suggest another place to stay. He replied that he had a special deal with the hotel in question, and that I should have paid only $20 per night. He apologized for not being able to get me a refund, but he promised that I would get the lower rate for the remainder of my stay. He was good to his word. I remained in the same room, in the same hotel, but for a cost of only $20 per night. In this instance, the discount was a full 50 percent.

Certain of the larger motel chains offer special "corporate rates" which must be approved by the head office. These are usually obtained through arrangements made by industry trade associations with the motel. In order to receive this type of corporate consideration from the desk clerk, you will be required either to present a card or give your corporate number.

Occasionally, these reduced rates are more illusion than reality. Through affiliation with a trade organization in the fashion industry, our company was issued a "corporate number" and a directory giving the locations for a particular chain of motels and their "discounted" rates. A location-by-location comparison of this directory with one from their closest competitor showed that the discounted rates of the first were, on the average, comparable to the standard rates of the second. Having stayed at several different locations of both motel chains in various cities, we knew that their respective lodgings and facilities were comparable. Therefore, we concluded that the "discounted commercial rates" of this particular innkeeper were more a promotional gimmick than anything else.

If your business travel requires that you attend industry tradeshows which often last more than a week, you should look for accommodations which offer a weekly rate. The savings can really be significant, and weekly rates are available at more places than many people realize.

My wife and I participate in five women's apparel markets in Dallas each year. Including the time it takes to prepare the showroom and set up our samples before the market and then take everything down after the show is over, we spend 7 or 8 days in Dallas for each market.

When we initially started going to Dallas, the room situation was a real problem. On our first trip, we found that the most desirable motels in terms of clean, comfortable facilities, reasonable rates, and convenient location were booked solid *for the actual market dates for an entire year in advance!* We were able to get a room for Thursday and Friday, but come Saturday morning we had to get out. On that trip, we stayed at three different places during the time we were there. It was awful. I packed and unpacked our little rented car so many times, I felt like a professional porter.

There had to be a better way, and I was determined to find it. Before the market ended, I sat down with the Dallas phone book and a map and began my search for a place to stay during the next market. During this search, I discovered that weekly rates *were* available at various hotels and motels in the Dallas area. Some were places that we felt would have been undesirable at any price, but there were a couple of places comparable to the best AAA-rated motels. Up until this time, I had always equated "weekly rates" with the Main Street–flophouse type of establishment. But, that isn't necessarily the case at all.

For a one-night stay in a particular city, it really doesn't pay to scurry from one motel to the next in an attempt to save a few dollars. For me, the price extracted by the search in time and energy seems to usually outweigh minor monetary savings. Although if you happen to be at an FBO or a terminal which sports one of those illuminated advertising boards with direct phone lines to several competing motels, a little comparison shopping might still be worth the effort.

Almost all the establishments listed on this board will provide the business pilot with "free" transportation from the airport. If your particular business can be successfully conducted from your motel, obviating the need for a rental car, then the availability of a "courtesy car" can be a meaningful consideration in your selection of a place to stay. You should be aware, however, that the motel van might not be available on a 24-hour basis. If you plan a takeoff at 5:30 A.M.—check with the desk clerk to see whether someone will be available to drive you back to the airport at that time in the morning.

If your plans for departure from a given city are predicated on the weather as seen from the motel window upon awakening and low clouds, wind, and rain have weighed heavily for a decision to stay another day, then plan to do so. The least expensive route to take under these circumstances is to request a *late* checkout, planning to leave later in the day if the weather improves. If you contact the desk clerk early in the morning with your request, it will often be granted. Should the weather continue below your personal minimums, simply inform the clerk that you will be staying on.

There will be times when the weather is poor and the motel where you are staying will be unable to allow you a late checkout. The options then are to either commit for another night or checkout and have them cart you to the airport where you can reload the airplane while waiting for the weather to clear. Occasionally, you will be forced into getting another motel room, but far more often, the weather will improve sufficiently sometime during the day to allow you to head out for your next destination.

Many of the motel chains have toll-free 800 numbers for reservations, just like the car rental firms. In addition, some have a teletype or computer-based reservation system which allows you to book a room at your next stop as you check out from your present location. Both of these are extremely convenient and work well everywhere—except on the East Coast where you can have a confirmed and *guaranteed* reservation and still end up without a room. This is particularly troublesome in New York and Providence when the jewelry shows are in progress.

The dividing line between *expensive* and *reasonable* in motels generally seems to be marked by the opulence of the adjacent restaurant and cocktail lounge. It's as if the curriculum at the school for motel management decreed that "boozers" are big spenders and big eaters who are unmindfully free with corporate money. One can almost estimate the room rates and the cost of a "continental breakfast" by noting the number and quality of the vinyl upholstered stools at the bar. Where a single might cost $40 per night in a motel with a "restaurant" and cocktail lounge, you can often find a comparable room across the street for only $18, but you will have to forego the pleasures of the bar and settle for a coffee shop.

RENTAL CARS

If you go by air, be it TWA or Piper Lance, when you get to your destination city, you will be needing some form of ground transportation. Since a collapsible moped is hardly in keeping with the status and image of a successful business pilot, you will probably end up with a rented car.

At every major airline terminal, there will always be several competing companies in the car rental business. At least, one would assume that those colorful kiosks, attended by uniformed personnel, were placed in terminal lobbies for the purpose of competing for your car-rental business. Experience, however, tends to indicate that on a value-for-value basis, there is precious little competition between "number one" and the "we-try-harder" bunch. Most of the distinctions between the two will be found *only* in the ad copy used for their respective TV commercials.

A rate comparison on a cost-per-mile basis between the companies represented at a given terminal might suggest to a cynical traveler that the prices were established by mutual agreement between the various companies. Making this comparison, however, would test the mathematical capabilities of an Einstein, since the rate formulas are practically incomprehensible. It was probably a situation like this in the banking industry which led to the laws requiring disclosure of the annual percentage rate (APR) on loans so that consumers might make intelligent comparisons when seeking a loan.

Although it might seem, considering the foregoing, that one would end up in the same place financially even if he selected a car-rental company on the basis of which had the shortest line or the most attractive attendant, it isn't necessarily so. There are other considerations, such as your preference for driving a Dodge, a Ford, or a Chevrolet *and* which company is offering what *promotional rate* in *this* city on *this* day. For most of us, the make of the rental car is pretty much a meaningless thing, but those promotional rates can offer some dollar savings on your car-rental bills.

There are weekend rates, unlimited mileage rates, and some companies even offer special rates for senior citizens. In addition to the special rates available, most of the major rental firms offer discounts for any number of reasons. Hertz offers a 30 percent discount off their regular rates and a 10 percent discount off their special rates to AOPA members. Thrifty Car Rentals offers a dollar a day off their rates to those with an AOPA card. Almost all the companies have some sort of corporate discount, which has to be obtained through the head office, but this is usually only available to large corporate customers.

Sometimes there are special arrangements between car-rental firms and motels in which you can obtain a discount on one or the other, dependent upon the specific deal. Generally, these seem to be local arrangements, completely apart from the national policies of the firms involved. For example, we received a reduction of $5 a night in our room rate at one Holiday Inn when we rented our car from Thrifty. We still were allowed our dollar-a-day discount on the car rental for being a member of AOPA, but unfortunately, this arrangement existed in only one city in Michigan, and we were unable to duplicate it elsewhere. Some of the Ramada Inns also have a discounted combination room and car-rental deal.

Variations on the discount theme at car-rental counters are many and sometimes seemingly illogical. I have actually received discounts from National for being a former member of the U.S. Air Force. The one thing that seems to be consistent about all the car-rental companies is that in order to get these discounts, you must be aware of them and *you must ask for them.*

In many respects, the business pilot enjoys advantages over his air-line-traveling counterpart when it comes to renting a car. Not only will he receive cash discounts from several of the companies on the basis of being a pilot but he can also arrange to avoid those long lines at the car-rental counter which plague the airline traveler. These slow-moving lines are the natural product of schedules which seemed designed to land a 747 or DC-10 from *each* of the airlines at the same airport, at precisely the same minute past the same hour. This practice not only creates a "crowded sky" but also generates chaos and delay at the car-rental counters. Fortunately, with a little bit of planning, the business executive who flies his own airplane can avoid both of these problems.

The tendency for most business executives is to stick to one particular car-rental company across the entire country. Certainly this can be the easiest route, but it won't provide the best service and rates. The same company in various cities can be so different that it is difficult to believe that the separate locations are part of the same corporate structure.

Don't overlook the independent car-rental companies. In certain locations they can offer more in terms of rates and service than the national firms. In San Diego, for instance, there is a small rental company formed by a couple of airline captains which has competitive rates and provides service superior to any of the bigger companies. Such operations are not always easy to find, but they do exist.

Amazing as it may seem, none of the car-rental companies likes cash. If you're one of those unusual business executives who shuns the convenience of paying with plastic cards and prefers to carry large bundles of money, you will probably be required to leave a very large deposit of that cash when you want to rent a car. In fact, you may find that it is impossible to even rent a car for cash. The reason usually given is the large number of times that the car-rental company has been burned on cash deals. It seems that far too many of the customers who paid with cash overlooked that part of the rental agreement which states that the car is to be *returned* to its owner.

Almost all the major car-rental companies have a toll-free 800 number which can be used to make reservations. Use these whenever they are available and be sure to obtain a guaranteed rate and confirmation number from the operator who takes your call. Make a note of the details of your call and get the name of the person with whom you talked, if it is at all possible. Such information can help swing things your way should there ever be a mix-up at your destination about rates or availability of a car.

If you need a large trunk or a hatchback to accommodate your sample line, make a point of asking about this when you make your reservation. Ask the operator to type your request into the "remarks" section of the contract. This will sometimes help you get what you want at the destination airport. Unfortunately, there are times when it won't help at all.

If your territory requires that you call on customers in several small towns which are relatively close to one another, you should check the mileages involved to determine the best way to solve the problem. You may find that it is more economical in both time and money to land at a central airport, rent a car, and drive to the surrounding towns than it would be to fly the relatively short distances involved and then be faced with renting a second car or even a third car. In this type of situation, it really pays to shop around until you find a car with a simple day rate which includes unlimited miles and with which you have the responsibility of paying for the gas.

For frequent users of their rental cars, Avis has a computer-based service which can be a real time-saver. By having a data file in the Avis central computer containing the customer's name, address, driver's license number, and other such information which is required for the rental contract, counter personnel need only key the customer's "wizard number" into a remote terminal to obtain an automatically printed contract in a matter of seconds. All the pertinent information is filled in by the computer, so the customer simply presents his credit card, initials a couple of blocks on the contract, and is quickly on his way. Certainly there are times when this type of convenience is worth more than the few dollars which might be saved by shopping around.

Regardless of how you approach the car-rental problem, it is going to be an expensive proposition. Perhaps it is a great deal more expensive than most business executives realize. For example, let's look at the cost per mile for renting a *small* car as compared to a general aviation airplane. The following comparisons are based on actual figures and notes recorded in an expense diary covering the final months of 1977. Although the current prices are considerably higher than those used in the calculations, the relationships and percentage differences remain intact.

After shopping around for the best rate available at the time, we were able to find an AMC Pacer for only $14.95 a day with unlimited mileage. Of course, we had to buy the gas, but that certainly beats the competitor's Ford Granada at $22.95 a day and 19 cents a mile.

For our calculations, let's assume that we had to drive 65 miles and the gas cost was 69 cents per gallon. Churning these figures together, we come up with a total cost of $18.61 for a day in the Pacer, which includes gas and the inevitable 6 percent tax on the rental rate. To save money, we declined the optional insurance coverage which would have cost an additional dollar or two per day. Still, the cost for our *inexpensive* Pacer works out to 29 cents per mile, and the Granada, under the same circumstances, would have cost exactly twice that much.

As a comparison, let's assume that you don't even own your own airplane and you are renting a Beech Bonanza for $50 an hour, wet. This is a seemingly modest sum compared to current rates which factor in fuel costs approaching $2 per gallon, but it is consistent with the foregoing and therefore is valid for this exercise.

Using a 70% power setting on this single-engine airplane results in enough miles for that fifty bucks to give you a cost per mile of about 10.5 percent *less* than the rented Pacer and 55.2 percent *less* than the Granada. In either rented car, if the miles driven are reduced, the rented Bonanza becomes an even better bargain. The picture becomes still more favorable to the Bonanza when you consider that the hardware investment dollars you are leveraging are at least ten times greater for the airplane than they are for the car.

Looking at the economics of a rented airplane versus a rented medium-size car from a slightly different viewpoint reveals some other interesting information. In the rented Granada, your $50 will buy approximately 140 miles of travel. This amounts to some 26.3 percent *fewer* miles than the same money will buy in the Bonanza of our example. While costing considerably more on a per-mile basis, the rented car also extracts an enormous penalty in both time and energy, since traveling by car will require a 340 percent increase in the time needed to cover the same distance in the Bonanza.

Even without an attempt to quantify the elusive value of executive time and bring this very meaningful element into the equation, it is obvious from the foregoing exercises in elementary mathematics that on a value-for-value basis, a rented single-engine airplane can be a much better travel buy than a rented car. Unfortunately, this fact is neither well known nor appreciated by the general public, our legislators, or the pesky IRS agent who accepts car-rental expenses as "reasonable and necessary" and challenges anything which deals with an airplane.

This situation is clearly illogical and discriminatory. It seems the reason behind the negative attitudes concerning business aircraft held by everyone—stockholders, board members, and the Internal Revenue Service—is simply that the people flying them actually *enjoy* flying. It is as if the mere fact that there might be some pleasure attached to an endeavor automatically robs it of its validity as a justifiable business expense and a tax-deductible item. In view of this apparent prejudice against anything pleasurable, it seems strange that while most people will agree that the prelude to human gestation is, like flying, a pleasant activity, there is no one clamoring to do away with the dependency deduction for children.

Unfortunately, government employees and corporate stockholders do not have a monopoly on irrational behavior. There are those in the business world who are equally adept in this area.

At the 1977 "ritual" at Reading, one of the major car-rental companies reportedly demonstrated more than their standard measure of avariciousness when they offered to rent a foreign compact car for $24 per day and 24 cents per mile. The usual charge for this same car from the same company was $15.95 per day and 18 cents a mile, while a competitor would have had it available at only $14.95 per day and *no* mileage charge at all. So it would seem that those who decide such things figured that pilots, like oil sheiks, are all multimillionaires and the pricing policy for Reading should be "get the maximum this rich traffic will bear."

Working the figures into a calculator and assuming a use of 50 miles per day in each case, it appears that this particular car-rental agency felt that Reading warranted about a 44 percent premium over their own standard rate and 118 percent premium over the standard rate of their competition. Regional price variations are normal in the car-rental industry, but the situation at the 28th National Maintenance and Operations Meeting suggests something possibly just a cut beyond that.

As pilots and consumers, we are not blameless in those situations where we have been "short-changed" in a value-for-value exchange. For too long, we have given our consent to this type of thing. Because dollar amounts are so often relatively small and any attempt at gaining satisfaction is so frustrating and time-consuming, most of us take the easy way out, rationalizing our apathy by saying, "It isn't worth the hassle."

Certainly, that position is a valid one, but it doesn't require a hassle to withdraw from the situation. Simply refuse to deal with anyone who is unwilling to transact business on a legitimate value-for-value basis.

YOUR LITTLE BLACK BOOK

> Hell, when a Saberliner pulls up, I can pump a thousand gallons in the same time it takes to mess with a little airplane. I just give the jet pilot some ice and away he goes.
>
> Did you know, it takes pumping 35 gallons of avgas to just break even?
>
> Most little planes use 80, and they all fly off to the outlying airports to get it. Out there, the FBOs don't have to pay their help any-thing—those kids work and pump gas just to be around airplanes. Hell, our guys are *unionized,* and a line boy here gets more than five bucks an hour.
>
> *Little airplanes just aren't good business!*

The man speaking was the line service supervisor of a large airport service operation. He was speaking the truth as he saw it. Certainly, he had made some valid points, but his conclusion that "little airplanes just aren't good business" will be true only because his own attitude makes it so.

After paying for the paltry 80 gallons of 100 octane consumed by the Lance, I made some notes in my little black book, one of which was to find another place to buy gas on my next trip through St. Louis. It simply infuriates me to have someone tell me that taking my money creates some sort of an imposition on them. But I was cool; I didn't say a word.

It wouldn't have made any difference anyway. This man "knew" that little airplanes weren't good business, and he sincerely believed that he was doing everything he could for the best interests of his em-ployer. The thought would never enter his mind that pilots who fly little airplanes today are the ones who fly the big ones in the future, and they often determine *which* big airplane will be bought, *what* equip-ment will be in it, and *where* it will be serviced.

Originally, I began taking notes on the various people and opera-tions that I encountered on trips for the simple purpose of planning future flights. It was a means of keeping track of the good guys and the bad guys. My notes were an aid in deciding just where and with whom

I would spend my money in the future. Little by little, however, my notes became longer and more detailed, and I took more time to analyze each situation.

A sameness began to appear.

It seemed a common human failing to concentrate so hard on one aspect of a situation that the total picture was overlooked. This type of shortsightedness apparently can occur at any level, in any operation, and it is always detrimental to the best interests of the owners.

Being successful in business requires constant awareness of the total picture.

By consciously observing the attitudes and actions of line personnel, waiters, desk clerks, service managers, and suppliers, and then *making notes* of those things which especially please or displease you, an increased awareness of the strengths and weaknesses of your own business will develop. You will quickly come to recognize those situations in which you or one of your employees has dealt with a customer either very well or very poorly.

Since there are already so many record-keeping demands made on the business pilot by both the IRS and the FAA, you may feel that the addition of yet another paperwork item is more than you are willing to undertake. Certainly this is an understandable position. Your "little black book," however, can be something as simple as a one-letter grading of an FBO on the face of your gasoline charge slip or a few words in the "remarks" column of your personal logbook.

Do whatever is easiest for you. Use some form of existing paperwork to do double duty. The goal is not an exercise in record keeping; it's an attempt to develop a body of information which will aid you in planning and enjoying future trips. You may find that over a period of time, your little black book is collecting more marks in the plus column than in the negative one. That's good, and you will probably want to send thank-you notes to those folks who have made your life away from home a bit more pleasant.

CHAPTER EIGHT

Flying the Mission

ARE YOU READY?

It seems whenever some aviation writers address the problem of pilot proficiency, the discussion inevitably begins with a parcel of legalese plucked from the Federal Aviation Regulations. The recitation usually starts with a litany concerned with how many landings and how many takeoffs and how many approaches are required within some previous period of time *in order to be legal.* Holy weight is given to this ritual by including copious quotes from the source material, giving the part, subpart, paragraph, and subparagraph where the specific items may be found in the FARs.

This is good stuff for a writer trying to beef up his word count in an article or a lawyer trying to make a legal point in an accident case; but the serious, thinking pilot is advised to recognize that these rules are simply the line drawn between that which is considered legal, and that which is not. Aviation safety cannot be guaranteed by rules and legislation. The pilot who measures his experience and skills against the currency requirements of the FARs stands a good chance of eventually "busting his butt!"

It is a regrettable fact of life that in our society, from the first day of kindergarten until that last day which results in a college degree, our teachers seem prone to indoctrinate us to equate government decree with *good* and bureaucratic regimentation with *adequacy.* It is this brand of teaching and thinking that leads to the situation in which an individual allows greater value to the judgments of a "higher authority" than he does to the commonsense product of his own mind. This is a grievous error, and in an airplane it can be fatal.

It is this fallacious notion pertaining to the wisdom of a higher authority which prompts a 300-hour instrument-rated pilot, who is legal within the demands of FAR 61.57(e)(1), to launch a flight into weather which his common sense probably told him was over his head:

> After all [he rationalized], if I weren't a capable and competent instrument pilot, the FAA [read: *higher authority*] would not have issued me the instrument rating. Hell, I passed the check ride the first time around, and my instructor [another: *higher authority*] recommended me when I only had 41 hours. He said I was the best student he ever had, and he's been teaching for 22 years! He ought to know. Besides, compared to that combination tax shelter and corporate merger I put together last month, this instrument-flying stuff is duck soup.

For the first hour and a half, the flight progressed very well. Feelings of anxiety slowly eased into a sense of cautious confidence for the pilot. Even when the turbulence began and the rain pounded furiously against the windshield, he managed to maintain control of the situation. In the radio silence between tense communications with ATC, he offered words of assurance to his frightened wife. It wasn't until a series of exceptionally severe vertical gusts wrenched the airframe violently, causing the cabin door to pop open, that the flight situation began to deteriorate. Then, in the terrifying noise and confusion which filled the cockpit, cautious confidence gave way to growing panic, setting the stage for the inevitable chain of circumstances which followed. Spatial disorientation came first, quickly followed by panic. The pilot lost control of his airspeed, and in a last-ditch attempt to salvage the situation, he exceeded the design limitations of the aircraft. The countdown to disaster which began long before the door popped open came to an end within seconds after the twin-engine aircraft emerged from the base of the clouds in an inverted spiral.

This pilot was a bright, energetic overachiever. He was the senior partner in his law firm, earning somewhere between $65,000 and $80,000 per year over the past several years. He was 41 years old, married, and had two sons. He and his family lived in a lovely $150,000 home in the suburbs. When he graduated from college, his grade point average placed him in the top ten of his class. He was a moderate smoker and occasionally would have a drink, but rarely more than two. His score on the Private Pilot Written Exam was 96, and he made an 87 on the Instrument. His logbook showed that he had been involved in flying for about 4½ years. It also confirmed that he was *current* in accordance with the applicable FARs and was, therefore, *legal* at the time of his death. This will, of course, be a great source of consolation to his two orphaned sons who lost both father and mother in this "tragic plane crash."

The aftermath of this *unnecessary* tragedy involved the usual estate-raping litigation. There was also a product liability suit filed against the aircraft manufacturer due to the problem involving the cabin door. Attorneys met and hassled, attempting to set the blame for what had happened, but now, years later, the only positive things resulting from this crash are a few minor improvements in the latching mechanism of some aircraft doors.

Setting the legal aspects of the question aside and addressing it with the pure and simple intent of learning in order to prevent recurrence, let's ask—"Who was to blame?"

The most obvious answer, of course, would be the airframe manufacturer who made the faulty door latch. Some might indict the pilot's flight instructor or the FAA examiner who issued the man an instrument rating. Others may call what happened an "act of God." Frightening as it may seem to a rational being, there are even those who would

The tendency for many pilots is to accept that those ATC fellows in the glass cab of a control tower are the "bosses." Many FAA employees have also come to regard themselves as the "higher authorities" of flying since they represent the power of the federal government. Don't you believe it! The FARs are very clear on this point. When it comes to the safety of an aircraft in flight, the final authority is the pilot in command.

blame the regulators for allowing a man to legally venture into circumstances which could overpower his abilities. Finally, there are those few who, even with due respect for the dead, would place the responsibility squarely on the pilot himself.

Certainly, the door problem was contributory to the accident, but thousands of pilots could have been presented with that same circumstance and then flown on to a safe landing. Neither the flight instructor nor the examiner could have known with certainty when and if this man would meet a stressful situation which would be insurmountable for him. Only the pilot could know the limits of his own capabilities, but it is obvious from what happened that he did not, in fact, know his limitations.

It seems a very human trait to overestimate one's abilities and underestimate the severity of unseen problems, bolstering false confidence with the *implied* judgments of "experts." Perhaps, this develops as a part of that same social conditioning which often leads people to be more concerned with what is *legal,* than with that which is safe, or right, or moral. From the first day of awareness, we are taught that "mother knows best," which was perhaps true at the time but unfortunately serves long into the future as a base from which experts manipulate us. We become both the seducer and the seduced in this scenario which recurs so often in a lifetime. We wish to believe what the experts say because they have the wisdom of higher authority, and we constantly encourage them to tell us *what we want to hear.*

In aviation, our "experts" are the certified flight instructors (CFIs) who incessantly quote the FARs by chapter and verse, the bureaucrats who keep them supplied with new material, and the aviation magazines which peddle the wares of Wichita. In addition, there are also the FAA examiners, designees, and check pilots. Some of these experts are truly masters in the field of aviation and have a great deal to offer in the way of experience, knowledge, and understanding of the world of flight. The wise pilot will "pick the brains" of the valid expert for everything that he can possibly learn, but he will always make *his own* decisions when he's laying his life on the line.

Flight instructors are not gods, and the FAA is not infallible. One should never be overly impressed or intimidated by credentials. Airplanes are not impressed by the number of hours a pilot has in his logbook, nor will a thunderstorm be intimidated by a list of certificates a pilot carries in his wallet. The world of flight is governed by laws that the bureaucrat cannot change, and these are the laws which should be of prime concern to the pilot who wants to survive.

There are times when a pilot must say: "No, this is not for me. It is not in keeping with what I know and understand about flight. It is not safe, and I *will* not do it."

For Robert Buck, the author of *Flying Know-How,* one such time occurred for him during an instrument check ride in a Lockheed Constellation. Describing the incident in his book, Buck relates that is was "a winter day of gusty winds, low gray racing clouds that spit snow showers, and that down-in-the-seat, up-against-the-belt kind of turbulence."

The flight was set up to make a three-engine landing, which Buck felt was "pretty interesting under the conditions." Then the check pilot pulled another engine, leaving the Connie with only two developing power. It was to be a *two-engine* approach and landing.

"I wasn't about to do something as silly as that," Buck relates. "Without stopping to think for long, I can count five friends who were killed during checks or checkouts in the years I was with an airline."

Buck refused to play the check pilot's game; and when the latter insisted that the maneuver was part of the check, Buck replied, "Well . . . I've just busted the check, so let's turn on that other fan and go back home."

For a pilot whose livelihood depends upon passing check rides, that decision not to participate in something which he judged to be "silly" took a great deal of courage. Bob Buck was not intimidated by the credentials of a check pilot. He analyzed the situation, made a judgment and a decision based on his knowledge and his experience, and proceeded to function in accordance with that decision. With 30,000 hours logged, during which he never even put a scratch on an airplane, the quality of this man's decisions pertaining to flying seems totally beyond reproach.

At the time of this incident, Buck was already a wise and very experienced pilot; he had a wealth of knowledge and background upon which to make his decision. There are occasions for the low-time pilot, however, when his lack of background and his total trust in a flight instructor can lead him into a dangerous situation. The student's innocence generally prevents him from making any assertive decisions simply because he is not aware that such action might be appropriate to the circumstances. He also fears, even if he wants to make a decision, that his lack of knowledge might lead him to some very wrong conclusions. My confrontation with this problem occurred early in my flying career.

Thirty-four days after my first hour of dual instruction, I was a licensed private pilot. I was in a hurry; I had made a handshake deal with a new friend.

"You get your private ticket," he had said, "and *then* I'll teach you how to fly."

This promise was the incentive behind my drive. Where the jump-plane pilots of my previous skydiving experience might be considered house painters, my new friend, Richard Bach, was a master artist with an airplane. Since I had decided to embark on a journey into this exceedingly dangerous activity in which one goes aloft *without* a parachute, it was only common sense that I would want the very best teacher and guide available. With his background of military training and his extraordinary ability to work with ideas and communicate them to others, Bach seemed a perfect choice.

During the 90 days following the issuance of my certificate, I logged 123 hours, checked out in eight different models of single-engine aircraft, began my formation and aerobatic training, and flew with six different flight instructors. Included in this group was Bach's former military instructor, a man for whom Richard had almost as much respect as I did for my teacher. This varied experience was good for me; and it proved, at least to my satisfaction, that if Bach had an equal as a flight instructor, I had not yet met him.

At Richard's insistence, I took some aerobatic dual and other "advanced training" from his former military instructor. The experience was invariably educational, exciting, and a good bit more dangerous than a training flight ought to be. I had implicit faith in Bach, and on the basis of their previous association, I unconsciously transferred much of this trust to the other man. On the sixth of June, however, one of our flights together came very close to being a final one for both of us. Barely 4 months after my first flight as a student, that day marked the end of my aeronautical innocence.

We were enroute from Merced to Santa Monica, and I was flying a dilapidated old Luscombe while Bach's former C-119 instuctor slept in the right seat. Approaching the mountains surrounding the San Fernando Valley, the patchy clouds beneath us turned into a broken layer. Ahead of us, well beyond the mountain range, I saw an area which appeared to be a hole in the cloud deck.

Arriving over the hole, I pulled the power back and began a steeply banked spiral. The change in sound and attitude disturbed my sleeping companion. He sat upright in his seat and queried me about the situation. I briefed him about the conditions at the Newhall Pass and related my plan to descend through the hole and proceed under the cloud deck to Santa Monica via the San Diego Freeway. If necessary, we could always divert to Van Nuys.

He nodded his agreement, shook the control stick to indicate his desire to fly the airplane. "I've got it," he said as he took the stick. "We'll spin down."

We entered the spin at 6500 feet above a residential area just south of the Ventura Freeway. We were directly above a home with a swimming pool; I used this as a reference to count off the turns. After six revolutions, the instructor attempted to recover from the spin, but we continued to turn and I continued to count. The swimming pool was becoming larger. Curiously, there was no appearance of "ground rush" as I had seen once when my parachute had malfunctioned, letting me fall to within less than 500 feet of the ground before I was able to get it open. This seemed such a strange thought to be having while I sat in an airplane spinning toward the earth, more a spectator to a movie drama than a participant in reality.

After thirteen turns, it was evident that my companion was both confused and concerned. He had repeatedly applied the standard spin recovery techniques without success. After the tenth turn, he began application of full power along with his control movements. His brow was furrowed in intense concentration, like the stereotyped taxpayer puzzling over his Form 1040 on April fifteenth. He was mumbling something about this airplane; it was an A Model Luscombe which had been converted to an E.

Now I was beginning to get quite concerned. We had both spun Luscombes before—many times. They had always reacted predictably, but he had recently acquired this machine, and it was chilling to learn that he had never spun this one before!

"I just don't understand it," he said. "I just don't understand what could be causing this."

At seventeen turns the swimming pool had become much larger. Still there was no "ground rush," but, of course, there shouldn't have been since our rate of descent in the spinning Luscombe was nothing near the 183 feet per second I had experienced as a falling skydiver.

"Wonder what that last quarter-turn will look like?" The question was asked in a calm, even manner; it was devoid of fear, but the message was clear—the flight instructor had resigned himself to dying in the immediate future. But, I had not!

The rudder pedals under my feet were completely without resistance. It was as if the cables had been cut. There was nothing there.

In an act of pure desperation, I slammed the control stick forward with such force and violence that the stick itself was bent and my knuckles left an impression in the aluminum of the instrument panel. Following the instructor's previous actions, I firewalled the throttle and then kicked the left rudder pedal viciously.

The little airplane responded by pitching forward in a grotesque, negative-G maneuver resembling something like an outside snap roll. We went inverted and then rolled into level flight with a slight nose-down pitch. The altimeter read 1600 feet. We had lost 4900 feet during this episode. After *nineteen turns*, we were barely 700 feet above the terrain.

We both were emotionally shaken. This had been an experience of the type which rarely allows the participants to examine its nature, its cause, and its meaning. Usually this chore is relegated to the experts of the FAA and NTSB, due to the demise of those who played the major roles in the incident. We were lucky, I suppose. It wasn't skill, knowledge, or experience which saved us from almost certain death, although proper application of these three items would have prevented the situation in the first place.

A snap-in canvas sling which served as a luggage compartment had torn loose, apparently due to the forces involved in our abrupt spin entry. The small camera bag, shaving kit, and two sleeping bags which had been packed there were released into the metal megaphone of the Luscombe's fuselage. We were never able to decide if our problem was the result of an unfavorable CG situation or simply physical interference with the control cables and pulleys by our errant luggage. Long discussions, however, led to agreement that something in the aircraft configuration and flight path resulted in "blanking out" the tail surfaces of the Luscombe. We had been flapping the controls around in which must have been a virtual vacuum.

Having survived an involuntary nineteen-turn spin, I duly recorded the incident in my logbook; and I made a vow that such a thing would never happen to me again. No one would ever fly an airplane, containing my precious being, into a situation or circumstance from which it would require more than my own abilities to extract us. If I were to risk death in an airplane due to errors in judgment, those errors would be my own.

Although it is popular and many in our society have found logical-sounding rationalizations to disavow personal reponsibility for their fate and circumstance, we cannot, as pilots, afford such irrational behavior. We must assume direct responsibility for our lives and those of our passengers. We choose to be what we are; therefore, we must assume the responsibilities that go along with that choice. If you or I die as the result of someone else's mistake, we have committed an error which exceeds theirs.

When those comforting words of a controller confirm "radar contact," if you relax and mentally transfer *your* responsibilities to him, you're setting yourself up. He is a highly trained, intelligent, and very competent human being who will do everything he can to ensure the safety of your flight, but *if* he makes a mistake and vectors you into a mountain, *it's still your fault.* You are the pilot in command, and it is your responsibility to know where you are, the appropriate altitude for your position, and when you can safely begin a descent for an approach.

That ATC controller is an accepted "higher authority," but he is not infallible; nor is he the final authority concerning the operational safety of your flight. You are. Do not let his credentials intimidate you into doing something which is hazardous to your health and longevity. He cannot know all the circumstances involved in your flight. He can't feel the way the engine is running, how fast the ice is building, or how limited your climb capability might be. You are simply a blip on a radar screen to him, and his scope can't feel the extent of the turbulence that might be shaking your eyeballs right out of your head. Without knowing these things, he *cannot* be the final authority—you *must* be.

The responsibility is yours; make no mistake about that. When you fly, you must be prepared to make your own decisions. The experts cannot make them for you. No flight instructor, FAA examiner, or written test can determine if you are capable of coping with the situation at hand. Only you can look inside yourself and evaluate your capability to meet a given task. This is a fluid situation that is ever-changing with the weather and the ebb and flow of the pressures in your life.

Making proper decisions requires facts, knowledge, and understanding of the elements involved. These do not come without hard work, practice, and continuing study. Nor can they be transferred from another field. Your MD or MBA are of little value when shooting a turbulent approach down to minimums. Far too often, the NTSB reports detail the tragic conclusion of a flight undertaken by a brilliant doctor or lawyer who allowed himself to believe that his expertise in an operating room or a courtroom would automatically follow him and be of value in the cockpit of an airplane. This can be a fatal error. It is an unfortunate fact that the very characteristics which allow an individual to become a successful business executive, doctor, or lawyer are the very same ones found on the psychological profile of the aviation statistic.

With proper regard for the qualifying clauses, 6 hours in 6 months will make a legal instrument pilot, but this will hardly make him safe. These few hours might suffice to keep the rust from gathering on the skills of a man like Robert Buck, but for those of us with just a fraction of his experience, it will not be enough. We must work harder. We must be more than just "current," because our lives depend upon being *skilled*, not just *legal*.

For the business pilot, recurrent flight training should become a way of life. It should not be a haphazard thing. It should be planned on a continuing basis, and perhaps occur more often than it does for the corporate and airline pilot to compensate for the business executive's usually irregular pattern of accumulating flight time.

Are you really sharp on needle, ball, and airspeed? When was the last time you practiced with a partial panel? Were your last unusual attitude recoveries the day that you took your instrument check ride? Have you ever made a no-gyro approach? Could you handle one if you had to? If circumstance were to ask—"Are you really ready?"—can you look inside yourself and honestly reply, without bravado, "You're damned right I am"?

THE RECURRENT-TRAINING PROBLEM

Business executives invariably have time problems. They usually work exceptionally long hours, and they still are faced with more to do than time allows. Historically, family life suffers; and for the business pilot, the very meaningful and necessary demands for recurrent flight training are not met. The usual excuse is "I simply haven't got the time."

This is a very real problem, perhaps not as real as some business executives would have us believe, but it seriously compromises a valid recurrent-training program for many business pilots.

It is not only very expensive to hire an instructor and grind around holding patterns in the company's high-performance aircraft but it also takes one heck of a lot of time. It's almost impossible to get an hour of instrument dual without losing more than half a day to do it. For a busy person, this can be quite a deterrent. To make things even worse, the actual "learning time" involved will probably be counted in minutes. This is a terribly inefficient use of time.

The AOPA Air Safety Foundation offers a multitude of weekend courses directed at recurrent training for just about every level of pilot experience. Probably the most important of these to the business pilot would be the Mountain Flying Course, the Multi-Engine Refresher Course, and the Instrument Pilot Refresher Course. Each of these involves both ground school and in-flight instruction. For the business pilot who has let his instrument proficiency slip from lack of use, the AOPA Instrument Refresher will allow you to spend a pleasant weekend with other pilots and become legally current again. This would provide a good first step at gaining or regaining important instrument skills necessary for the business pilot.

One of the most important possessions of any pilot will be his aviation library. Reading is a means of constantly adding to and refreshing your aeronautical knowledge. It can be done almost anywhere and at any hour. It is not dependent upon the cooperation of any other person, nor does it require time in large chunks to be effective. Fifteen or twenty minutes spent studying a specific topic in a book, such as Richard Taylor's excellent *Instrument Flying,* is something that even the busiest business person could manage several times a week. If you commute to the office, you can obtain material on tape cassettes. A fine example of this type of thing is the *IFR Safety Seminar* from Aviation Training Enterprises (ATE) which sells for about $35. It contains tremendous amounts of information concerned with flight planning, departure procedures, enroute and arrival procedures, and a great deal more of interest to the business pilot.

An alternate solution to the instrument recurrent-training problem for the time-limited pilot can be found in the use of flight simulators, either the commercial units available at certain training centers or the desk-top variety intended for home and office use. With either one, the productive "learning time" for each hour invested by the business executive will greatly exceed that which can be obtained from a comparable amount of time in the company airplane. Not only will simulator training result in more effective time utilization for the business executive but it will probably cost less than comparable time spent in an airplane.

According to former NTSB chairman Webster Todd, "The flight simulator is the single most under-utilized piece of equipment that aviation has available to it today." Perhaps this is true, in part at least, due to the historical composition of the pilot population. The vast majority of general aviation pilots are VFR-only types, whose association with aviation has been generally in the area of "fun flying." The primary attraction of flying to these people has always been the more sensual aspects of flight—the ability to manipulate and control a gravity-defying machine while simultaneously enjoying a closer communion with the wonder and beauty of our physical universe. Since *lots of flight time* equates to *lots of pleasure* for these folks, the efficiency and time-saving attributes of the simulator hold little appeal for them. These electromechanical devices simply cannot duplicate the pleasures of flight on a bright, clear morning in spring.

These "facts" cut an enormous chunk out of the potential 814,667-

pilot market for personal flight simulators which existed at the end of 1979. The statistics, however, have been changing, with a heavy upswing in the number of pilots becoming instrument qualified. Coupled with this pilot response to the increasing complexity of the ATC system and the demand for more productive work from business aircraft, the current fuel problems will probably be a boon to the popularity of the personal flight simulator.

"But it still doesn't fly like an airplane!" This is the most common complaint levied against the low-cost, personal flight simulators. Although this criticism is a statement of fact—the simulators do not fly like any airplane—it in no way invalidates the simulator as a meaningful training device for the instrument pilot. In fact, this cross between a pinball machine and a computer is probably a *better* training tool than any airplane will ever be.

Coupled with a recording plotter device, the simulator allows the pilot the advantage of working on holding patterns, approaches, procedure turns, and ADF orientation problems without the added complications of wind and turbulence. "Not realistic," you say. Well, so much the better. Too much realism at the wrong time can go a long way in inhibiting the learning process. The goal is for the pilot to really learn the relationship between the indications on the instrument panel and his position over the ground. The ability to stop a procedure in "midair" and then analyze the instrument indications and the ground track as drawn by the plotter is something impossible to duplicate in an airplane.

Being able to fly a procedure first without any wind, and then immediately repeating this same procedure with a wind of known direction and velocity quickly illustrates this "reality" of flight. Comparing the plotter ground track as recorded by the two flights graphically illustrates the effects of wind at the various stages of the procedure and aids in visualization of the problem and the necessary corrections.

Positional awareness is what the instrument pilot is trying at all times to obtain from the abstract indications of the needles and dials on his panel. Consistent and repetitive practice on a simulator with a ground-track plotter is probably the best training aid available to develop strong positional awareness.

It is my opinion that without the ground-track plotter, the value of an instrument simulator decreases drastically. This is particularly true for the pilot who wishes to use the simulator in his home without the services of a flight instructor. Certainly, the pilot can get a lot of practice on the various approaches, but it is not until he studies the meandering of the plotter track that he can realistically evaluate his performance. It will be very surprising to many "competent and current" instrument pilots just how much room there is for improvement in their present level of skills. Just as it is prudent for any business to keep good records so that the health of the enterprise can be objectively evaluated, the wise business pilot ought to consider frequent use of an instrument trainer with a ground-track plotter.

The current market availability of units which will allow the convenience and affordability of personal ownership is limited. Only one manufacturer at this time offers a unit with a ground-track plotter, and that comes with a price of approximately $6000 for a complete unit. Even figuring the per-hour value of the business person and plotting that against the time waste in traveling to the airport and back, it will take a bunch of training hours on a simulator to cost-justify such a purchase.

An enterprising distributor for ATC flight simulators in the Los Angeles area has come up with a program which gets around the high cost of ownership: rentals. He offers the ATC-610 with a plotter on an extremely flexible rental basis. The package is available by the hour, day, week, or month. A special weekend rate gives you around-the-clock availability at a price which works out to be an excellent training bargain. By planning your recurrent training for a specific weekend, this rental program can cut the per-hour cost to an easily affordable and cost-effective amount.

To get a feeling of just how much actual use a personal flight simulator might get in the home of a typical business pilot, I rented an ATC-610J with a ground-track plotter for a month. The machine was set up in an out-of-the-way corner of my house so that it would be instantly available whenever time and the desire to "fly" presented themselves. This was done during a period in which demands upon my time were particularly heavy; still the tabulation at the end of the month showed that I had been able to work in 26.4 hours and twenty-eight approaches with the simulator. The cost for this experiment was $275.60, including the inevitable tax bite. This worked out to be $10.44 per hour of use, slightly more than the usual hourly rental rate for the ATC-610J.

It took about 4 or 5 hours with the ATC unit before I felt that I was concentrating on the problems of instrument interpretation rather than constantly being distracted by the fact that the unit does not fly like an airplane. It was this same type of experience in the Frasca and GAT-1 simulators which originally led me to believe, like many other pilots, that flight simulators were, at best, very expensive toys.

By the end of a month with the 610, my opinion had definitely swung in the opposite direction. In spite of its penny-arcade appearance and woefully inadequate course-ware, the position-based ATC-610J can be a very important learning and recurrent-training tool for the business pilot. In order to get the most out of it, however, requires that the pilot exercises both discipline and imagination in creating challenging flight situations for himself on this personal flight simulator.

Regardless of the specific approach taken, every business pilot should have a continuing program for skill maintenance and recurrent training. This is not something to be left to chance or worked into your schedule when you can find the time. You must *make the time available* for this important task on a regular basis. You can't afford not to.

GETTING DOWN TO BUSINESS

In 1969, Richard Bach wrote a book titled *Nothing by Chance*. His premise was that all things happen in accordance with some sort of master plan. Having shared with Richard the experiences recorded in his book and having been a witness to an impressive string of "coincidences," I have grudgingly allowed a minor possibility, though little plausibility, to his thesis. I am convinced, with no concession to any metaphysical concept, that each of us makes his own luck, for the most part, and personally forges the chain of circumstance link by link. In my view, the participant of a situation builds the controlling circumstances by his own acts of commission or omission.

Certainly, there is not an experienced pilot alive today who, if he searched with honesty, could not find at least one flight in his logbook where the balance between survival and personal disaster was held in check by a clevis pin, a prop shank, or the stability of the temperature-dewpoint spread. But why does one pilot succumb to a situation, becoming a statistic, while another lives on to become respected for his wisdom, knowledge, and experience? What makes this difference? We have been told for years that there are no *bold* pilots who are also *old* pilots, but is this truism really true? If it is, how do we explain away the likes of Bob Hoover and a few others like him? Are they just lucky?

Perhaps this apparent contradiction concerning old and bold pilots is due to sloppy semantics. There are no connotations of reckless disregard for the facts in the term *bold;* these belong to the word *foolhardy.* One must be bold to be a pilot. One must be bold to be a successful business person; but if one is foolhardy and disregards the facts, either as a business person or a pilot, he is on a one-way trip to disaster.

The physical universe extracts painful penalties from those who violate its laws and separate themselves from its truths. When Hoover does those spectacular routines in his P-51 or the Shrike Commander, his boldness stems from an understanding of these laws and confidence in his own flying skills, not from a reckless disregard of the facts.

Brinkmanship may be an accepted strategy in business, but it is the benchmark of foolishness in flying. Although some of the basic tenets of business can apply to your flight operations, a blanket transfer of many accepted business practices across to flying would be detrimental to flight safety. The usual standards of acceptable performance in business, even the best-managed ones, are far below those which must be achieved and maintained by the business pilot. For him to accept the cliché "to err is human" as an excuse for poor performance (which is so often done in business), rather than as a red flag demanding great caution and vigilance, would be a gross judgmental error. Complacency in the cockpit concerning a person's capacity to make mistakes is a luxury the pilot cannot afford. The price is simply too high.

Something which we can borrow from business is the common five-step procedure used in creating a business plan. Some managers are able to complicate this basic list by adding innumerable subdivisions and qualifiers, but there are still only five steps. These ideas are not imbued with any special magic; they are simply the most direct, commonsense approach one can use to define, organize, and execute any project from the simplest to the most complex. Because they are general, these steps can apply equally as well to an aviation problem as they can to one of a business nature.

1. SPECIFY THE GOAL

Expansion of the product line in order to increase gross sales by 15 percent next year. . . . The destination of our flight is Salt Lake City— Where are we trying to go? What are we trying to achieve?

2. SET A SCHEDULE

*To introduce the new line in the fall fashion market, fabric orders will have to be placed by April 1. . . . Victor 16 from ELP to SFL and then on to INK. . . . The annual inspection is due at the end of March, but we need the airplane in Dallas then, so we'll—*When must it be done? How will this timetable fit in with other parts of the plan? How will we get there?

3. PLAN FOR AN EXPECTED RESULT

With twenty sales representatives calling on five customers a day, sales on the new product should run about. . . . If our groundspeed holds, we will arrive over the Palm Springs VOR at 1821 Zulu—How will we know we have arrived? What are the mile markers? How much will this alter our cash flows and bank balance? How's the project going?

4. ANTICIPATE THE UNEXPECTED

If Congress passes the new minimum-wage bill, our costs will go up by. . . . If we encounter headwinds exceeding 25 knots, what will the fuel reserve be at—This is the one that covers—"What if?"

5. HAVE AN ALTERNATE PLAN

If the deal in Denver falls through, we will have cash shortages in November, but our open line of credit will provide. . . . It's 2346 and we just crossed San Simon; that means we will land at Deming for fuel and overfly El Paso—It doesn't matter how much things change enroute, Plans B, C, D, and E are ready to be executed. The analysis and the decisions have already been made. If we wait until the need arises before we make an alternate plan, it may be that we have waited far too long.

Although they may not have ever formalized it, practically every business executive uses some variant of this five-step procedure. It is a basic approach to the planning phase of problem solving, and problem solving, in some form, is the primary activity of any business executive. For the business executive or the pilot, the problem-solving routine remains the same: Gather all the facts available, analyze this information within the framework of specific goals, make the appropriate decisions, and translate those decisions into action.

Now, in addition to our five-step planning procedure, we have a four-step problem solver:

1. Gather all the facts available on the subject.
2. Analyze the facts within the framework of specific goals.
3. Make your decisions based upon the facts and your goals.
4. Translate those decisions into action.

Used systematically, these two commonsense procedures for project planning and problem solving will provide a structure within which highly complex situations can be organized into manageable segments, allowing rational decisions to be made.

Clear thinking and logical procedures if persistently applied will ultimately convert a problem into a solution. The by-product of this exercise will be a thing called *learning*.

Sufficient learning, invariably, results in behavioral modifications. The behavioral patterns, or habits, which develop from specific learning experiences will either be "good" or "bad" depending upon the depth and quality of the learning involved. Superficial learning might well create *good* habit patterns, but the lack of in-depth understanding will prevent the learner from correlating known facts when they are presented under unfamiliar circumstances. Maybe, in this we have an answer to that question concerning what is the difference when two pilots are thrust into potentially fatal circumstances and one becomes an NTSB statistic while the other is "lucky."

Perhaps the lucky one was better able to cope simply because he had mentally prepared himself. He had exercised his ability to visualize this situation; he had accepted that it *could* happen to him, and he was mentally ready to execute his alternate plan. Possibly, mental attitudes and habits acquired over a long period of time allowed him faster adaptation to his changing circumstance; and just conceivably, practiced mental discipline shut out distracting irrelevancies, permitting him to focus all his capabilities on the primary problem.

In addition to the foregoing, it is possible that the circumstances of an engine failure on takeoff, for example, will be perceived by the lucky fellow as a totally different thing than it is by the NTSB statistic. To the former, this situation might be perceived in this way: *The engine quit; what caused it? Boost pump—ON . . . everything forward, switch tanks . . . watch the airspeed. . . . Where will I land?* For the latter, the same objective reality might be perceived in this manner: *The engine quit! Oh my God, we're going to die! Help—I need help . . . call the tower . . . emergency checklist, where's the checklist? There's no place to land; we're going to crash!*

Perhaps this comparison will strike many as being grossly exaggerated. It may be, but before you dismiss it entirely, reflect upon your own training experiences as a manager in business. It will be a rare individual who works in a management capacity that has not been confronted with a bright, well-meaning employee who incessantly scurries from one nonproductive project to another simply because he is unable to establish valid priorities and visualize the meaning of his efforts within the framework of company goals. Now put this employee in the cockpit of an airplane, add a valid emergency, then speculate on his reactions and the result.

There is the force of a lifetime of "training" behind the *mind-set* that any person brings to the cockpit of an airplane. Basic beliefs and attitudes are formed early in life, perhaps as soon as 7 or 8 years of age. Unfortunately, governmental paternalism and the ineptness of our educational system have created an atmosphere permeated with disincentives to the growth of individual responsibility and self-reliance, which are both indispensable attributes for a pilot. The maturing process and true education will alter these products of social indoctrination somewhat, but they are extremely resistant to change.

We are all the sum total of our experiences and beliefs. Under stress we will draw upon our previous experiences and basic beliefs in order to process new information, correlate this with old information, and develop a plan to deal with the threatening circumstance. It has been demonstrated that emotional stress interferes with both thinking and memory recall, but those things which will most strongly influence our actions are those known longest and those with emotional imprints. Therefore, it is conceivable that environmental indoctrination which results in a mind-set denying the concepts of self-reliance and individual responsibility might prevent the pilot concerned from extricating himself from his predicament. He will function on that which he believes most strongly. If that belief has always placed responsibility for his well-being in the hands of others—his parents, his teacher, his instructor, the government, a controller—he will not believe that he can save himself; and this will become a self-fulfilling prophecy. One simply cannot do that which he sincerely believes is impossible for him.

When faced with an emergency, superficial learning vaporizes, leaving only those things which have slowly and over a period of time become a part of the person's awareness. For a pilot, superficial learning is usually comprised of all that stuff that we learn to pass a test and never use again, or the rote-memory garbage that a flight instructor wants us to spit back at him verbatim, even though it can be found in a book and the need for it will never occur in flight. Unfortunately, for some pilots, the drill of learning what they feel is busy-work memorization creates an attitude toward learning which they carry over to more important items. The result is that many bits of important information, items which could mean the difference between life and death in an emergency, are learned superficially instead of being *internalized* by the pilot.

To delineate between superficial learning and the internalization of information, let's look at a couple of illustrations.

First, there is the dictionary. It is filled with words and their definitions. If a person were to memorize all the words in the dictionary, he would have achieved a monumental feat in the area of superficial learning. If he were able to organize a small portion of those words into a meaningful piece of literature or a poem, then he would have demonstrated that he had internalized those selected words.

Another example would be the middle-aged man who catches the reflection of his paunchy image in the plate-glass window of a bookstore. He enters and buys several books on diet, exercise, and jogging. After months of reading these books, he "knows" all there is to know about these subjects, but he has never ventured from his comfortable chair to internalize this information by actually performing any of the memorized exercises, running, or pushing back from the table at dinner time.

To be of any real value to a pilot, the "dos" and "don'ts" of flying and the entire body of "facts" pertaining to his area of flight operations must be internalized. It is not enough to simply read about things; you must actively think about them and how they might apply to you in your airplane and your particular operation. You must gather new information, analyze it, correlate that which is meaningful in it to what you already know, and develop insights as to how this will apply to you and your flying.

Start with your checklists. Sit down with the manufacturer's manual for your airplane and go through the checklist for each operation as it is given by them. Play the "What if?" game for each item listed. Make notes about any question which comes to your mind during this process. Review your notes, and analyze the alternatives available to you under the various circumstances. If a question comes up about a particular system, make a note of it and then pursue the answer until you are satisfied that you understand the situation completely. If the manual description of a system is too brief, talk to a mechanic or call the manufacturer—don't quit until you have an answer.

Take your notes and go sit in the cockpit of your airplane. Go over the checklists again. Touch the items called out. *Rehearse* the actions you would take in the case of an engine failure. Close your eyes and try to visualize the situation. Mentally move your hand to the boost pump switch, the carb heat, the throttle, and the fuel selector valve. Create a mental picture of your actions in response to your imagined emergency. If you can't hold the mental picture, open your eyes, read the checklist, and go through the procedure again, slowly and carefully.

Watch your hands as they move from one switch or lever to another, and then try to hold a mental picture of this entire procedure. Practice until you can do it. This is an important part of internalizing this knowledge. You are working to create an emotional imprint on your memory. Talk to yourself. Direct your mental image the same way that a movie director creates a scene for the screen.

Become emotional over this. Imagine the reactions of a frightened passenger. Listen for the sounds of your airplane *after* the roar of the engine stops. Conjure up the sweaty palms, the dry mouth, and yes— the fear—that would surely be there if your charade becomes a reality. Emotion is a powerful memory stimulus; use it.

Get lots of cockpit time on the ground. Sit there for hours; learn the position of every switch, handle, lever, and dial with your eyes closed. Fly an entire mission completely in your mind. Visualize how the course deviation indicator (CDI) will look as you are about to intercept the localizer. Hold a mental image of the automatic direction finder (ADF) as you pass the marker inbound. See your hand on the gear switch, on the throttle, and on the mixture control. Step outside yourself, and visualize *you* successfully handling both the emergency and the routine flight.

If this game of "pretend" seems childish and silly to you, reflect upon the fact that the airlines have millions of dollars invested in what is just a slightly more sophisticated version of the same game. Your "simulator" just requires greater imagination and more mental discipline, but it can achieve the same training goals as theirs at a savings to you of several million dollars.

When you get back to the office with your notes and annotated checklists, go over all the material again. Organize and simplify it before you type up your personalized checklists and numbers notebook. Don't have your secretary do this chore unless your secretary is also going to be the pilot in command during your hours of business flying. Don't rely on the thought that "it's all in the operator's manual." That's very true, but until you internalize that information, that knowledge is not really yours.

After you have completed each actual flight, sit in the cockpit for a few minutes. Think back over the time you have just spent in the air, and ask some questions of yourself:

What could I have done better on this flight?

Where could I have been smoother, more professional?

How can I better organize a flight or the cockpit to reduce my workload?

What could I have done to improve the safety of this flight?

Write down the circumstances, the questions, and, finally, your answers. Writing things down tends to crystallize them, making them more clear and understandable. It helps to internalize the facts, making the knowledge a meaningful and usable part of your awareness. This is an exercise in mind development. To become better pilots, we must first become better thinkers. Flying is not an act of daredevilry; it is a highly complex activity which takes place in a stressful and demanding environment and, therefore, deserves the highest level of thinking and mental discipline we can bring to it.

All of this, of course, is one hell of a lot of work, and it takes a bunch of time. But those are the facts—if you wanted to do something easy, you should have taken up the violin instead of becoming a business pilot.

RADIO TECHNIQUE

There was a time in years gone by when I was dating a woman who would rarely say a word at any social gathering. She would sit quietly and smile in response to whatever was being said, offering only an occasional polite word of encouragement or agreement to the conversation. Everybody liked her and all our friends called her "an excellent conversationalist." Once when we were alone, I questioned why she was always so quiet at a party or in a group. With a smile, she patiently explained her somewhat unconventional conversational technique: "If I'm quiet, there may be some who will *assume* that I'm not too bright; but if I open my mouth, there's the strong possibility that I will *prove* their suspicions right."

The average general aviation pilot should probably give serious thought to this woman's philosophy about keeping one's mouth closed. It is an unfortunate fact that when the mike button goes down and the mouth comes open—that's the time when poor thinking or total lack of same is most often demonstrated by the average pilot.

The business pilot is not the average pilot. Flying is an important and serious part of his total business plan, and he treats it as such. He recognizes the importance of clear, concise communications, both on the ground and in the air, and his years of experience as a manager have taught him that the key to good communication is *listening*.

Listen before you *ever* punch the mike button. No one likes someone else "stepping on his lines." Listen, because you will probably learn the answers to the questions that you were going to ask. Listen, and you will quickly find out who is doing what and where in the airport traffic area. Listen to the Automatic Terminal Information Service (ATIS), and you will "have the information" when you contact the tower. Listen to Flight Watch and the various Transcribed Weather Enroute Broadcast (TWEB) outlets to gather weather information. Listening and learning go together; a good pilot should do a bunch of both.

There are times when a pilot must talk, but before you do, know exactly what you want to say. Be prepared to say it precisely. Write it down if necessary, but don't key the mike and broadcast "Ahhh . . . Well, ahhh . . . " unless you're asking for a DF steer.

If you are making a request for information or service, know what it is that you want. Make the request in the appropriate language. The ATC system is not "good buddy" land and there is no place within it for CB slang. Conveying precise meanings with word-symbols can be confusing under the best of circumstances, so we must do everything we can to prevent confusion and misunderstanding in our transmissions. The NTSB reports on the Lear Jet accident which killed Frank Sinatra's mother and the Dulles crash both demonstrate the dangers of confused communications between pilots and controllers.

A multiband radio, such as this one from Sony, can provide the business pilot with the ability to listen to the transcribed weather broadcasts on both the VHF and LF/MF bands while still at the motel. If the airport and motel are close enough, you can sometimes even get the local ATIS on a unit such as this. The short-wave bands also allow the pilot to monitor WWV on the 5-meter band. This is the broadcast of the "universal coordinated time" (Greenwich mean time; GMT).

Never argue on the radio. It doesn't matter who's right and who's wrong: If you argue on the radio or render a VHF tongue-lashing to a controller—*you are wrong.* It does not matter if the controller made an error; it is of no consequence that he has possibly rendered you an injustice. Bite your tongue. Count to ten. Reconsider the angry words, and address him with a nonsarcastic "sir" *regardless* of what he says or does. If you must argue the point, do it on the ground. Write a letter or make a phone call, but don't subject everyone on the frequency to your diatribe.

If you happen to make a mistake and a controller comes down on you for it, there is only one appropriate response: With all the humility that you can possibly stuff into two words, key the mike and contritely reply, "Sorry, sir." There is really no need to defend yourself; if your actions were such that the controller decides a violation is appropriate, any defensive prattle from you which is recorded on the tape will probably do you more harm than good.

As a pilot, it is distressing to me to admit that the average controller is far more professional than the average pilot. Most of the time, but not always, when there is a confrontation between a pilot and a controller, it is because the pilot involved really didn't know what it was that he wanted, didn't know how to ask for it, or didn't know that the regulations governing the controller's actions prohibited it. To successfully function in the ATC world, we should probably know a little bit more about it than most of us do. The best way to learn is to make an appointment for a visit at an approach control or center facility. Spend some time with these people, learn what their problems are, and find out what pilots do that they find upsetting. Go there to learn, not to rehash some old beef you had with a controller in the past. If you leave your belligerence at home, ask intelligent questions, and listen very hard, you will probably learn a few things which will make life easier for you in the cockpit.

In the field of law, they have an axiom which states that something which looks like a duck, walks like a duck, and quacks like a duck most probably is a duck. This same logic can be used to good advantage when dealing with controllers: If you make sounds like a professional and indicate that your thoughts are those of a professional, you will be treated like a professional by the professional with whom you are dealing.

To that controller you are a voice in his headset and a data block on his radar screen. He cannot see the ratings in your wallet, the diplomas on your wall, or the seven-figure balance in your bank account, but he can size you up as a pilot in a great big hurry by the sounds you make in his ear. He is a trained listener, and he can just about peg the level of your professionalism by the sound of your voice, the things you say, and the way that you say them.

PIREPS *AND* EFAS

One of the most frustrating experiences for a conscientious pilot occurs when he has found the actual weather along a specific route to vary significantly from what is being forecast; and after properly reporting his observations to Flight Service, he later hears the same Flight Service Station (FSS) specialist read off the erroneous forecast to another pilot approaching the area. To make matters even worse, the FSS specialist doesn't even mention the pilot report (PIREP) to the second pilot. This has happened to me innumerable times, and I am certain that many other pilots have had the same experience. The net result has been that pilots simply stop making PIREPs, and the FAA wonders why.

The reasons for this haphazard approach to the dissemination of PIREP information are hidden somewhere deep within the FAA bureaucracy, but they now seem to be aware of the problem as they have instituted a program to standardize the format for pilot reports so they may punch them into their computer system. This certainly seems like a step in the right direction, but it's also the standard bureaucratic procedure of closing the barn door after the horse is gone. After years of bungling the PIREP situation, the FAA has seriously damaged its credibility concerning this program with the source of information—the pilot.

Several years of what I am sure was expensive study have convinced the FAA that pilot weather reports might just be the most valuable indication of in-flight conditions, trends, and the validity of weather forecasts. Based upon this conclusion is the Enroute Flight Advisory Service (EFAS) network, which is heavily dependent upon PIREPs for its successful operation.

The EFAS network is planned to include about forty stations across the country. Each will have one or more remote antenna sites, allowing practically coast-to-coast radio coverage for this important service. A complete listing of EFAS facilities which are currently operational can be found in the *Airman's Information Manual*. EFAS stations operate from 0600 to 2200 hours local time on the frequency of 122.0 MHz and utilize the call sign *Flight Watch*.

Flight Watch is one of the most meaningful services that is currently available to the general aviation pilot. Properly used and with strong pilot participation, the EFAS network allows, for the first time, pilots to share real-time weather information. With inputs from the airlines, calling the weather as they see it from the perspective of the higher altitudes, and PIREPS from the general aviation types that are usually plowing through the stuff, a very realistic and timely picture can be drawn of any given weather system.

PIREPs are the backbone of EFAS, and we pilots should support the Flight Watch program with in-flight weather reports, regardless of how poorly they have been handled in the past. This is one of the few FAA programs that has been designed with the general aviation pilot as the primary beneficiary, so it really deserves our wholehearted cooperation.

The new standardized format for giving a pilot report is *location, flight level, type of aircraft, sky cover, temperature, winds, turbulence, icing,* and, finally, *remarks.* It is not mandatory to give your pilot report in this format, but it will save time and speed it into the system if you do.

Unfortunately, there are those pilots who still have not received the message concerning the purpose and intent of the EFAS network. They insist upon trying to use 122.0 as just another FSS frequency to open or close or file their VFR flight plans. Don't make this mistake. If you need the services provided by Flight Service, then call Flight Service on an appropriate FSS frequency.

Flight Watch is for weather only! It is *not* to be used to file flight plans, or obtain approach control frequencies, or to have someone call Uncle Harry with the news that his loving nephew will be 7 minutes late for dinner.

When you tune to 122.0 MHz, remember the purpose of Flight Watch is the dissemination of real-time weather to pilots in the air. It is not another flight service frequency. Please do not attempt to use 122.0 for the usual flight service business.

EFAS is intended to augment the current FSS preflight weather-briefing services, not replace them. You will still want to get a complete briefing before your flight, looking at the synoptic outlook, forecasts, and the sequence reports. If you are going IFR, remember that the most important weather information could be the direction from your route of flight to the nearest VFR conditions. This would be comforting information if you were to have a complete electrical failure while totally immersed in clouds.

WEIGHT AND BALANCE

One of the best overall compromises in light general aviation aircraft today is the Cessna 182 Skylane. It is a pleasant and comfortable machine to fly, and it combines good range with respectable cruise speed and load-carrying capacity. These characteristics make it an extremely popular airplane with business executives who are venturing into business flying for the first time.

The particular balance of design considerations which gives the 182 its popularity also contributes a basis for the folklore that has developed about this machine. The most prevalent and cherished belief amongst the Skylane clan is "This airplane will take off and fly with *anything* you can stuff in it!" The happy combination of power specifics and wing on the Skylane just about turns this bit of folklore into valid fact; unfortunately, there are some real dangers encountered when this belief is put into practice. They are *not* the ones generally *stressed* by aviation educators in their books directed at the private pilot.

In October 1976, Joyce and I departed Dallas for San Antonio in our Skylane. It was solid IFR for the entire trip with 300 and one-half at Love (LUE) and 500 and a mile at San Antonio International (SAT). In between there was 2.2 hours of negotiating moderate to heavy rain and matching turbulence by means of a panel full of bouncing dials and gauges. The airplane had been loaded carefully. It was definitely within the CG envelope and *forward of the aft limits;* yet I was unable to trim it for level flight! Every bump would send the nose either into a screaming dive or up into an approach to the stall. I couldn't take my hands from the yoke for a second.

Flying a heavily loaded airplane in turbulence was not new to me. With almost 1000 hours in various Skylanes, and most of that right at gross weight, I was reasonably familiar with the flight characteristics of this airplane, but I had never encountered anything quite like that trip. At San Antonio we confirmed the weight and balance data. There had been no mistake. The CG was well within the legal limits; but the flight from LUE to SAT was neither comfortable nor safe.

This experience was sufficiently interesting to inspire a thorough rereading of all my books on the subjects of weight and balance and aircraft stability. According to the experts, what happened to us just doesn't happen unless you exceed the aircraft's gross weight and CG range limitations. It was the classic contradiction of the immovable object and the irresistible force—it couldn't possibly happen, but it did.

This situation that experts say "doesn't happen" struck me as something which could easily lead to a loss of control and subsequently overstressing the airframe during turbulent IFR conditions, so I turned my study to the accident reports.

In an extremely comprehensive statistical study done on the Cessna 182's involvement in accidents, it was discovered that the Skylane suffered a significantly higher-than-normal amount of "hard-landing" accidents. The occurrence of catastrophic airframe failures for the 182, however, was lower than the average for the entire general aviation fleet. Although they may appear to be so at first glance, these two bits of interesting information about the Skylane are not unrelated; nor would it be going out into left field to point out that during the period between 1970 and 1974, the Bonanza ranked highest in the general aviation fleet for fatal accidents due to airframe failure.

The unifying elements which will tie these facts pertaining to the Skylane and the Bonanza together are a couple of things called *stick force* and *stick-force gradient*. The first, stick force, is a seat-of-the-pants type of term used by some pilots to describe the *feel* of the elevator control of a given airplane during normal flight maneuvers. It is usually expressed in subjective terms, such as "light" or "heavy." On the other hand, stick-force gradient is a technical phrase applied to the measurement of the relationship between control-column back pressure in pounds and aircraft loading in G's. Although these two terms are not precisely the same, they are directly related, and many times they are used interchangeably.

There is a direct correlation between the stick-force gradient of any given aircraft and the propensity of that airplane to shed its wings or other structural members due to overstressing of the airframe. Usually, an aircraft with a *lower* specific stick-force gradient will be involved in catastrophic in-flight component-failure accidents more often than a comparable machine which has a *higher specific stick-force gradient*. Under identical circumstances, a frightened pilot trying to recover from a spiraling dive by hauling back on the yoke with all his strength might pull the wings off one airplane and not another. The deciding factor will probably be the specific stick-force gradient of the airplanes involved.

Stick-force gradient is a design consideration, and the pilot's only tool for affecting it is aircraft loading. As the airplane's center of gravity moves aft, the back pressure required on the yoke to pull a given number of G's will be considerably less.

As any experienced Skylane pilot knows, the 182 is easiest to land when there is someone in the back seat. It requires a lot of muscle on the Skylane's yoke and generous application of nose-up trim, however, to make a good full-stall landing out of a full-flap approach when the pilot in the left seat is the total payload. Under this condition, the required stick force to execute a full-stall landing is very heavy. With passengers or baggage in the rear, which moves the CG aft, the stick forces required are much lighter and closer to what most pilots would consider being normal.

The solo pilot in the Bonanza will find that his airplane is very responsive to rearward movement of the control column and the stick force required for a full-stall landing is light. There are many other factors which could be involved in comparing these two airplanes, such as glide-path steepness with full flaps, pitch-up versus pitch-down with flap deployment, and fixed versus retractable gear; but even those items which have bearing on the stick-force comparison are peripheral to the main points of this discussion. The primary concern here is the comparative stick forces required to execute a full-stall landing in these airplanes when they are loaded with just a pilot.

Under the specified conditions, the stick force for the Bonanza will be light, while that for the Skylane will be heavy. The Bonanza pilot will be satisfied that this is precisely as it should be when one is flying a refined, well-made machine like this one from Beech. He will interpret the very light stick force of his Bonanza as a desirable characteristic of an airplane which is, under most circumstances, "an absolute joy to fly." This same pilot would probably describe the Skylane's handling as "trucklike," and he would correctly surmise that the high incidence of hard-landing and nose-gear accidents are due to the 182's "nose heaviness."

This subjective evaluation by the Bonanza pilot of the Skylane's elevator response, under the conditions stated, would be "conditionally correct." Compared to the Bonanza, the Skylane would seem trucklike, and the correlation between its nose heaviness and the specifics of the Skylane accident history is too great to be ignored. To conclude that these facts represent undesirable flight characteristics, however, would be completely wrong.

Although the relatively frequent nosewheel type of accident might be termed a "design-induced" pilot error by some, to a pilot reared in taildraggers, it is just plain sloppy flying technique, due to improper or inadequate training. The heavy stick forces required under certain CG conditions in the Skylane are a by-product of the factors which allow a pilot to "takeoff and fly this airplane with anything you can stuff in it." The previously mentioned dangers associated with this practice will develop from aft-CG conditions which reduce the stick force to a level where aircraft control will be difficult or even impossible.

It is important to note that this condition can occur *even when the aircraft is loaded within the legal limits of the CG range and gross weight limitations!* Equally important to remember is that the Skylane is less affected by this situation than many other airplanes are. This conclusion would tend to be verified by the statistics which show the Skylane to have a "lower-than-average" involvement with in-flight catastrophic airframe failures.

Here again, the message is very clear—just being *legal* does not make it safe. Pushing weight and balance considerations right to the edge of an airplane's CG envelope is something that some "expert" pilots do upon occasion, but it certainly is not a good, safe practice. Generally, they do this knowingly, and they "get away with it." Remember, however, when flying VFR in smooth air, you can do a lot of things with impunity that have the potential for disaster in turbulent IFR conditions.

The area dealing with the relationship between CG location and stick-force gradient is one where the unwary pilot can be extremely vulnerable. The business pilot who must occasionally carry very heavy loads in his airplane should run some actual tests in smooth air with various loading configurations *before* venturing into rough weather with comparable loads. The "book" is not necessarily the final word on what will fly well under all conditions. It would probably be wise to consider the caution often given to multiengine pilots about "book figures" pertaining to single-engine performance: "These figures were developed by experienced test pilots under ideal conditions with equipment that was in perfect condition." The implication, of course, is that the average twin pilot may not be as sharp as the test pilot and will be unable to extract comparable performance from the machine under identical conditions, let alone under *less favorable* ones.

The comparison made between the Skylane and the venerable Bonanza was not intended to imply that either airplane is more safe than the other. These particular machines were selected for illustration purposes simply because they represent specific design compromises which place them at opposite poles of the question of stick-force gradient. Certainly, there are as many Bonanza pilots who haven't pulled the wings off their airplanes as there are Skylane pilots who haven't pranged a nosewheel, but the statistics do indicate that each of these airplanes does have a proclivity for the specific type of accident mentioned. The primary point for consideration by the business pilot is that different airplanes are different; and you cannot always transfer "knowledge" about one machine to the operation of another. This caution is most valid in the area of weight and balance and its effect on the safety of your flight.

SCUD RUNNING

Scud running is not of itself dangerous. It can be done under certain circumstances with a limited amount of safety. The tool, however, must be appropriate to the job. The *scud runner special* should be able to fly forward at walking speeds, hover motionless in the air, turn on its own vertical axis, ascend and descend vertically, and, of course—back up. Even with a limited understanding of the problem, it is easy to see that a Beech Bonanza or a Cessna 210 hardly fits the description of the tool for the job.

Due to relatively slow speeds and a high degree of maneuverability, such aircraft as the J-3 Cub, the T-Craft, the Luscombe, and even the Cessna 150 have been used successfully for a moderate amount of scud running. Pilots who have trained in these machines will occasionally believe that they can continue to follow the same practice of pushing ceiling and visibility minimums after they have stepped up to high-performance retractables. Often, you can read about these pilots in an NTSB report which says that the pilot concerned "continued VFR flight into instrument meteorological conditions." This type of report usually concludes with a statement of the number of fatal injuries sustained in the accident.

If you find that you occasionally play this dangerous game and your *rationalization* is that VFR is faster and less trouble, then recognize that you are taking unnecessary risks with your airplane and your life. On the other hand, if it is a matter of scud running or not being able to go because you're not instrument-rated, or really current, then place a bookmark right here, get yourself to the telephone, and make an appointment to do something about that today.

Scud running in the average traveling machine used by the business pilot is like playing Russian roulette—the question is not *if* you are going to get hurt; it is simply a question of *when* it will happen.

THE DEADLY SIN

Something which has become almost traditional in our society is the use of alcohol as a social cement and a lubricant to the machinations of business. The custom is so deep-rooted and firmly set with some people that refusal to participate in this rite of conviviality is looked upon with great suspicion. For the business pilot, there are occasions where this presents a situation of damned if you do and damned if you don't.

The easiest way to handle the dilemma of drinks before dinner is to take the initiative when the cocktail waiter comes to your table. Don't hem and haw and make excuses about flying in the morning. Simply smile pleasantly and order your drink:

"Make mine a Virgin Mary, please—What are you going to have Mr. Erickson?"

Even if he knows that a Virgin Mary is just a glass of tomato juice, he will feel free to order whatever it is that he likes without any sense of guilt. This is an important consideration. A customer who is in the habit of having a drink before dinner or lunch may well refrain from satisfying his desire for a drink if you don't join him, but the relationship could suffer as a result of this denial. Fully two-thirds of the population in the United States drink alcoholic beverages, yet many are extremely sensitive to any word or action that might hint at disapproval of their drinking.

Regardless of its effect on customer relations, the business pilot should never allow himself to be pressured into "having just one." Alcohol and altitude can only add up to one thing—an extremely dangerous situation. Even a couple of beers contain sufficient alcohol, when mixed with the effects of altitude, to seriously degrade a pilot's judgment and performance. If you believe that a little wine with dinner would constitute an acceptable level of alcohol consumption for an aviator, consider the fact that wine usually contains 18 percent alcohol, more than three times the amount found in beer.

Alcohol does not require any digestive action before it can be absorbed into the bloodstream. The presence of fatty foods in the stomach will delay absorption, but the usual routine for two business executives at lunch or dinner is to have several drinks before even ordering their meal. Disposal of alcohol from the body is an extremely slow process, and the detrimental effects continue for the entire detoxification period.

The effects of alcohol are often misunderstood due to the manner in which they take place and misinterpretation of the lack of observable changes in motor reflexes as evidence that the drinker has not been affected by his consumption of small quantities of this intoxicant. Compounding this problem is the fact that some highly intelligent and well-trained individuals can actually perform better in certain limited problem-solving tasks involving symbolic logic after consuming a small amount of alcohol. Unfortunately, this has often been misconstrued to mean that they are "thinking better" after a couple of drinks, which on a general level is not true.

The most immediate action of alcohol is an impairment of the highest functions of the brain, those which require complex reactions and the simultaneous processing of more than one type of incoming information. These are precisely the functions most needed by a pilot, and they are degraded by blood-alcohol concentrations too low to affect simple reflexes and reaction times. It is this anomaly that makes the drinker assume that there has been no effect on his efficiency. Laboratory experiments have shown that extremely small blood-alcohol concentrations increase the willingness of the subjects to take risks, even when there were no other distinguishable manifestations of alcohol consumption. Good judgment seems to be the first thing that is affected by any amount of alcohol.

The rarefied atmosphere of an unpressurized cockpit adds to the problem. Lack of oxygen will multiply the deleterious effects of alcohol on the pilot. The undetectable effects of one drink on the ground can become the equivalent of several when the pilot goes to 10,000 feet. The result, of course, is a serious degradation of the pilot's judgmental and functional capabilities. At night, the combined effects of subtle hypoxia and alcohol will be devastating to the pilot's vision. Add some cigarette smoke and fatigue and the total effect on the pilot can be lethal.

FATIGUE

Everyone gets tired; no one is immune to fatigue. Certain extremely well trained and disciplined individuals, however, can function in a semisomnambulant state, performing routine duties with amazing efficiency, but their ability to establish priorities and generate alternate solutions to problems is almost completely compromised. The mechanism which allows them to handle routine matters during a state of total fatigue seems to also create an intellectual tunnel vision.

This *one-answer* type of thinking settled into the cockpit with me several years ago during a flight which started in Little Rock and ended in Van Nuys (VNY). That's a long haul in a Cessna 182 which is bucking a constant headwind. It was after dark when I landed in El Paso (ELP), and I was tired. I had planned to stay there for the night. Unfortunately, the Shriners were in town; and there wasn't a room available anywhere in the city. My first thought was to press on to Tucson or Phoenix, but the dark night and the mountains made me reconsider.

It was 3 A.M. in El Paso. I had tried unsuccessfully to sleep both in the pilot's lounge and in the rear of the airplane. The situation was aggravating, and I was somewhat concerned about the fact that my telephone calls to my home in Los Angeles continued to go unanswered. The idea that my wife and daughter had experienced an auto accident became an obsession; I had to get home.

Dawn caught my westbound Skylane at Gila Bend. I was extremely hungry and tired, but with daylight I knew that the hard part was behind me. With its long-range tanks, the Skylane could just about make the trip from ELP to VNY, but I elected to land at Blythe for fuel. I had been awake for 27 hours and had logged 10.7 hours of flight time since leaving Little Rock. I tried calling home again—still no answer. It was too early to call the factory; no one would be there yet. In less than 2 hours I could be home, so I decided to press on.

The L.A. Basin was socked in as usual. I couldn't get a report for Oxnard (OXR), but with the conditions existing at Los Angeles (LAX) and Santa Monica (SMO), the chances were that OXR was also suffering from a solid stratus cover. It would probably clear before I arrived; but if it didn't, I would go to Van Nuys which was calling marginal VFR. I had decided that I was simply too tired and mentally dull to attempt to go IFR and make an approach. It didn't occur to me at the time that if I were too tired to shoot an approach, I was certainly too exhausted to be flying an airplane at all.

Wanting to avoid the jets descending into LAX and an extended flight over a city covered by a stratus layer, I proceeded north behind the mountains, via Palmdale to Fillmore. Oxnard was still IFR with 200 and one-half, so I returned to Van Nuys, where it was "sky partially obscured, 3 miles, haze and smoke—report the hospital on final."

As the familiar shape of the hospital passed beneath the airplane, I made the appropriate report and was cleared to land. I was now within minutes of home, and I was really ready for something to eat and 20 hours of sleep. But—I couldn't find the airport! I was over landmarks that I had been using for almost 15 years, and I was *completely lost*.

The well-known freeways beneath me had become an indecipherable confusion of cars, junctions, and off-ramps. Nothing was where it was supposed to be. The inputs were all wrong, and I was shaken.

I stopped my descent immediately and informed the tower that I was executing a climbing left turn.

"Roger—Cessna 45 Kilo, contact Burbank Approach Control for vectors."

That became unnecessary. As I made my turn, the runway that I couldn't find magically appeared outside my window. *I had been lost while flying directly over the airport, barely 200 feet to the left of the runway centerline.* It had been legally VFR, but I couldn't find the runway, and the men in the tower could not see me. The atmospheric conditions, the angle of the light, and the position of the aircraft over the ground had managed to make an enormous dual-runway airport completely invisible.

Joyce was at the factory when I called; our home phone had been out of order for several days. I was extremely relieved. There had never been any need for my anxiety. As I waited for her to come for me, I made notes about my flight. It had taken 14.6 hours of actual flight time on the tach for the trip from Little Rock to Van Nuys, and I had been awake for almost 32 hours. With all my wandering around included, the less-than-2-hour flight from Blythe had taken 3.9 hours, so the decision to refuel had been a good one.

For weeks I pondered my notes and questioned why an experienced instrument-rated pilot would blunder around the sky as I had done, becoming lost over the runway and completely ignoring the fact that Van Nuys had both a localizer approach available and a very-high-frequency omnirange (VOR) at the end of the runway. I hadn't even turned on the nav radios! It didn't occur to me to do so; I was maintaining a VFR operation. Everything I needed to know was outside the window.

It was evident that I had been functioning on long-established habits which prevented me from making any fatal mistakes, *but I wasn't thinking.* I had been suffering from an extreme case of mental rigidity. In retrospect it seemed incomprehensible that I had been so determined to remain VFR. It was a classic case of got to get there, compounded by extreme fatigue which caused a mental fixation on the VFR operation. In my mind there was no alternate plan; there simply were no other choices that I could see.

It would have been an easy matter to label my actions as "stupid," and then dismiss them; but that seemed to be a very simplistic answer to the questions created by this experience. I was intrigued by the many similarities between my flight and that of other pilots whom I had read about in accident reports. The details always showed that there were innumerable opportunities to alter the final outcome of the ill-fated flights, but the pilots involved were seemingly blind to all the choices which were quite obvious to any knowledgeable and thinking pilot who read about their mistakes. In the past, confident in a self-righteous knowledge that I would never make such mistakes, it was simple to second-guess these errant pilots and find them stupid. That was before I had made some of them and survived to reflect upon this fact.

Why would experienced and knowledgeable pilots be blind to things which are obvious to a student? What would cause such individuals to fixate on a single item to the exclusion of all other data inputs? What is the cause of this mental rigidity? Is there a relationship between this and the circadian rhythms, the biological clock, and the "jet" syndrome? What effect do blood-sugar levels have on mental flexibility, and how does what a pilot eats alter his performance capability? How does the accumulation of fatigue toxins specifically depress activity in the central nervous system? What bearing would this phenomena have on the pilot's ability to see, know, and remember? How does the bodily chemical balance, which is affected by both flight and fatigue, influence the electrochemical functioning of the synapses, and how would the transmission of nerve impulses alter or inhibit problem-solving abilities?

There are so many questions which we still cannot answer pertaining to the functioning of the human mind that it seems presumptuous to conclude pilots involve themselves in accidents simply because they are stupid. Even though we do not have all the answers relative to the physiological conditions which influence pilot thinking, common sense tells us that a healthy, well-fed, and rested pilot performs better than one who is not. Fatigue is a very real problem, and every pilot should be aware of its potential impact upon flight safety. The debilitating effects of fatigue cannot be overcome by sheer determination and will. There is an extreme danger for the business pilot who attempts to do so. As an entrepreneur, he is accustomed to driving himself beyond the limits normally accepted by others, but this practice must never be carried over to flying where even little mistakes can be fatal.

CRASHING

The two most deficient areas of pilot training for the general aviation pilot are flying thunderstorms and crashing airplanes. The reasons for this extend from simple lack of knowledge to a fear that mention of some of the realities of flying will discourage potential pilots and *aircraft buyers* from becoming involved in aviation. In many ways, the industry's handling of these two subjects parallels the position held by some folks concerning sex education for children: If we don't talk about it and we don't teach them, they won't do it! Statistics for both aircraft accidents and illegitimate births tend to indicate that this sacred philosophical position is not being taken too seriously by either the pilots or the teenagers.

Certainly the best advice pertaining to either crashing or flying through a thunderstorm would be "Don't!" A great deal of our current training is directed at teaching pilots how to follow this advice and avoid becoming involved in either of these potentially catastrophic situations. For the average pilot, the avoidance of thunderstorms is really easy—when Mother Nature rolls up a bunch of those 40,000-foot monsters, he locks the airplane in the hangar and watches TV. Since the only 100 percent way of avoiding an unscheduled return to earth would be to give up flying, let's take a look at what is known about the subject of crashing in an airplane.

The National Transportation Safety Board's statistical data shows that about 25 percent of all general aviation accidents are associated with emergency landings. It also appears that the mechanical malfunctioning of the modern airplane is less often a factor in emergency landings than are such pilot-induced items as flight planning, fuel mismanagement, and penetration of marginal weather. In view of these facts, it is evident that the majority of crashes could be prevented with better preflight planning and a general improvement in pilot habits and skill levels. Our present training programs are directed at this, and the recent improvement in accident statistics tends to confirm their effectiveness. However, we still have not done much about teaching pilots how to crash and survive when a collision between his airplane and the earth is inevitable.

So much stress has been placed on finding a "suitable landing area" that some pilots will not even entertain the idea of a precautionary landing unless they are convinced that they can save the aircraft. This desire to save the machine, regardless of the risks involved, probably stems from several factors: the large financial investment involved in the airplane, the strong belief that an undamaged airframe will preclude bodily harm, and fear of bureaucratic retribution. Certainly, many of the fatal weather accidents found under the heading of "continued VFR into IFR conditions" can be attributed to desperate attempts to get to an airport because the terrain below would not allow an emergency landing without some damage to the machine.

If you have stumbled along and find that there are simply a few minutes between you and a *forced* landing, then a *precautionary* landing while you still have power to help will be the better choice. This will generally be less hazardous than a forced landing because you will have more time for terrain selection and planning your approach. In addition, you will still have power to compensate for any errors in judgment or technique.

Should a forced landing become inevitable, the goal becomes surviving the impact; the airframe is expendable. It becomes an asset to use in preserving life. Research into aircraft crashes shows that the amount of *crushable* structure between the occupants and the principle point of impact on the airframe has a direct bearing on the severity of the transmitted crash forces and, therefore, the extent of occupant injury. It is imperative to keep the vital structure of the cabin area relatively intact, using dispensable structure, such as the wings and landing gear, to absorb the violence of the stopping process before it affects the passengers. Experience has shown that a collision with obstacles at the end of a ground roll or slide is much less devastating than striking something at flying speed before a touchdown is made.

Speed is the watchword. With too little airspeed during the approach, you may become another classic stall-spin statistic; maintain the optimum glide speed for your airplane. If you have a controllable prop and it is windmilling, you can stretch the glide by pulling back on the prop control. You can adjust the glide with prop pitch almost like using a spoiler since it is adjustable in both directions. The degree of control that can be exercised over the glide in this manner will be very surprising to most pilots.

Contrary to the opinion of many pilots and pilot writers who insist upon stating that a "frozen prop will increase the drag and, thereby, decrease your ability to glide," an airplane will glide farther with a stopped prop than it will with one which is windmilling. The effective drag area for the windmilling prop is much greater than its "frozen" counterpart and, therefore, exerts significantly greater *unfavorable* influence on glide range.

Positive aircraft control during the final part of the approach has priority over all other considerations, including aircraft configuration and cockpit checks. It is very unlikely that you will survive a stall and a spin which results in nose-first contact with the ground. You must maintain your airspeed and control over the situation. You will want to get out of the wreck, so it is probably a good idea to unlatch and prop open a door. Use a shoe or a folded chart.

Have your passengers tightly secure both seat and shoulder belts.

Have them remove all sharp articles from their pockets and remove their glasses if they wear them. Then they should be instructed to cover their faces and heads with any cushioning material or extra clothing which may be available. Tell the rear-seat passengers to assume a bent-forward position like that described in the safety literature on the airlines. These precautions will reduce the severity of the "second collision," which occurs when the occupants collide with the interior structure.

Find the wind, and attempt to land into it as every knot of reduction in groundspeed lowers the dangers resulting from final impact. The prime factors to consider in the approach are wind direction and velocity, the size and slope of the selected crash site, and obstacles in the final approach path. These will most probably present themselves in a manner in which some compromise will be necessary. Generally, the best choice will be a combination of wind, obstacle, and terrain which allows a final approach with some margin for error in judgment or technique.

The need for the lowest possible touchdown speed cannot be overemphasized as the severity of the deceleration process is governed by speed and stopping distance. The most critical of these is speed. Even a small change in groundspeed at touchdown will affect the outcome of a controlled crash. Doubling the speed will quadruple the total destructive energy of the crash. For instance, an impact at 85 mph is twice as hazardous as one at 60 mph. It is three times safer to crash at 60 mph than it would be if you were traveling at 104 mph at the time of the impact.

The typical general aviation aircraft today is designed to provide protection in a crash landing which results in deceleration forces of 9G's in a forward direction. Assuming that a uniform force of 9G's could be maintained, it would require a distance of 9.4 feet to decelerate from 50 mph, and it would require four times that distance to decelerate from 100 mph.

When a normal touchdown is assured and there is ample stopping distance, a gear-up landing on level, but soft, terrain, such as a plowed field, may result in less aircraft damage than a gear-down landing. A hard-and-fast rule, however, concerning the best position of a retractable landing gear cannot be given. I believe that I would elect to leave the gear in the UP position in most instances. Although there are some very good arguments about having the gear down to absorb a lot of the energy from the impact as it collapses, my reservation stems from the feeling that in the tricycle-geared airplane, those forces which would shear off the gear would also have a strong influence on whether the airplane would flip over on its back or cartwheel. Both of these situations, of course, would be less than desirable.

If your airplane is one of those which is equipped with an automatic gear extension system, the first action you must take when the engine stops is to engage the override mechanism. You will not want all that extra drag to be thrust upon you at the discretion of the system's sensors.

Crashing is at best an unpleasant subject, but every pilot should give some thought to it and occasionally review the considerations offered here. Being mentally prepared can increase the odds in your favor should you be subjected to one of those extremely rare mechanical malfunctions which results in engine failure.

CHAPTER NINE

The Survival Situation

Survival is cursing the darkness in an act of defiance when there are no candles left to light. It is the determination to endure. It is the will to live—the commitment to continue the process of life for just one minute more.

The single constant which spans time and species is the will to live. It is this which links the Wall Street broker with the Neanderthal. Passed along in the genes and chromosomes from generation to generation, this inherent quality has endured. The transient skills of hunting, tanning hides, and blacksmithing have given way to checkbook balancing and tax-form preparation in adaptation to the requirements of the times. The prime force, however, remains unchanged.

It is this *will to live* which allows the individual to adapt to his changing environment. This is the wellhead of resourcefulness. It is the great compensator which allows a human being to overcome his lack of specific skills and provisions and participate in the documented "miracles" of wilderness survival.

For example, Ralph Flores, a California pilot, and Helen Klaben, a New York student, crashed a small plane in the desolation of British Columbia. They endured the driving snow and temperatures of 40 degrees below zero for 7 weeks before they were rescued. They had both suffered severe injuries.

"We never gave up at any time," said Flores, carrying a Bible and a volume of Robert Service poems which he and Klaben had read from cover to cover during their ordeal.

Flores and Klaben were not prepared for survival. Their entire store of provisions consisted of two cans of sardines, two cans of fruit salad, and a box of crackers; yet, they survived for 6 weeks after the food was gone. They chopped wood with a hammer and chisel and melted snow for water.

"It was water for breakfast, water for lunch, and water for supper," said Klaben. They had tried to catch rabbits to supplement their meager supply of food, but they had failed. They had used the supreme survival tool—the human mind. These people survived because they had a strong will to live. This man and woman preserved and nurtured their problem-solving capabilities, using what few resources they had to protect themselves from two real enemies of life—hypothermia and dehydration.

HYPOTHERMIA

In news reports detailing the failure of some unfortunate to survive the trial of wilderness existence, the saga usually concludes that the person involved had died due to "exposure." This is the media term for hypothermia, the number-one killer of those who blunder into the wilderness, unknowing and unprepared.

Cold is a killer and the inner-core temperature of the human body has a very narrow range within which it can change without adversely affecting both the physical and mental capabilities of the organism. The span is approximately 12° ranging from a low of 92°F to a high of 104°F. Any reduction in the temperature of the vital organs below the normal 98.6°F marks the onset of hypothermia.

As the inner-core temperature drops, the body's defense mechanism diverts the flow of warm blood from the hands, feet, and outer skin. This automatic action is an attempt to preserve life by marshaling the available resources to protect the more vital organs at the expense of the extremities. The usual result is an increase in the possibility of frostbite.

Below 96°F, shivering becomes uncontrollable; and if the temperature drop is allowed to continue, the victim soon becomes irrational, incapable of doing anything to help himself. At just below 80°F, the respiratory and cardiac centers fail, immediately followed by death.

The onset of hypothermia is insidious; it can creep up without fanfare. You will simply feel a bit drowsy. Therefore, it is imperative that you take immediate action to protect yourself. You *must* preserve your problem-solving capabilities.

Seek shelter from the weather and the wind. If you are wet, strip off the wet clothing and replace it with dry. Remember that cotton, which is excellent when dry, tends to wick up moisture, losing heat 200 times faster when it is wet. Wear wool if at all possible. Build a fire and drink hot liquids. Heating the body to keep it within the very limited temperature range at which it functions rationally and efficiently is mandatory. Stay awake!

Don't use the airplane as a shelter except on a very temporary basis. The metal skin provides very poor insulation, making it difficult to heat. In winter, frost and wind can combine to turn it into a large refrigerator.

A shelter should be just big enough for the number of people it must hold. It should be well-insulated and provide protection from wind and rain.

Put on a hat! If you don't have one, make one. Take a sectional chart and fold it into a paper hat. Find something with which to cover your head and neck. Heat escapes from the top of your head at a tremendous rate. This is true for both men and women. It is of equal importance to the fellow with the shaggy long locks or the man with a totally bald head.

Remember that any loss in body heat will cause an automatic diversion of blood to the critical organs, reducing circulation to the hands and feet and increasing the potential of frostbite. It may sound silly; but if your feet are cold, put on a hat. For warmth and protection, nothing can equal an old-fashioned, wool-stocking cap which can be pulled down to cover the ears.

Gather firewood to build and feed your fire. Rig a reflector behind the fire to maximize the benefit of its heat. Don't allow yourself to become overheated while you are working. Dress in layers and remove the outer garment during work periods. Overexertion causes perspiration which can freeze inside clothing, reducing its effective value as an insulator. Work slowly and breathe steadily. When the work period ends, put your outer garments back on and rest.

Unfortunately, most business pilots dress for the client conference at their destination. They fly over the winter mountains dressed in a suit, tie, and street shoes. Rarely is consideration given to the terrain over which they will fly. It should be considered, however, and adequate clothing should be aboard to provide protection from the most severe environmental exposure you would experience should you be forced down. Of course, it would be impractical to carry the appropriate gear for an arctic expedition for a flight from Los Angeles to Seattle, but some thought and survival preparation should be given to such a flight.

IT REALLY CAN HAPPEN

It is difficult, sitting in the den, currently healthy, warm, and well-fed, to project forward in time and circumstance and see yourself injured, in pain, suffering from acute stress, dehydration, hypothermia, inadequate nutrition, and quickly losing the capability of rational thought.

To the uninformed, it seems farfetched to consider that the span of a few days and the lack of a few quarts of water could totally disable the human mind and body. However, those who work in search and rescue can verify the debilitating and often fatal results of hypothermia and dehydration.

Perhaps it is this difficulty of visualizing and personalizing the survival situation which prevents most pilots from taking proper steps to be prepared should the *unthinkable* ever actually happen. It is so simple for the self-examining *self* to support the concept of it always happens to the other fellow. Almost without exception, newspaper and magazine accounts of a survival ordeal point out that the participants provoked the situation by breaking one or more commonsense rules of flying. The NTSB statistics confirm that it is very uncommon for fate to conspire against a careful pilot and throw him and his passengers into a hostile environment and the survival situation.

But, it does happen.

A balky fuel pump, a broken oil line, or a fractured crankshaft can transform a methodical systems manager in the controlled environment of his airplane into a frightened, vulnerable being in an alien, uncompromising world. The transition requires but a few minutes.

In necktie and Gucci loafers, a frozen propeller will transport you to a set of problems not covered in your college classes on managerial accounting and business statistics. The problem now is primal—providing the necessities of life—shelter, water, warmth, and food. Whatever you need and don't have, you must make, kill, or find.

Our pioneer ancestors would have been more at ease under these adverse circumstances. It was a daily task for them to wrench a meager existence from the earth. They were hardy, strong, and versatile. The same individual plowed the ground, grew the food, chopped wood, and slaughtered the pig. He built fences and cabins and milked his cow. These people were so much closer than we to the prehistoric ones who fought the wild animals, discovered fire, lived in caves, and came to terms with the world they were trying to conquer.

Today's business executive is still faced with a hostile environment. His problems are of taxes and finance, material costs and labor strife.

Our modern civilization and economic structure have been built on increased productivity through specialization. We have continued to learn more and more about less and less, until most of us can no longer do little things that were commonplace to everyone less than 50 years ago.

Four out of five people today cannot make a fire out-of-doors, even if they have a match. For their entire lives, fire was available with the twisting of a knob on the range; water was always abundant at the tap.

In our homes, offices, cars, and even some of our airplanes, the internal environment is completely controlled. If it is too hot or too cold— simply turn the thermostat to another temperature. The automatic whatevers will provide the appropriate atmosphere and comfort shortly. We have gained much in creature comforts, but we have lost our skills to survive in the wilderness.

FOOD

When considering the aftermath of an airplane crash in a desolate wasteland, the minds of most people turn to food and the fear of starvation. They recall the Donner Party, bound for California in 1846, who due to severe weather and hardships turned to cannibalism to survive. This fear is more firmly engraved in the minds of many as a result of the current exploitation film which details the cannibalistic experiences of sixteen Uruguayan rugby players, who survived a 1973 crash in the Andes.

Sensationalized stories of survival and the entire genre of disaster films and books paint distorted pictures of horrible extremes and total hopelessness. In the typical survival situation, however, the choice is not between cannibalism and starvation. *Food will be one of the least important items.*

You can survive for extended periods of time with little or no food. This was amply demonstrated by Ralph Flores and Helen Klaben who survived for 7 weeks with practically nothing to eat.

Certainly, nutrition is important and energy will be required should you try to walk out. However, you would probably be better off to stay with the wreck and conserve your energy. Realize that the greater amount of food you eat, the more water your body will need. In fact, if you don't have water, even if you *do* have food, the best advice is "Don't eat!"

An individual can survive very well on 700 calories a day, considerably less than most of us consume. When maintenance of the inner-core temperature is aided by having adequate shelter, warm clothing, and consumption of warm liquids, the need for food will be reduced even more. The prime problem will be one of obtaining something which approximates a proper balance of carbohydrates, proteins, vitamins, and minerals.

This situation has been dramatically demonstrated in many instances where the quantity of food has been more than ample but completely lacking in nutritional balance. Perhaps one of the more startling instances is that pertaining to rabbits. Along with the danger of tularemia, it has been found that a diet consisting of nothing but this high-protein, low-fat meat, if followed for an extended period, will result in kidney collapse and death. Groups of arctic explorers have also encountered dietary-deficiency disease and death when circumstance forced them to eat unaccustomed foods which were adequate in caloric terms but nutritionally unbalanced.

Survival rations can be carried as part of your basic survival kit or separately but should include both a multivitamin supplement and vitamin C tablets.

There has been a great deal of controversial dialogue pertaining to the exact needs and benefits of vitamin C between the American Medical Association and several eminent research doctors; however, the clinical data available tends to support the position taken by the vitamin C advocates. Even professional mountain climbers have entered this controversy, stating that lack of this vitamin can create unfavorable personality changes under environmental and emotional stresses, such as those encountered during an assault on the ice-covered slopes of Alaska's Mt. McKinley. Expedition experience has shown that climbers, lacking vitamin C, become belligerent, more self-centered, and intolerant. Most dangerously, they become careless about safety considerations and their personal habits.

Experimental stress has been produced in laboratory animals by subjecting them to extreme cold and enforced fasting, circumstances similar to those encountered by the person facing a wilderness survival situation. Under these circumstances, the nutritional needs of these animals soar beyond that of the control group by enormous multiples. Under stress, the need for vitamin C is increased so greatly that a deficiency can be created in a matter of hours. Rats subjected to swimming in ice water quickly died unless they received massive amounts of vitamin C. These laboratory experiments seemed to indicate that huge amounts of this vitamin protected the experimental animals from every form of stress.

Since the survival situation is sure to be a stressful experience, and your rations will probably not include fresh oranges, it would seem reasonable to include an ample supply of this very important vitamin in your store of emergency rations. It may not cure the common cold, but the known benefits of adequate vitamin C certainly make inclusion in your survival gear a worthwhile consideration.

Survival food is available in many forms. Backpacking stores can supply a wide variety which will provide the needed calories in the proper balance. There are space-food sticks, tropical chocolate bars, malt tabs, and trail cookies. There are literally hundreds of powdered, freeze-dried, and dehydrated foods which are nonspoiling and fit the requirements for emergency rations.

Traveling will require about twice as much food to maintain the same physical condition as it will to remain with the aircraft. The situation is very straightforward—the more work you do, the more food you will require. Likewise, the more food you eat, the greater amount of water your body will need to process that food. If you have less than one quart of water daily, eat sparingly, avoiding dry, starchy foods. The best foods under these circumstances would be hard candy or fruit bars.

There are two distinct positions held pertaining to the concept of live off the land. The first states that the survivor should hunt game and forage for edible plants from the onset, saving the on-board rations for an emergency. The second takes the opposite view, suggesting that the survivor uses his rations and conserve his energy. The latter would theoretically forego the possibility of intestinal problems and discomforts due to an abrupt and dramatic change in the diet. Realistically, however, if the survival situation goes beyond the average time span before rescue, there will be no choice. Once the rations are gone, the survivor will either live off the land or do without.

WATER

If given the choice between 20 pounds of food or the same weight in water, the wise survivor will choose the water. All authorities and reports from successful survivors place water high on the list of "must have" items. Dehydration is a major problem in the survival situation and can render a person completely helpless in a very short time.

Water is the elixir of life. It is the means by which the body regulates both the chemical balance in the cells and the internal temperature.

The human body itself is approximately 65 percent water. The balance between the intake and output of water is critical and must be properly maintained so that the life processes can continue and the vital organs can fulfill their normal functions. Deprivation of water can lead to gradual dehydration and loss of the body's capabilities to perform. With a water intake of less than the required minimum of 2 quarts daily, dehydration is inevitable and will ultimately lead to a loss of rationality.

You must guard your problem-solving abilities. This is one of an individual's most powerful weapons in the fight for survival. It is second only to the will to survive itself. When the ability to reason and think logically is lost, the will to live also weakens and dies. Without the will to live, death is inevitable.

When you are thirsty—drink! Remember, however, that thirst is not an indication of your body's water needs. You may drink enough to satisfy your thirst, and it is still possible to slowly dehydrate. Drink

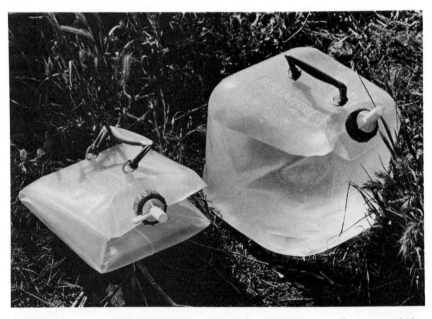

Although there are 330 million cubic miles of water on the Earth, it is still a very good idea to bring some of the precious liquid along with you if your flight path crosses the desert areas of our country. The collapsible plastic water bag shown here is an excellent lightweight container for water.

plenty of water whenever it is available; utilize your body's capacity for water storage.

Reduce your losses of body water by rationing your sweat, as you cannot stretch your available survival time by rationing your water. Life is maintained by the water in your body, not by the water in your canteen.

Research indicates that a person subjected to temperatures of 110°F in the shade, resting, and having only 1 quart of water has a maximum survival potential of 3 days. With an increase of the water available to 2 quarts, there is no increase in the potential life expectancy. It is not until the water available increases to 4 quarts that the anticipated survival time is extended to 4 days. Remember these estimates are based on an individual resting. If you are working or hiking, with commensurate increases in water losses, the survival period could be cut in half. Lower temperatures, on the other hand, will extend the survival period.

The primary processes resulting in water loss from the human body are perspiration, respiration, and urination. The first two remove excess heat from the body, and the latter removes the waste products of food oxidation and energy production. Although you can do little to control these processes themselves, you can control some of the conditions which affect these processes and the resulting water losses. By observing the following rules, water losses can be minimized:

1. Keep your mouth closed, breathe through your nose, and do not smoke. This reduces water loss from the drying of mucous membranes.

2. Movements and breathing should be slow and steady.

3. Do not drink any form of alcoholic beverage.

4. When water is limited, the consumption of food should be kept to a bare minimum.

5. Do not remove your clothes. Keep a layer of clothing on at all times, including a hat and some sort of protection for the neck. Wear long pants and long sleeves—no shorts. This will slow down the evaporation of sweat and prolong the cooling effect.

6. Protect your body from the sun. Remain under shelter during daylight hours, and work only in the cool evening or early morning hours. If at all possible, sit or lie 12 to 18

inches above the ground or dig a depression 18 to 24 inches into the sand; the temperature may be as much as 30 degrees cooler than it is at the surface.

7. Cover your lips with a protective coating of Chap-Stick, grease, or oil.

If your routine mission involves carrying three people in the airplane, your minimum water requirements for 4 days would be 12 quarts. This amounts to about 25 pounds of water, not including the weight of the container. At 2.09 pounds per quart, water is heavy, but it is an absolute necessity for the maintenance of human life.

Although there are 330 million *cubic miles* of water on the surface of the Earth, 97 percent of that water is salt water and another 2 percent is frozen in ice caps and glaciers. Of the remaining less than 1 percent, only a small portion is available to humans to support their needs. Therefore, it is probably wise to figure some way to bring a certain amount of this precious liquid along with you.

THE SOLAR STILL

Some pilots, unfortunately, are gamblers. Water is simply too heavy to carry, and the survival situation is *never* going to happen to them. To hedge against even the remote possibility of death due to slow dehydration, these intrepid risk-managers figure that even 0.5 percent of 330 million cubic miles is still one hell of a lot of water; and if the need arises, they're going to find some of it.

Generally, the place to look is in loose sediment rather than in rocks. Dry stream beds sometimes have water just below the surface; and if there is green vegetation, chances are good that there is water nearby. If there are animal trails, where they come together, the forks will point to the location of water.

The greatest drawback to the concept of find the water and live off the land is that it further complicates the survival situation. It does not take into consideration the possibility that the location of the crash may be miles away from any source of water. It does not consider the problem that would be presented should the person involved be injured in the crash or the cost of an extensive search in terms of water loss from the body. Hiking over rough terrain in desert conditions can cause a body-water loss as high as 2 quarts an hour.

Of course, one can always squeeze some water right out of the dirt. Dust is not necessarily as dry as it might at first appear. Seemingly dry dirt may contain as much as 15 percent water by weight. Soil in which plants can grow will contain an even greater percentage of extractable moisture. The trick is getting that moisture out of that dry dust and into your cup.

Two physicists from the U.S. Water Conservation Laboratory in Phoenix looked at the problem of wringing water out of the dust and came up with an answer—the solar still. The idea is so simple that it is astounding someone had not put it to work solving the world's water problem years ago.

The materials of construction are few and simple. The basic components are a square of plastic, a small container, a plastic tube, and something with which to dig a hole.

The plastic should be tough, about 1 mm thick, and of the rough-surfaced type. Preferably, it should be clear and about a 6-foot square. Colored plastics reduce the efficiency of the still, and smooth-surfaced types will only work if one side is abraded with sand or fine sandpaper. The condensation droplets formed in the still will not adhere properly to a smooth surface, so be sure that the roughened side is placed down.

The site for the still should be in the full sun. Be careful not to place it where it will be shaded in the morning or late afternoon. The most productive area is usually in a dry wash, but the water yield will largely be determined by the temperature—the hotter the better. An established still, however, will often produce some water even at night. The first still set up in the Phoenix area, back in 1965, produced a quart of water daily for more than a month. Recall, the daily water requirement per person is 2 quarts, so even a productive still will not completely satisfy that need. If you are able to line the still with cactus chunks or other vegetation, water yield may be as much as four times as great as it would be from the earth alone.

Although one must not drink urine, this body waste can be purified by the action of the solar still. In fact, any form of contaminated water other than that containing antifreeze compounds can be used to prime the still and increase production.

Construction of a solar still simply requires digging a pit with sloping walls and a position at the bottom for your collector vessel. A wide-mouthed pot would probably be best. The plastic drinking tube is placed into the collector and secured. This will allow you to suck the water out of the still without disassembly and the resultant loss of production.

The plastic sheet is stretched over the hole and secured with dirt. A rock is then placed in the center of the plastic sheet causing it to sag into an inverted cone. Care must be taken to assure that the plastic does not touch the walls of the pit.

The sun's heat will evaporate the moisture from the soil. The air volume within the pit becomes saturated and condenses on the underside of the plastic sheet. The moisture droplets adhere to the rough surface of the plastic until reaching the apex of the inverted cone and then drop into the collector vessel. In this manner, a productive still will collect between a pint and a quart of water every 24 hours. Additionally, the still may become a source of food as lizards, snakes, and other small animals may fall into the cone, becoming entrapped.

Several such installations may be necessary to provide sufficient water for your needs. The solar still is a valuable tool; its ability to extract water from the soil can make the difference between life and death on the desert.

To this point our attention has been focused on the problems of obtaining water in a desert environment. Dehydration, on the other hand, can be just as threatening on the slopes of a mountain in the middle of winter as it is on the desert floor. Colder temperatures will, of course, reduce the amount of body-water loss due to perspiration. Just the same, total water deprivation will ultimately lead to dehydration and its resultant problems. Fortunately, water availability is usually greater in the mountains due to the freshwater springs that generally can be found there. If there is snow and ice and you have the ability to make a fire, the problem of water procurement is solved. You must not, however, attempt to eat snow for its water content. You will waste too much energy that could be used for body upkeep. Using the mouth to melt snow could lead to the onset of hypothermia.

FIRE

In the wilderness environment, fire is undoubtedly one of a person's best friends. It should be considered with shelter since it protects the body by providing warmth. This warmth also extends your food supply by aiding in maintenance of the inner-core temperature. This is heat which would otherwise have to be provided by the body through the metabolic processes.

In addition to the body warmth it provides, fire gives light, dries wet clothing, and can be used for cooking and the purification of water. It is one of the best signaling devices, and perhaps most important, it gives a meaningful lift to the morale. The sight, sound, and feel of a warm, crackling fire offers a sense of security and reassurance. It is a known in the midst of a multitude of unknowns.

To derive these benefits, you must know how to build a fire. Unfortunately, when the need for fire is greatest, such as when it is cold, windy, and raining, the conditions for fire building are most adverse. Still, if all the materials required to support a fire are brought together, a fire may be built even under the most difficult conditions.

There are three necessary elements for a fire: oxygen, fuel, and heat. Oxygen is needed since burning is simply very rapid oxidation. You must have fuel—something to burn; and there must be sufficient heat to bring that fuel to its kindling point. All three items are essential; you cannot have a fire if one is missing.

Before attempting to build a fire, an appropriate site should be found. It should be a place free from wind and overhanging flammable materials. You must also be careful not to build your fire on nor around porous rocks, nor under a snow-ladened tree. Never try to build a fire directly on the snow or ice; build a platform under it.

Prepare everything before you start. Gather your tinder, kindling, and fuel. Make three piles of the materials. Be sure to keep everything dry.

Tinder is anything which will ignite on contact with a spark or minute flame. The kindling point for tinder is very low. Tinder may be cotton balls, scrapped cloth, dry grass, fine wood shavings, bird down, or even lint from your pockets.

Kindling is the next category of fuel. It has a slightly higher kindling point. This fuel should be broken, shaved, or split to increase its flammability. Small, dead twigs, dry branches which are finely split or broken, or a fuzz stick carved with a knife all make good kindling.

Almost anything can be used for fuel. Caution should be used with man-made materials as many of them will release poisonous fumes when they are burned; some may even explode. Standing dead trees will almost always be dry inside. If you can push one over, the center wood will make excellent fuel. Indians used the bark of the ponderosa pine and dried dung for fuels. Anything will burn—if it is finely split— even green wood, provided sufficient heat is applied. Generally, it is better to select fuels from deciduous growth rather than from evergreens as these fuels will produce more heat and less smoke.

In very cold weather, several small fires will be more beneficial than one large one. The best way to increase the efficiency of any fire is with a reflector. Almost any sort of reflector behind your fire will direct greater warmth into your shelter. The silver side of a space blanket

The versatile Swiss army knife, a metal match, and some dry cotton balls create what could be very basic survival kit that will fit into any jacket pocket.

makes an excellent heat reflector. Care should be taken to ensure that there is no danger of the space blanket catching fire. Cooking fires should be walled in to concentrate the heat in the same manner as a stove.

Generating that first spark to ignite your tinder can be done with anything from an ordinary match to a bit of broken glass used to concentrate the rays of the sun. But, there are easy ways, and there are more difficult ways.

Perhaps the most difficult and frustrating method is the well-known system of rubbing two sticks together. This ancient art was all but impossible for me as a boy scout, and I find that neither the method nor I have improved with age. Next on the list of trying experiences is attempting to start a fire with a magnifying glass. It can be done, given ample sunlight, perfectly dry tinder, and abundant patience, but I prefer the easier ways. For example—matches.

Every survival kit should have a generous supply of waterproof, strike-anywhere matches. The kit should also include a metal match along with some dry cotton balls. For even greater versatility in the fire-starting supplies, consideration should be given to several pads of 0000-size steelwool. This can be ignited with the heat generated by a flashlight battery; and if it gets wet, you simply shake the water out and try again. For wet-weather fire starting, there is miner's carbide which combined with water, rain, urine—any liquid—produces acetylene. The harder it rains; the better it works. One small spark and you've got fire. The carbide can be carried safely in an airtight, metal, 35mm film can.

FILE A FLIGHT PLAN

Fortunately, 95 percent of all survival situations are resolved in 24 hours. Only a very small percentage go beyond 3 days; but weather may hold up the search or you may be missed on the first sweep, so you should consider the possibility of staying for a while. Of course, none of this means a great deal if you failed to file a flight plan.

Although I have neither been an advocate nor a consistent user of VFR flight plans, the statistics show that with a flight plan, an *alert notice* will be issued within 3 hours *after* your ETA, and the average time for search and rescue (SAR) recovery is 33 hours. Without a flight plan, the issuance of the SAR alert notice will be delayed, and the average time for recovery is extended to 73 hours. Your chances of still being alive when search and rescue arrive are also more than double if you take the time to file.

My own practice has been to monitor the appropriate center frequencies along the route, obtaining advisories when possible, and maintaining radio contact in this manner. The idea being that should an emergency arise, I could instantly advise center of my problem, and location, and squawk *7700* on the transponder. The SAR statistics, however, still indicate that a filed flight plan does the most to enhance one's chances of successful rescue.

It is best to wait at the crash site for rescue. To aid the search and rescue crews in finding your location, you will need some sort of signaling capability. If you filed a flight plan and followed your planned route, SAR will have a general area in which to search. Finding you and the wrecked aircraft, on the other hand, can still be difficult due to the variables of weather and terrain. Give SAR all the help you can.

SIGNALING

People in distress often wait until they see or hear rescue aircraft before they start their signal efforts. Generally, this is wrong. Start your signal fires right away. Do everything you can to disturb the natural look of the terrain. Use reflective parts of the aircraft to spell out an SOS. Remember, the larger you make your signal, the easier it will be to see from the air.

Set several fires. Use the tires from the aircraft, the seats and upholstery, or anything else that will not be needed for life support during your ordeal. Make large, bright fires at night and smokey ones during the day. The addition of oil-soaked rags or bits of rubber will produce black smoke, while green leaves, moss, or other damp foliage will produce white smoke. Plan your fires to contrast with the terrain.

The aircraft radios will be the most effective device for signaling, if they are still operable after the crash. Check both the radios and the aircraft battery. If you were flying on or near an airway, attempt to contact overflying aircraft on the appropriate center frequency. If unable to do this, you might try periodic calls on 121.5, particularly if you can see or hear a commercial airliner. The chances are very good that they will be monitoring this frequency.

Despite the fact that the emergency locator transmitter (ELT) was forced upon us and we've been plagued with false alarms and battery problems, in a crash it can still be the most important piece of equipment on the airplane. If impact did not activate the G-switch on the ELT, turn it on manually; then, check for proper operation on the aircraft radio, if possible.

The most common signaling device is the signal mirror. Most commercial survival kits contain some form of this item, and it is usually poor. It would be an excellent idea to shop around the army surplus stores, looking for the *glass* military version of the signaling mirror. These are superior to the metal types in ability to draw attention from airborne searchers.

During the AOPA Survival Training Course, our class was given a demonstration of the various types of mirrors and how to use them. The difference in signal brilliance between the smaller metal mirrors packed in most survival kits and the larger glass military mirrors was impressive. On a slightly cloudy or hazy day, the metal mirror might not be seen at all.

Proper use of the signal mirror is not difficult; however, being able to follow an aircraft as the angles between it, the mirror, and the sun continue to change, does take some practice. Since your life may depend upon it someday, the time invested in this practice is time well-spent.

SURVIVAL KITS

There is no one single answer to the survival problem, nor is there one single survival kit which covers all situations. If such a kit did exist, it would probably require that you leave your passengers behind in order to accommodate your emergency equipment. Balance must be achieved as complete preparedness for all contingencies becomes totally impractical. Common sense dictates that we prepare for the most likely occurrence. It is foolish for a fellow who flies weekly from El Paso to Phoenix in a two-place Grumman to be carrying a four-person life raft.

Survival kits are available in a variety of concepts, sizes, and costs. They range from something that can be stuck in a jacket pocket to heavy dufflebags crammed with hundreds of items and weighing enough to consume the total baggage allowance of most general aviation airplanes. For most business pilots, it will probably be the weight penalty rather than cost that determines selection.

Because the most appropriate contents for a particular survival kit will depend upon the needs of the person who will be using it, logic suggests that this person should be the one to choose those contents. The selection of each item should be evaluated carefully on the basis of its versatility, the routes and terrain generally flown, and the number of people the kit will need to support. The items should be categorized as *must have, useful,* and *luxury.* This will aid in making decisions about what will be included and what will be left behind. It takes a great deal of time and critical thought to put together a "good" survival kit. It

Survival kits come in all sizes and range from inexpensive to very costly. The best survival kit will be the one put together by the pilot himself, but every kit should contain items which will provide the victim with (1) instant body shelter, (2) fire-making capability, (3) signal capability, and (4) inducement to drink hot liquids.

requires a lot of introspection and understanding of one's own strengths and weaknesses. The better-trained and more knowledgeable person can probably make do with less equipment and fewer rations.

Any survival kit should contain items which fulfill these four functions:

1. Instant body shelter
2. Fire-making capability
3. Signal capability
4. Inducement to drink hot liquids

Just how elaborate you may wish to be in selecting items to provide these basics is up to you and the amount of money you wish to leave at the local backpacker's store.

Some of the more expensive survival kits contain a collapsible rifle. The question about the inclusion of firearms is, How well does a gun meet the actual needs of the potential survivor? Will it provide shelter? Will it aid in the collection of firewood and water? Its use as an inducement to drink hot liquids seems remote, and its signaling capabilities are limited at best. A rifle might have some usefulness in providing small game for the dinner pot, but it is probably just extra weight that should go into more important items—like tools.

On the top of some mountain slope after a crash, the person who had not thought about it before would probably trade a bunch of dollars for a small tool kit containing some tin snips, a set of screwdrivers, a pair of Vise-Grip pliers, a hacksaw blade, and perhaps a small ax. A small shovel or even a trowel could prove to be very useful.

A wrecked airplane is a storehouse of materials, but these precious items will be unavailable without a key. The key to this warehouse, which generally must be disassembled to be worthwhile, is your tool kit. In selecting your individual tools, be guided by the question: Will this tool allow me to make other tools should I need them? Being unable, as a practical matter, to take everything with you desirable to sustain life in the wilderness, any item included in your kit should be as versatile as possible.

Toilet paper is a very lightweight and versatile item. Several rolls can be carried in the airplane at all times without gouging into your useful load. It can be used as a signaling device, in the manner of mischevious kids who use this material as streamers to occasionally decorate the neighborhood trees. It makes good tinder to start a fire; and, of course, it can also be used for its customary purpose.

Observation of commonsense measures pertaining to personal hygiene is imperative in the wilderness. Disposal of human waste should not be conducted in a haphazard manner. A proper latrine should be dug to a depth of 12 to 15 inches; the wastes must be covered with a layer of soil after each use to avoid attracting flies, other insects, and small animals.

In a survival situation, maintaining your health is extremely important. Keep your body, clothing, and camp clean, constantly guarding against any unsanitary condition which might lead to internal sickness. Always cook your food and purify *all* your water. It is imperative to treat all injuries which break the skin. Use an antiseptic, regardless of how minor the cut. Left unattended, even the smallest scratch can become infected. In the wild, infection can quickly become uncontrollable, resulting in fever and loss of rational thought.

You must save your strength and get adequate rest, as fatigue reduces the body's tolerance to stress, creating nutritional needs beyond your ability to provide.

After you have done all you can to acquire the necessities of life, seek to expand your comfort zone. This is important for your morale. Each discomfort adds to the psychological burden that must be carried. Small things can build into devastating proportions, and you will find that one more mosquito bite, or one more itch, or pain, is more than you are ready to endure.

No one can be prepared for all possibilities, but you can recognize and prepare for those things which will rank highest in probability. Train yourself to respond to the potential emergency. Sitting in your living room is the place to make that plan. Go through the complete thing from the time that the engine gasps and the prop flips through the last time.

Close your eyes and draw the picture in your mind. Imagine that you have managed to bring your aircraft down in the desert without having it flip over. There has been no fire. From the time the engine quit, you have managed to do everything just about right. It certainly was a noisy experience, but it is quiet now and both you and your passenger seem to be in one piece.

Having survived the initial impact of your unscheduled return to the earth, it is time to logically assess the actual circumstances. Realization of the need to survive in an unfriendly environment induces fears and stresses. Although fear is a vital part of the self-preservation mechanism, if allowed to cloud thinking, the result will be self-destructive.

Hating yourself, turning aggression inward due to mistakes you made before the survival situation occurred, is just making another mistake. It is one, however, with the power to kill. To lock your thinking into a circle of recriminations is a foolishness you can no longer afford. Now is the time to readjust your goals. It is no longer important to think about some merger or closing some significant deal. Now, there is but one priority—to stay alive. Your heart is still pounding, and you are aware of your own rapid breathing. You begin to feel nauseous. Clammy sweat breaks out on your forehead. You can't seem to get enough air. Consciousness seems tenuous; and you become frightened, more frightened than you were during the crash itself. You've got to do something. Quickly—you've got to get out of the plane. This need to *escape* is overwhelming.

Releasing the seat belt was a complex chore. It shouldn't have been so difficult. *What's wrong?* Pain knifes into your left shoulder and chest as the belt reels back into its retainer. All is not so well as it seemed. Pain flashes a message to your brain; your collarbone is broken. Vision blurs—sight fades into a red fog that quickly turns gray. Consciousness is slipping away, and the nausea can no longer be controlled.

You vomit—choke, and fight to retain your awareness of the world around you. Sight returns and you look into the face of your passenger. His eyes tell the story of uncomprehending bewilderment. His face is pale, gray, and moist with perspiration.

"Help me," he says. His voice is frightened, plaintive, and barely audible.

You are both suffering symptoms of shock. This is the body's automatic reaction to trauma. Messages have been sent to the vascular system, constricting blood vessels, slowing or stopping the normal flow of blood to the vital organs.

It is not always possible to immediately identify shock in yourself or others, but you can expect some degree of shock to develop after any injury. The usual symptoms are pale skin, rapid breathing, sweating, a weak pulse, and cold, clammy skin. Persons who exhibit these symptoms should be laid flat with the feet raised 12 to 18 inches *if the nature of the injury permits.* The victim should be made as comfortable as possible and kept warm. If no abdominal injury is present, warm liquids will aid in recovery. No alcoholic drinks should be given, and the victim should not smoke. If oxygen is available, it should be administered.

If allowed to advance, shock can become irreversible and result in death. Therefore, shock must be treated immediately, second only to problems involving profuse bleeding or cessation of breathing. Stopping the loss of blood is always the most important task. It can also be the most difficult and distasteful.

If these fictions from your imagination were to some day take on the substance of reality, would you be able to cope?

If the noisy, comforting din of your cockpit were to be shattered by silence—will you be prepared? Will you be ready to execute the forced landing? Will you be able to keep your terrified passengers alive until someone comes to your rescue? Will there be a survival kit on board, and will you have the knowledge to use it?

Take the time and make the effort to learn. The American Red Cross offers first aid classes which will cover the type of material most useful to you in a survival situation. If you travel with your family in your airplane, it would probably be an excellent thought to have all members of the family take the class together. Not only will this increase the learning value through interfamily participation but it will also be very meaningful should you be rendered unconscious in an accident. Even a 12-year-old can be very effective in first aid matters *if* that child has been properly trained.

Both the Aircraft Owners and Pilots Association and the National Rifle Association (NRA) sponsor survival training schools. The course curriculum differs between these two, but either one would be of great benefit to the pilot. Cost is nominal as compared to the benefits to be derived. Information concerning either course can be obtained by writing to the AOPA or NRA at the addresses listed in the back of this book.

Your aviation library should contain several good books on wilderness survival and first aid. Both you and your family should read them and tuck away bits of information that may serve you well should you be forced down. You shouldn't try to include this library in your survival kit, but you can obtain either a set of plastic-enclosed cards with the most pertinent survival information on them or a set of small wilderness survival books which will fit nicely into the glove box of the airplane.

It really doesn't matter if the location is an Alaskan glacier or the hills behind Bakersfield, California, the problems of wilderness survival are equally demanding, and the costs of failure just as high. Although your chances of individual involvement are remote, no one is totally exempt. To be unprepared is both foolish and irresponsible.

On your next flight between Phoenix and El Paso, or Los Angeles and Portland, look down for a few minutes . . . and think about it.

CHAPTER TEN

Night, IFR, and the Weakest Link

THE FIRST QUESTION

With reference to night and IFR flight in general aviation aircraft, there are those who do and those who don't and those who might under very specific circumstances. Generally, the qualifying circumstance for those of the latter group is a matter of power-plant redundancy—if it doesn't have two, they won't go.

This question is a highly emotional one; and like most emotional questions, it generates a certain lack of harmony when the proponents gather to discuss the merits of their respective positions. Confrontations are frequent, and I was unsuspectingly drawn into such a situation while trying to sell our company Skylane, shortly after we acquired our Lance.

Cessna 4645K was the finest, cleanest, and best-maintained Skylane on the used-airplane market. It was the used airplane that pilots dream of finding. Every mechanical and electronic gremlin had been discovered and dealt with. The airplane was literally better than new. I wanted this beautiful machine, my airplane, to go to a new owner who would appreciate it and continue the loving care to which the Skylane was accustomed.

My first prospect was a professional pilot. He looked at the airplane with the knowing eye that comes only from experience. To impress this prospective buyer with the mechanical soundness of the machine and the care with which it had been maintained, I related that I had flown all the hours recorded on the tach except those few when the airplane was ferried from the factory. Emphasizing my faith in this particular airplane, I added that many of those hours were IFR or at night. The intent had been to communicate my complete confidence in Skylane 45K, but the result was something else.

"That you've survived certainly speaks well for the maintenance program you've followed," the professional pilot conceded. "But it doesn't say much for your level of intelligence. Anyone who flies night and IFR in a single-engine airplane is crazy."

This young man was certainly forthright and positive in his opinion. He was also very disturbed by this brief portion of our conversation. He became visibly uncomfortable and obviously wanted to be somewhere else. His face displayed a vague mixture of amazement, revulsion, and fear. Perhaps he felt that standing so close to one afflicted with this form of insanity might threaten his own well-being.

Obviously, the sales interview was over. With a thump of the stair door on his Cessna 340, the young, professional pilot was gone, leaving me alone on the ramp with the Skylane and my thoughts.

The last time I had been faced with this sort of thing had been in Evansville, Indiana. The situation was somewhat different, but the essence was the same. Fortunately, that time, I was simply an observer.

Two professional pilots—a man and a woman—were sitting in the lounge discussing the weather, airplanes, and the foolishness of those who penetrate the clouds in single-engine machines. The man was very well-dressed in a conservative gray suit and tie. He was the perfect image of a corporate pilot. The woman with whom he had been swapping bits of wisdom was a vital, energetic, grandmother-type. She reminded me of that idealized woman on television who always makes a great cup of coffee and then modestly gives all the credit to her brand of freeze-dried coffee crystals.

They were visually an odd couple to find passing a rainy Indiana afternoon with tales of ice accumulation, dark nights, thunderstorms, and engine failures. But, these two very experienced pilots were of one mind on the subject of one engine:

> Singles are toys, and those who fly them should be restricted to flight on bright, spring mornings. At any other time, pilots of single-engine airplanes are a threat not only to themselves and people on the ground but also to the professional, multiengine pilots for whom the sky was created.

It was unnerving to listen to experienced pilots expound such ideas with total sincerity and conviction. The temptation to interject some comments defending singles and their pilots was strong, but previous confrontations and the trip up from Kentucky had taken a bit of the starch from my sails.

It had been solid IFR from a few moments after lift-off until we broke out beneath the clouds in moderate rain while making the VOR approach into Evansville. There had been sufficient turbulence that I had to hand fly the entire trip, and I was tired. In the terminal area, we were given four revised clearances and then sent off to hold at the VOR. A Lear Jet was speeding around the murky skies, and the controller decided that jets deserve preferential treatment, so the Lear was cleared down the ILS (instrument landing system), relegating us to a nonprecision approach. It had been a busy flight. My shirt was completely soaked with perspiration even before my soggy dash across the rain-whipped ramp between the airplane and the pilot's lounge.

Rumpled, wet, and with my confidence slightly wilted by the fact that I was still wondering if my teardrop entry into holding had been the proper choice, it seemed inappropriate for me to disagree about anything with such well-groomed and obviously knowledgeable pilots. That their mutually shared opinions were biased folk wisdom contrary to the documented facts was insufficient to overcome my emotional inertia. I had long ago learned that attempting to persuade a devoted twin-driver of the utility, efficiency, economy, and safety of a single-engine airplane is an exercise in futility. Multiengine pilots are as enamored of those sleek twin nacelles as the sixteenth century dandy was with his padded codpiece. Reason, facts, and practicality seem invariably to fall before the throne of the "Great God Safety."

Unfortunately, when all the NTSB figures are tallied and summarized, completely contrary to what "common sense" would infer, recorded history indicates that "twin-engined safety" in reality may be a myth. Certainly, the redundancy should create a greater measure of safety, but the statistics indicate that it doesn't. Twin advocates charge this off to "lack of pilot proficiency." This assumption may be true, but it does not alter the facts: *Your chance of being involved in a fatal accident is greater in a twin than in a single.* Although NTSB studies show that singles have twice as many engine-failure accidents as twins, four times as many twin accidents are fatal.

Richard Collins, editor of *Flying,* in his 1977 book, *Flying Safely,* examines the question of relative safety between twins and singles in a very thorough manner. After sifting through the NTSB numbers, Collins concludes that in terms of real risk to life, the statistics might well favor the single over the twin by a 10 to 1 margin. In another study, done by *Business and Commercial Aviation (BC/A),* involving IFR engine-failure accidents over a 3-year period, that same figure of 10 to 1 emerged. Again, the results were favorable to the single-engine machine.

Statistics, of course, are strange things. They can either prove anything or nothing. The fault is not with the statistical method, but rather with those people who either through ignorance or malicious design lead the unwary astray with statistical presentations developed from technically true data which is structured in such a way as to lead the recipient to false conclusions. Certainly, this is not the case with Collins and *BC/A*. If either of these two had an "economic axe to grind," the light twin would probably have been presented in a far more favorable light. The enthusiastic supporter of single-engine airplanes should, however, still draw his conclusions with caution unless he is a competent statistician and has access to all the raw data on the subject.

For the reader who is interested in the use and abuse of statistics, McGraw-Hill has published an extremely interesting and informative book, *The Figure Finaglers*. The author, Robert S. Reichard, cuts through the usual jargon and obtuseness found in most books on statistics. He has written a very readable text for the person who would like to separate the sense from the nonsense found in the large number of statistical presentations encountered in daily life. Geared to the non-mathematician, this book will show the business pilot how to look at the NTSB statistics with new understanding. Armed with insight as to what the accident figures really mean, the single-engine pilots who fly night and IFR can confidently meet the twin-drivers eye to eye and ask that primal question: "Who's crazy?"

A WORD OF CAUTION

Now that we have addressed the question of sanity as it pertains to those who penetrate the dark and cloudy skies in a single-engine craft, we are free to explore some of the more pertinent aspects of this realm of flight.

Based upon my own experience as a pilot, and some research into the probable cause of night accidents, I find it difficult to separate night and IFR flight. The two types of operations share so many common factors that to separate them seems nonsensical. Except under very specific and limited conditions, night flight is most definitely IFR, regardless of how some government regulation defines it. Simply because something is accepted by the FAA as being legal does not make such an operation safe.

Unless you are flying over a major metropolitan area, black-night flight is an IFR operation regardless of what some lawyer might call it and should be undertaken only by an instrument-qualified pilot. Certainly, under a full moon and a cloudless sky, it is possible to fly an airplane using visual cues. To the business person wanting to use his airplane as a meaningful transportation tool, however, waiting for the full moon before planning a sales trip might just limit his airplane's utility quotient right out of any reasonable area of cost-effectiveness.

There is nothing inherently dangerous about flight through darkness and cloud. The airplane couldn't care less about either one, but the limitations placed on the pilot's capability to see can certainly complicate the situation arising from even a minor mechanical malfunction or lapse of good judgment. An occurrence which might be considered a minor inconvenience under day VFR conditions can quickly become a catapult to disaster for a flight conducted at night or IFR. The statistics, on the other hand, indicate that the highest percentage of mishaps under these conditions of flight are a result of *judgmental* errors rather than mechanical failures. Therefore, the major risks are potentially under the control of the pilot, and the fatal accident record can be improved by better pilot planning and higher levels of proficiency.

Night flight is extremely important to the business pilot. It allows him to work a full business day after a full night's rest. It is a valuable time expander, but it requires a careful, competent instrument pilot who can separate his roles of business executive and aircraft commander.

At some time every business executive is probably faced with faltering sales. Generally, this condition is accompanied by soaring costs or the unexpected resignation of a key employee. Problems always seem of such a gregarious nature. They never come singly. First it is one thing and then it is six others. The pressures can become almost unbearable. If you're like most business executives, at a time like this you will look inward, seeking to find an answer. You may even discover that some of your problems were due to errors in your own decisions. You may even feel just a twinge of guilt.

Don't compound your problems. Stay on the ground. Spend another night where you are. Take in a movie. Relax. Whatever you do, don't file IFR for that 4-hour trip back home. The weather *this time* will probably be far worse than forecast.

Sort out your business problems before you enter the cockpit, even if that means waiting a day. Stress, fatigue, and night IFR just don't add up to anything but living dangerously. If you really have to get back, fly commercial. Do not allow your business problems to make you the weakest link in the system and a potential NTSB statistic.

OXYGEN—SOMETHING EVERYBODY NEEDS

The ability to think clearly and logically while controlling the many systems involved in single-pilot IFR operations depends on the normal chemical balance being maintained in the body. Stress, anxiety, and smoking all create chemical imbalances in the body, making clear thought more difficult. Subtle hypoxia often begins as low as 5000 feet, degrading both the visual and mental capacities of the pilot. Yet, the confirmed smoker will invariably light up another cigarette the moment he is confronted with a stressful situation.

Although the long-term dangers of smoking have been widely publicized (the first report detailing the correlation between smoking and cancer was issued in 1859), very little has been said about smoking and the carbon monoxide (CO) problem.

As student pilots, we were all taught about the dangers of CO poisoning and how faulty exhaust systems can lead to disaster by leaking this highly toxic, colorless, and odorless gas into the cockpit. Our teachers, however, failed to tell us that one of the largest components of cigarette smoke is that same poisonous carbon monoxide gas. Smokers will claim that a comparison between cigarettes and a faulty exhaust system is ridiculous. Perhaps it is, but research has shown that even nonsmokers subjected to several hours in a room with several average smokers had signs of definite carbon monoxide poisoning.

The FAA publication *Medical Handbook for Pilots* points out that the most common source of carbon monoxide in an airplane is tobacco smoke. This book goes on to state that for a pilot "whether he is hypoxic because of low oxygen availability or whether he is poisoned by carbon monoxide, the effect is the same."

Since hemoglobin, the oxygen-carrying substance in the blood, has a much greater affinity for carbon monoxide than it does for oxygen, the smoker is probably suffering subtle hypoxia at all times. Additionally, nicotine increases the body's heat production, creating even greater oxygen demands while carbon monoxide is attaching itself to the hemoglobin in the blood, depriving the body of its normal ability to supply the brain with oxygen-rich blood. Oxygen starvation strikes the brain first so the victim is generally the poorest judge of his capabilities to function as a pilot. The previously mentioned FAA publication likens the hypoxic pilot to the person who has several drinks too many and then insists upon driving home when he can hardly walk.

Enroute to the Reno Air Races in 1964, the effects of smoking on a pilot's altitude tolerance were demonstrated most effectively to me. I was in the left seat of a rented Cessna Skylane; my companion in the right seat was Richard Bach.

At the time Richard was the West Coast editor of *Flying*, and I was working for him as a free-lance photographer. We were both relatively young and healthy. In terms of physical condition, the average observer would have probably awarded me the prize since it was visually obvious that along with lugging heavy camera cases, I had also spent a lot of time lifting weights. What was not obvious was the fact that under my well-muscled facade were lungs which had been subjected to 15 years of abuse from a cigarette habit of two packs a day. Richard, on the other hand, had *never* partaken of the poison weed. In retrospect, I feel very strongly that this single distinction prevented our Skylane from becoming a NTSB statistic that night.

It is never a single thing that leads a flight to disaster. It is invariably a combination of circumstances. For us, the situation began with very high terrain, an unforecast headwind that dropped our groundspeed down to 95 mph, and prolonged flight above 14,000 feet. From this beginning, our flight progressed at a snail's pace into darkness and an unexpected snow storm. The final element in our drama was hypoxia.

My head was throbbing and my eyes burned. I found it difficult to concentrate on the instruments. Technically, we were VFR, but we were definitely flying on instruments. Richard looked as if he were asleep, but in the red glow of the cockpit interior, it was difficult to know for certain. I knew that I was beginning to suffer the effects of hypoxia. I didn't want to say anything to Richard about this as it would result in a 30-minute diatribe concerning my stupidity for continuing with my "self-destructive, idiotic, and obnoxious passion for nicotine." Such was the theme of Bach's "gentle" chidings pertaining to my cigarette habit.

It was continually disconcerting to me that this dear friend with whom I spent so much time could hold such a narrow view of one of life's great pleasures. Wasn't he aware that cigarettes have long been a part of the aviator's mystique? Had he missed the social significance and meaning of cigarettes and their associated paraphernalia to the pilot-heroes of *Dive Bombers* and other early World War II films starring the likes of Fred MacMurray, Pat O'Brien, and James Cagney?

My mind, filled with nostalgic thoughts about an earlier day when movie heroes were truly heroic and invariably punctuated every dramatic moment by lighting another cigarette, drifted back to the curious sight of my blue fingernails which looked black in the red light of the cockpit interior. The directional gyro was turning lazily to the left and the engine sound was muted. There was something strange about these circumstances, but I couldn't figure out exactly what. My face tingled with an eerie but somewhat pleasant sensation, and then I felt a split second of absolute terror as reality intruded momentarily into my dreamlike state. We were in a spiraling descent to the left. It was night in the mountains, and I was floating back and forth on the edge of consciousness. This was a serious situation, but I couldn't keep my eyes open and my mind was too busy reminiscing about B-grade movies and cigarettes to evaluate the messages being presented by the instruments. I wasn't even sure if this was real or a dream or if it even mattered much one way or the other.

Consciousness eventually returned with an excruciating headache and the blinding glare of our landing light reflecting back at us from wind-driven snowflakes that formed almost horizontal streaks of white against the surrounding blackness. The wind was not only strong but it was gusting, making it very difficult for Bach to land our Skylane even after we found the runway at Bishop, California. We made several abortive attempts at landing before Richard managed to successfully cope with the turbulent crosswind.

Certainly Bach and I had been lucky that night. We had pushed a lot of the rules right to the limit and still managed to survive. Had I been alone, or if Richard Bach had been a cigarette smoker, I am now convinced that our flight would have ended as a ball of crumpled aluminum on the side of a mountain. The NTSB report would have first stated that we were not on a flight plan and then cited weather, darkness, and spacial disorientation as the cause of our crash and resulting demise. The text would go on to include improper preflight planning and poor in-flight decisions as causative factors. Nowhere in the report would there be a mention of the true cause:

> The pilot in command lost consciousness due to hypoxia and carbon monoxide poisoning resulting from continued flight above 5000 feet without supplemental oxygen while suffering from a chronic physiological deficiency brought about by a cigarette habit of two packs a day. All aircraft systems were operating properly at the time of the accident, and the probable cause was pilot incapacitation resulting from the previously mentioned factors.

Hypoxia is also a danger to the nonsmoker, resulting in the same diminishment of both physical and mental capabilities. The prime difference is simply a matter of degree and absolute altitude tolerance. The nonsmoker is certainly not immune to hypoxia.

It is important for the business pilot to understand that the only reliable indicator for use of supplemental oxygen is the altimeter. There are, of course, FARs which regulate when various classes of aircraft occupants must use oxygen, but the best rule is to use it at any altitude if such use results in an increase in alertness and your feeling of well-being.

The regulations don't make any distinction between day or night operations; and if you plan all your oxygen use according to the regulations, you are most probably starving your brain of much needed oxygen-laden blood just when you need it the most. I personally find that extended night flights are considerably less fatiguing if I use oxygen continuously from the ground right on up to cruising altitude. During daylight hours, I have rarely felt the need for supplemental oxygen below 11,000 feet; however, my wife becomes irritable and develops a mild headache after only an hour above 9500 feet. Because of this, we have adopted the practice of donning oxygen masks for any extended flight above 9500 feet. Although it did not seem necessary for me below 11,000 feet, I now find that by following the practice of using oxygen at 9500 feet, I arrive at our destination feeling a great deal less fatigued. Faced with a difficult approach down to minimums, this added personal reserve can be extremely important.

Another consideration pertaining to hypoxia and the use of supplemental oxygen is the equipment, in particular—the mask. In 1974 John W. Brantigan, who is both a pilot and a medical doctor, conducted a series of experiments to measure the efficiency of the various oxygen systems available to the general aviation pilot. His research indicates that there are significant differences between the various masks available and that the Hudson type of mask, which is supplied with several low-cost oxygen systems, "was not designed for aviation and should be left in the hospital, where it belongs."

The underlying implication in the article presented by Dr. Brantigan was that a pilot could be using oxygen and still have an inadequate supply due to an ill-fitting, unsuitable mask or an inoperative reservoir bag. He points out that the Hudson type of mask makes poor use of the reservoir bag "which was often seen to collapse into total uselessness as exhaled moisture caused the sides of the bag to stick together." This type of failure of the reservoir function, according to Dr. Brantigan, creates "a sudden loss of 10,000 feet of protection without warning." This might not be critical to those of us who fly nonturboed airplanes in the 10,000- to 15,000-foot altitude range, but it could be an extremely important matter to a pilot of a turbocharged machine cruising along at flight level 290.

Although our Piper Lance can barely struggle up to 14,000 feet, the oxygen bottle is ever present in the cabin and filled. The lessons learned from that incident above the Owen's Valley more than 16 years ago have not faded with time. Hypoxia is an insidious enemy of every high-flying pilot and a still greater threat to the smoker who is probably hypoxic even on the ground.

SINGLE-PILOT IFR AND THE AUTOPILOT

For the single pilot flying serious IFR, the autopilot is an absolute must. There are those who scorn the use of the autopilot by the neophyte instrument pilot stating that he will never learn if he relies upon a black box to do his flying. These critics of the autopilot are usually flight instructors to whom a flight from Long Beach to Bakersfield is a long cross-country IFR flight. They will also tell horror stories about the doctor who regularly filed IFR in his Bonanza until that fateful flight when the autopilot quit and the doctor and his family perished. Like so many other general statements, there are elements of both fact and fancy in this position pertaining to autopilots.

Certainly an instrument pilot must be proficient at hand flying his airplane with reference to the gauges. To break into the clouds and darkness without this basic skill is flirting with suicide. As business pilots, however, our prime concern is with the safe and efficient use of an expensive company asset, not to participate in some macho fantasy by our ability to endure hardship. Instrument flight is a "thinking man's" game. It is an exercise in self-discipline, not masochism. And, for the single pilot flying IFR, the autopilot is an absolute must. Even if one wants to hand fly for the practice during long enroute legs, being able to let "George" keep it straight and level while copying a revised clearance leaves you free to do what the autopilot can't do—think!

Another of the must-have items for the single pilot plying the dark and cloudy skies is the boom mike. Distractions in the cockpit are extremely dangerous, and fumbling for a conventional microphone while executing a difficult approach in turbulence is a ridiculous and unnecessary addition to the cockpit workload. Those last two words are the key to decisions pertaining to equipment selection. Does the addition of this item to the airplane panel add to or subtract from the *cockpit workload*? If the gadget adds to the cockpit workload, you certainly

One of the most important items for the pilot undertaking single-pilot IFR is the boom mike. A lightweight unit, such as the one being worn by the author in the cockpit of this 1946 Navion, is a great aid in reducing cockpit workload. When the weather is rough and the approach is going to minimums, a conventional microphone is a nuisance and a dangerous distraction from the important job of flying the airplane.

should keep your money and forget it. If the item in question can significantly reduce the cockpit chores, then you might consider mortgaging your father-in-law, if need be, to obtain the desired item.

Until recently, for example, I felt very comfortable flying without distance-measuring equipment (DME) and looked upon this electronic marvel as a real luxury. The panel of our Skylane had a digital VOR (DVOR) which gave a constant readout of the radial from an off-course station, so it seemed almost the same as having a DME. Of course, this required a little measurement on the chart and a spin on the computer, but it was certainly a lot less expensive than even the cheapest DME. When we bought our Lance, however, it came with a Narco 195 which has taught me just how much I had been missing. For the IFR pilot, a good DME really reduces the cockpit workload. In many ways, I have come to feel that I would rather have a single nav receiver and a DME with a "hold" function than the customary dual VORs.

DISCIPLINE AND PERSPECTIVES

To the pilot flying night and IFR, cockpit organization is an important primary consideration. Being able to complete a flight of 600 to 700 nautical miles and arrive at the destination with the cockpit as orderly as it was at the departure requires a bit of ground planning and discipline.

Your charts and approach plates should be placed on your kneeboard in the order that they will be used, and then folded back up and placed at the bottom of the stack as the flight progresses to your destination. Certainly it is mandatory for the pilot to know his airplane extremely well. He should know the speeds and limitations of his machine to perfection. He should also be able to put his hand on every switch, knob, and control in the dark. Being able to put your hand on everything that you need without a frantic search for it is conducive to completing an uneventful flight. At night and IFR, an uneventful flight is always the goal.

Take your time. Check everything *before* you get out to the runway.

When it comes to cockpit organization, nothing is as handy as that magical stuff called *Velcro*. Using a patented "hook" and "loop," Velcro provides a means to attach just about anything just about anywhere in the cockpit of an airplane. Pencils, computers, approach plate holders, or stop watches can be secured to the control wheel, instrument panel, or side panels with Velcro. Items thus secured can be easily detached and then secured again almost instantly. Velcro is available at the notions counter of the local dime store or wherever sewing supplies are sold.

Establish a place for everything and then get everything set and in its place. Don't allow *anything* to rush you through your checklist. Exercise the required discipline needed to always use a checklist, and never let anyone or anything expedite you into the darkness or the clouds.

There are several logical approaches to prudent route planning for a night flight. The first would be a route selection, which travels from one airport to the next, giving consideration to the terrain, the possibility of an in-flight emergency, and the appropriate cruising altitudes. The weather is always a consideration in route selection, day or night.

The prime problem in planning for the flight off-airways is that you will not have the minimum enroute altitudes (MEAs) called out, and you will have to consult sectional charts for the entire flight in order to work out terrain-clearance altitudes. This takes a *lot* of time when you are going across the better part of the entire United States. This time penalty in the planning stage is one reason why I prefer to file IFR at night.

There are many knowledgeable pilots who insist that VFR is faster, but I have found for the stage lengths we usually fly, any time lost in following IFR procedures is more than compensated for in the time saved in the planning steps. On shorter legs, I am certain that this might not be true.

Even with my preference for filing IFR for night flights, there are combinations of terrain, weather, stage length, and MEAs which reduce the choices in my mind to going VFR or not at all. One such situation occurred on a trip from Los Angeles to Dallas.

We had diverted from our usual stop in Phoenix to Tucson due to some localized thunderstorms. Landing in Tucson in light rain, we refueled, ate, and checked the weather for the leg from Tucson to El Paso.

Like most everything in flying, it was a calculated risk, but the odds looked good. There was still an hour of daylight by the almanac, but the cloud cover would reduce that somewhat. The temperatures indicated that there might be ice in those clouds. There were no thunderstorms predicted, and El Paso was forecast to remain about 8000 broken for the night, but forecasts have been known to fall. My plan was to follow the interstate; most of the airports along this route are built very close to the road. This area from Tucson to El Paso is rugged country. I'd really like to spend the night in Tucson, but it is forecast to go down in the morning. So we leave.

The trip progressed through light and occasionally moderate rain. Luckily the air was smooth and the headlights from cars on the road below glistened from the wet asphalt. The visibility below the clouds was more than 20 miles, and the airport rotating beacons continued to appear in the expected places at precisely the expected times. We have made this trip many times via the airways, but the highway follows somewhat less threatening terrain.

At the north end of the mountains separating El Paso from the vast western desert, we encountered some moderate turbulence. It was a real shaker. We informed approach control of the situation as they vectored us to runway 22. The air smoothed out for the final 300 feet down to the runway, and then just above ground level the crosswind component became so great that even with full correction into the wind, we were still drifting slightly at touchdown. Even on the roll out, it was impossible to keep the Skylane pointed straight down the runway. This certainly was not the 6 knots from 170 degrees reported by the tower. Of course, at El Paso the tower is literally *miles* from the runway. We reported our findings to the tower, and an American Airlines captain who had preceded us radioed his agreement.

Off the runway taxiing to the ramp, the wind was dead calm. The wind had not diminished; it was simply a matter of a completely different set of circumstances existing on the taxiway a hundred yards south of the runway. The wind seems to do strange things in west Texas.

When the motel van came to pick us up, there were two young men already seated. From their conversation it was evident that they, too, had just arrived at El Paso. One remarked about running into "wake turbulence" on final approach. They had landed on runway 26 and found the wind at ground level to be calm. It was during the last few hundred feet that they had their problems.

It was an interesting conversation to me as it revealed that the one young man had just received his private license and his companion was a bit more experienced with "about a hundred hours." They were on their way to Florida; the more experienced pilot was building hours so that he could get a commercial ticket. They had departed Tucson right behind us in a Piper Arrow. They had elected to climb up on top and had made the trip in smooth air above a solid overcast. They had been at 11,500 for the past 3 hours without oxygen. Luckily they found a hole a little bit east of El Paso through which they had descended.

Sorting the details out in my mind, I tried to recall what I had felt was appropriate and safe when I had about a hundred hours. Certainly, a trip at night above a solid overcast covering the entire area from Tucson to El Paso was beyond the parameters that I would have felt comfortable with. To my mind, the two young pilots were really overextending their capabilities and pushing their luck. Since neither had an instrument rating, flying above an overcast which was both reported to exist and forecast to continue was putting too much faith in good fortune. They had closed too many doors. The mountains in this area often conspire with the moisture-laden air from the south to generate thunderstorms, even when they are not forecast. I had confronted this situation many times in the past, and these memories played heavily in the decision not to file IFR for this trip to El Paso. They were lucky in my opinion—nothing more. Change just one small item, and they could have become another binary bit of data for the NTSB computer.

FLIGHT LOGS AND FLIGHT PLANS

Preflight planning is required by the FARs, but the regulations do not explain exactly what that means. One of the required items for IFR flight is an "adequate" flight log for the trip. This can be anything from a few penciled notes on a napkin to an elaborately detailed itinerary for the proposed flight. What will be adequate for one pilot may be woefully inadequate for another.

In the real world of IFR flight, the individual who spent 3 hours working up a detailed flight log often finds that ATC's computer doesn't like his selected route of flight; and when he gets his clearance, it has made his flight log a complete waste of effort. Eventually this person stops working up a flight log at all and simply "wings it." This is a reasonable answer for a competent pilot so long as everything is going well. Should a problem arise due to an equipment failure, though, an accurately kept flight log can be a real help.

One answer to this dilemma, caused by conflict between your planned route and that specified by ATC, is to do some research before filing or working up your proposed flight log. Ask the local pilots or the flight service person if there is a preferred routing for your flight. Although it may not be listed under the heading of "Preferred Routes" in your *Jeppesen Airway Manual* or any of the government publications, you will find that every ATC facility has very specific routing between the airports under their control.

Should you be unable to get the desired information from the locals, go ahead and work up your plan, requesting the route which is best suited to your circumstances and equipment, and then file it. When your clearance comes through from ATC, write it down and *keep* it. This will become the basis for a future file of canned flight plans.

If you are like most business executives, your trips will generally be to the same cities again and again, so this flight plan file will become a great time-saver in the future. When your business schedule next requires that you travel from Grand Rapids to St. Louis, for example, all you will have to do is go to your file of flight plans, pull the appropriate page, copy the data onto a fresh flight log, and then give Flight Service a call. If the ATC computer liked the routing once, it will most probably be very happy to accept it again, provided there are no route segments involved which are dependent upon a temporarily out-of-service facility.

At Joyce Jewelry we have been using this method for the past 5 years with great success. Prior to that I had been a prime example of the diligent pilot who spent 4 hours working up a flight plan to cover a 2-hour trip only to have the whole thing reduced to an academic exercise by the frustratingly familiar words, "Cleared as filed except . . . " Continuing repetitions of this occurrence inevitably led to the decision to abandon formal flight logs for a few scribbled notes in a spiral-bound book and penciled estimates and arrival times on the face of my enroute charts.

Making the enroute chart serve a dual purpose seems an excellent idea at first glance, as it eliminates one piece of paper from the cockpit. When the flight is long enough to pass across two or more charts, however, this "simple" method starts developing a few complications and opportunities for errors. In order to keep track of the overall picture of how the flight is progressing in terms of changes in wind direction, groundspeed, and fuel consumption, you are now forced to consult the entire length of several enroute charts rather than a simple, well-organized flight log. Posting the data forward as you move from one chart to the next overcomes this objection, but it also increases the pilot workload and the chance for error. This is, of course, completely contrary to the desired goal.

Some readers, I suspect, may feel that the subject of flight logs is probably unworthy of such lengthy treatment. Right—I agree. So long as those electronic leprechauns that work in the hot, dark innards of the dual VORs and DME don't decide to stage a strike—the flight log is a superfluous bit of paperwork. But, should the magic elves elect to quit, thrusting the IFR pilot back to the dark ages of dead reckoning, the flight log becomes an extremely valuable asset. Coupled with the knowledge of the location of the nearest VFR weather, the flight log becomes a tool by which the flight may be concluded safely.

Being an essentially lazy person and a bargain hunter who wants the most value for the least effort, I wanted an easier way to cope with the problem of flight logs. Why not have all the advantages of the flight log and practically none of the effort usually required in preparing it?

The answer was simple—create a *master* flight plan file, including flight logs for every trip that our business would reasonably require. My personal logbook showed the trips which were made most often, and I had a collection of spiral-bound notebooks which contained the actual routing and clearances given by ATC. Together this information was used to flight plan each trip with all the attention to detail usually reserved for such projects as the Instrument Written Exam.

The result of this effort was a set of typewritten flight plans detailing the leg distances, magnetic courses, MEAs, and the other fixed data pertaining to the trips we make on a repetitive basis. Now, flight planning a trip from Los Angeles to Dallas and then on to Grand Rapids with a return via Oklahoma City and Albuquerque requires about 3 minutes at the copy machine. And best of all, we haven't been given a "Cleared as filed, except . . . " in months.

THE BIG GAMBLE

Perhaps it is all the years that I have spent in photographic darkrooms which allows me to feel comfortable in a dimly lit cockpit, but whatever the reason, I sincerely prefer to fly at night. For me, there are many positive aspects of night flight which weigh heavily against the reasons most generally given for avoiding the dark skies. Certainly, night flight is physically more comfortable than suffering in the greenhouse effect usually encountered during day VFR flight. The outside air temperatures at night are usually more agreeable to both airplane engines and to the occupants, allowing better performance and a more pleasant trip. Also the air is generally smoother, and there is a great deal less traffic and radio chatter. And the public servants at ATC are generally friendlier and more eager to serve during the quiet hours between darkness and dawn. The major drawback for many pilots is the constant specter of, What if the engine fails?

All of us in the aviation community are familiar with the clichés concerning the reliability of modern aircraft engines. We are equally familiar with the gruesome newspaper photos of the mangled wreckage of a general aviation aircraft, invariably captioned with a story of disaster which began when the engine failed. Those very reliable engines do occasionally fail, and we all know it. But we must also remember that those failures are more often than not induced by fuel starvation or mismanagement.

For some pilots, even the remote possibility of engine failure during a night or IFR flight is so frightening that they completely refuse to fly in most general aviation aircraft under those conditions. Speculating on the potential results of such an occurrence, it is easy to concede the prudence of their position. Unfortunately, if a company airplane is restricted to use during day VFR operations, it will be all but impossible to cost-justify the investment.

It is from this base that the twin advocates build the rationalizations for the expensive and comparatively inefficient multiengine airplanes. With two engines, IFR and night operations become "safe." We have now come full circle and are faced with the question again of one versus two. Of course, we have already answered that by laying out the results of the recorded accident reports. *Statistically, singles are safer.* But something continues to bother me about "facts" that are completely contrary to common sense.

Perhaps the question does not hinge on the number of engines at all. Maybe the general aviation fatality rates should be examined on the basis of *stall speeds,* regardless of the number of engines. What would result if the rate were figured on a comparison between twins and the heavy singles which have comparable stall speeds? After all, the destructive forces of a crash are directly related to speed and deceleration rates.

It is not my intent to tear down my previous arguments supporting the safety of the single-engine aircraft. I am simply attempting to point out how easy it is to overlook a pertinent and critical item by concentrating too hard on one aspect of a situation.

We all recognize that for any type of meaningful life there will always be some element of risk, no matter how small. As business executives, it is a routine matter for us to look at a situation on the basis of its cost, benefit, and risk. We approach our business problems in a logical and unemotional manner, and we must do the same thing in our flying, even if the problem is an engine failure.

You must consider the problem and the available solutions on the ground when there is no pressure of time and danger to cloud your thinking. If you wait until the situation arises to make your plan, chances are very good that you will be unable to meet the demands under the stress of an actual emergency.

Returning to the problem of engine failure at night or IFR, the first step would be to list all the reasons that your engine might quit cold under those conditions of flight. Is your engine fuel injected? Does your alternate air door open automatically if it gets clogged with snow, or must you do it manually? Does your engine have a carburetor? Is it extremely susceptible to carb ice? Do you always use carb heat in clouds? Do you have a carb temp gauge to help you handle this problem? Does your airplane have a complex fuel management system; and if so, do you know it cold—even blindfolded?

On your twin that you bought for supersafety, what could make them both give up? Were the temps too high just before they quit? Did the mechanic put in new plugs at the last maintenance? Were they the right plugs? Have you read the AD note about your aux tanks? Fuel vents—did you really check them during preflight? Was the tape removed after your son and his buddy washed the airplane last Sunday?

If you really become involved in this analysis and work to develop a comprehensive listing of all the conceivable problems which could occur and the appropriate action to take in each instance, the chances are good that you will never be called on to cope with a total power failure in your airplane—at any time. The simple act of doing the analysis will sharpen your awareness to the multitude of little things which so often compound themselves into engine failures and fatalities. Applying an ounce of prevention will become a habit for you, practically obviating the need for the proverbial pound of cure.

"That's great stuff for the jerk who does something stupid like trying to fly on gasoline fumes and wishful thinking," the skeptic retorts, "but what about the poor guy who's slogging through the clouds when the crankshaft snaps?"

The statistics, of course, indicate that engine malfunctions in well-maintained, modern aircraft due to internal failures are extremely rare, but I'm certain that statement offers damned little comfort to the pilot who must cope with one of those rare instances. Unquestionably, that pilot is in deep trouble; but the situation is not completely hopeless. With a cool head, it is possible to walk away from even a situation like this. The possibility is confirmed by the fact that it has been done before.

Recently, I questioned my mechanic about a Cessna 210 that was being worked on in the hangar. The crew was replacing the firewall, and I was curious about the story behind this repair. The mechanic related that the 210 had thrown a prop blade while IFR. The resulting vibration had deformed the firewall before the pilot could get the engine shut down, but he was able to get radar vectors to complete a no-power instrument approach, landing safely with no additional damage to the aircraft.

Due to the AD note on Hartzell propellers, which affects our Lance, my interest in accidents involving propeller failures is very keen. Looking into the NTSB figures, I learned that on the average the general aviation fleet suffers approximately thirty-one accidents involving prop failure each year, resulting in about four fatalities or serious injuries. For this specific type of mechanical-failure accident, the occurrence of a fatality is once every 7.7 million flight hours. This means that an individual pilot, even if he flew 24 hours a day, would probably die of old age before he would be involved in a fatal prop-failure accident.

Staying ahead in this game, where we are betting all the "blue chips" on every roll of the dice, demands that we concentrate our energies on the most important things—those things which we can directly control. In my opinion we have been "oversold" on the element of chance as it affects flight safety. Admittedly there is some small factor of chance involved in every flight, but allowing it undue importance will only frustrate our efforts to identify and deal with the risks of higher probability.

We must apply the same good business principles to our flight operations as we do to the areas of manufacturing, distribution, and finance, seeking always to optimize asset utilization, maximize benefits, and at the same time minimize costs and risks. To do this requires that we take a very hard look at the risks, categorizing them in terms of occurrence probability and the seriousness of such an occurrence.

An engine failure at night or IFR is an occurrence which would probably rank very high in terms of seriousness, but its probability value would be very low. If we were to eliminate fuel mismanagement and starvation as causative factors, the probability value of this occurrence would drop still lower.

For the instrument pilot, the failure which would rank next in seriousness would generally be that of the vacuum system. Here the probability value would increase since there are more instances of vacuum pump failures in the general aviation fleet than there are engine failures. The list would continue through the various aircraft systems in descending order of seriousness in the event of a failure of the particular system being examined. You should be seeking to find and understand the specific weak spot in each of your aircraft systems, and you should write your findings down.

The purpose behind this exercise is to enable you to identify, categorize, quantify, and evaluate the real risks being undertaken within the framework of your flight operations, your equipment, and your personal pilot skills. Once this has been accomplished, you can develop a program of risk management including preventative maintenance and equipment selection to reduce the probability value of failure within each specific system. From this basis, the next logical step is the creation of a series of alternate plans designed to reduce the seriousness of any in-flight system failure should it occur.

It is important for the business pilot to approach this analysis with the same or even greater interest than he gives to the results recorded on the month-end operating statement for his business. He must personally consider the problems, establish the priorities, and ask the questions:

What will happen if the alternator belt breaks . . . if the alternator or voltage regulator quits . . . what instruments will I lose . . . how much time will I have with reliable nav signals . . . can I get some sort of backup power source? What about the loss of the vacuum system . . . will I even know about it before the gyros spin down? Can I manage to fly the airplane on needle, ball, and airspeed? Will the autopilot be of any help, or will it create a dangerous situation when the gyros quit? If several systems fail, how will I conduct my plan with what is left? How serious is a complete comm failure, and how will I handle it if it happens?

The questions are almost endless, and the answers will depend upon the pilot and his airplane. Certainly there are some general answers to these questions, but I strongly feel that answers developed by the individual pilot will be better than any printed list of dos and don'ts that I might offer. The value of this study in risk management is to be derived from the headwork, research, and learning involved; packaged panaceas would not be an adequate substitute.

During my own research pertaining to the questions created by aircraft systems failures during IFR flight, I found that some of the more obvious alternate plans would not work in actual practice. Perhaps you will find my failures more enlightening than my successes, so let's look at a few of them.

In every ground school class that I have ever attended dealing with instrument flying, a great deal of time and consideration was given to the problem of lost communications. The instructor would generally list all the regulations dealing with what route to take, what altitude to fly, and when to start the approach. This was always very interesting information to me about what must be a very frightening occurrence. But surely, I thought, there must be some simple, inexpensive way to avoid the problem entirely.

As a neophyte instrument pilot, it occurred to me that perhaps an ounce of prevention might well be worth a pound of cure in this situation as it is in so many others. It seemed logical that the answer to this problem was a portable, battery-operated transceiver. There were not that many available at the time, so the selection came very easily. The only real decision was between a 10-channel or a 360-channel unit. Since it was to save my skin in IFR conditions, why not have the best?

Of course, that decision moved my answer out of the "inexpensive" category; but if I ever really needed it, that $1400 price tag would seem a bargain.

For months, I carried this 17-pound package along on every flight if there seemed even the slightest possibility of encountering clouds. It was very comforting to know that should the two aircraft radios quit simultaneously or the electrical system decide to die, I still had another 360 channels by which I could talk to someone on the ground. Finally, on a night flight from St. Louis to Tulsa, circumstance provided an opportunity to use that expensive portable.

Kansas City Center wasn't receiving our transmissions; this was evident by the controller's continuing request that we acknowledge. After repeatedly flipping switches and going back and forth between the two aircraft radios, the portable was brought into use. Immediately, the speaker was filled with a voice which could only belong to an airline captain. He informed Center that a "little Cessna" was trying to talk to

This compact and completely portable 360-channel transceiver packs a lot of communication capability into a neat, little package. As a backup for the aircraft radios in the event of communications failure during IFR conditions, however, tests demonstrated that without an external antenna, the radio was practically useless. If you plan to use such a unit as a backup system, discuss the problem with your avionics technician. He will be able to fit an external antenna onto your aircraft with a jack on the instrument panel. Such an arrangement makes this type of radio a meaningful piece of equipment. Without it, you're just carrying extra weight.

them and relayed our message. This led to a situation in which all our responses to Center were via the "Ident" feature of the transponder.

Later we discovered that the problem had been one of altitude, position, and something to do with Center's remote antenna site. Both of the aircraft radios were working fine. This incident, however, sparked a thorough investigation into the capabilities of our "emergency" radio. The results were extremely disappointing. Airborne tests showed that our transmission range was about a mile. The aircraft cabin was blocking the output of the little telescoping antenna, and to obtain better results would require mounting a permanent antenna on the outside of the airplane.

Very slowly realization began to form that the likelihood of losing both aircraft radios simultaneously was highly remote. If such were to occur, it would most probably be due to failure of some component in the system that lacked redundancy. Each transmitter had its own relay and separate power supply, and each radio had a separate antenna. So these items were scratched from the list of most probable problems.

In my thoughts, all the components were assessed for failure probability, and consideration was given to what items could be conveniently and affordably duplicated to build strength into the chain. Two microphones and a headset had already become standard equipment; so by the process of elimination it became clear that the weakest link was the electrical system itself. Reflecting upon the number of battery, alternator, and belt failures I have experienced in automobiles, it was sobering to acknowledge that my safety during IFR flight was secured by what is essentially the same type of electrical system.

Discussing this problem with mechanics and other pilots, I found that most agreed this was the *real* reason that sensible IFR and night flying is done in twins.

"Twins give you a lot more than just two engines, you know. You will also have two alternators and two vacuum pumps.

"And, flying night or IFR with anything less than this is not a gamble; it is idiocy."

Listening to the comments, I had the distinct feeling that I had heard all this before. Maybe I was simply being a blockhead, fighting a battle that inevitably I would lose. Perhaps the sensible thing for me to do was to buy a twin.

Over coffee in El Paso, I continued to conduct my personal poll pertaining to this problem. My companion was an ex-twin owner from Washington who was currently flying a Cessna T-210, and he was happy. He'd never go back to a twin.

"Too costly to run and too much maintenance," he said.

When I approached the electrical system problem, he just smiled. His airplane had been modified. He had *two* alternators . . . just like the twins.

What luck, meeting this man! I had just about given in, but here was someone with an answer, a viable compromise. The idea excited me. I was ready to buy a faster airplane; and if I went with the T-210, the problem of a supplemental type certificate (STC) for the dual alternators would be a cinch. At least one was already flying. In the meantime I would get one of those rechargeable battery packs that you plug into the cigarette lighter socket. Fantastic! I had a plan, and I was really pleased until a couple of seemingly unrelated incidents started punching holes in my plan.

The time span between the incidents stretched over a period of 2 years. The first occurred during the months immediately following the purchase of our Skylane. There would be occasions when the electrically operated flaps would not respond to the directions of the flap handle. This would always happen in flight and could not be duplicated on the ground. The mechanic worked and searched and could never find any reason for this phenomenon. Mysteriously, the problem magically "cured" itself and never reoccurred.

One night 2 years later Joyce and I boarded the Skylane preparing to return home from a sales trip covering central California. We had flown several legs that day, amounting to about 4 hours of flight time without any problems. Now, the Skylane's starter refused to budge. Although I heard the familiar sound of the battery contactor when I activated the master switch, neither the panel lights nor the rotating beacon would work, and the fuel gauges obstinately pointed to EMPTY. It seemed that the battery was dead.

Hand propping brought the engine to life, and all the electrical equipment was soon up and running. Going through my checklists, I marveled at the strong, steady output of energy from the alternator. This was certainly an improvement over the generator systems on the older aircraft that I had flown.

The flight back to Oxnard was pleasant and routine. Taxiing to the hangar, the Skylane's lights were strong and bright. It hardly seemed possible that a dead battery could rebuild so quickly and so well. Randy, the Cessna service manager, was working very late, and as he helped me pull the airplane into the hangar, I related what had happened. He checked the battery and wiring and said that he could find nothing wrong. The only thing that he could suggest was that the battery contactor might be faulty. He promised to thoroughly check this possibility the following day.

The final incidents occurred that following day. Joyce and I had made arrangements to rent a Cessna 150, in which I had agreed to give her some dual instruction. It was a new 1977 model with the bright red, white, and blue "Operation TakeOff" paint job. It was a beautiful day and a beautiful airplane, and my student-pilot wife was very excited. It had been several weeks since she had flown with her regular flight instructor; and since her last flight had been her first solo, she was really itching to fly again.

Her takeoff was a bit wobbly, but it was certainly safe. We flew out to the practice area where she did a surprisingly good job on the entire series of approach and departure stalls, steep turns, and simulated go-arounds. Satisfied with her airwork, I told her to take us back to the pattern for some touch-and-go landings. There was a brisk, steady crosswind blowing so this would be good practice.

Joyce was doing an excellent job. We had made about eight trips around the pattern, and she had handled the crosswind situation well. I was very pleased with her performance and had developed a good bit of admiration for her regular instructor. She could not have made a better choice.

We were making our final landing for the session; she had the crosswind under control, and we were tracking straight down the runway. She was holding it off nicely, just above the stall, when I decided to call for a go-around. With the practiced nonchalance of a flight instructor, I turned my head slightly to the right to appear properly disinterested in my student's actions while at the same time bringing the flap itself into the range of my peripheral vision. The little engine roared as my wife advanced the throttle, but the flap did not move. I waited, while the runway receded behind us, hoping my wife would realize her error before I was forced to intercede. Our Skylane would climb out of ground effect in a near-stalled condition with full flaps, but the Cessna 150 won't. I couldn't wait any longer.

"Flaps, Joyce," I commanded.

"But I did . . . " came the reply from a small, frightened, and terribly confused student pilot.

She was intent on flying the airplane down the runway. Her mind was racing, trying to understand this situation where she had done everything right, just as she had been taught to do, and yet something was still very wrong.

My full attention was now back inside the cockpit. Glancing across the panel, I verified that the flap handle had been raised to the 20° position and the master switch was on. I hadn't consciously looked at the fuel gauges, but as I pulled the power back to idle, their message prompted me to return the flap handle to the FULL-DOWN position. With as little runway as there was ahead of us, I wanted those flaps to stay right where they were for a few more minutes.

I knew this incident was somehow related to the situation we had experienced in the Skylane on the previous night. In both cases the fuel gauges had read EMPTY when there was plenty of fuel in the tanks. In each instance we had experienced a failure of the electrical system, and electric flaps just won't work without electricity. I was convinced that the reason the mechanic couldn't find anything wrong with the flaps on the Skylane 2 years before was simply that there was nothing wrong with the flaps. It had always been an electrical problem, an intermittent problem, but an electrical problem nonetheless.

We landed and came to a stop in the final quarter of the runway. Taxiing in to the ramp, I noticed the fuel gauges bouncing just below the HALF-FULL mark. I moved the flap handle to the UP position, and the flaps obediently complied. If my assumptions were correct, then my plans for a T-210 with dual alternators was another solution for the *wrong* problem. The weakest link in the electrical system was the *battery contactor;* you could have six alternators out there producing energy, but if the battery contactor failed, none of that energy could get to the radios and instruments where it was needed. That would also shoot a hole in the idea that dual alternators on the twin provided meaningful redundancy in the electrical system. Here was another fine example of an "insurance policy" which leads the pilot to believe that he has something that he doesn't. Dual alternators do not make a dual electrical system "fail safe" unless there are also dual battery contactors or a means of bypassing that part of the circuit.

Walking across the ramp to the hangar where a mechanic was working on the FBO's other 1977 Cessna 150, I reflected upon the details of an accident report I had recently read. A student pilot had been shooting touch-and-go landings; following one, he flew the airplane into the trees off the end of the runway. Witnesses reported that he had failed to retract the flaps. Reading that report, I felt that both the student and his instructor were a couple of dummies, but now I wasn't so sure. Maybe that student who crashed and died was a victim of the same thing which had occurred to us. Maybe he *had* done everything "right," just as he had been taught to do. If he were functioning mechanically, as most students are prone to do at first, it is easy to imagine how a systems failure like this coupled to a short grass strip with obstacles off the end could add up to disaster for a low-time pilot.

It was evident from all the open inspection covers that Dan, the mechanic, was conducting a 100-hour inspection on the green and white Cessna 150. When I asked if he had received any flap squawks on the new 150s, he replied that there had been several on both airplanes, but he had never been able to find anything wrong. The reason, of course, was obvious, at least to me. He had been checking the flap system when the culprit was actually an intermittent battery contactor.

Dan and I discussed the merits of my theory and other possibilities, but considering all the circumstances involved, it seemed my suspicions were probably correct.

Since the lighter socket was wired into the switched side of the circuit, a failure of the battery contactor solenoid would, unfortunately, make my planned auxiliary battery pack as useless as a second alternator under those circumstances. Of course, either one would be very helpful in the event of an alternator or belt failure, and my mechanic friend pointed out that due to its simplicity, the battery contactor is *generally* a very reliable component in the system. That might be true on a general basis, but I had just flown two airplanes on two successive days and experienced an electrical failure in both of them. Additionally, the squawk sheet on a third Cessna airplane, the one the mechanic was currently working on, indicated that several other pilots had experienced this same intermittent electrical system problem with that machine, so I was not convinced about that reliability. I tend to be more impressed with what I actually see happen than I am with what people say.

When we fly in general aviation airplanes, we are gambling on the reliability of our engines. Reviewing the statistics, we found the actual risks were small, making the risk-benefit relationship a favorable one. When we fly nights and IFR, as we must do to cost-justify our investment in an airplane, we are no longer gambling just on the reliability of

In the event of certain electrical problems, this rechargeable battery pack can provide sufficient energy to enable you to continue on to a suitable landing site and shoot an approach. The unit connects to the aircraft's electrical system by means of a plug which goes into the cigar lighter socket on the panel.

the engine but also on the performance of the various subsystems. In order to evaluate the true nature of the risk involved with the subsystems, it is imperative that the individual pilot dig deeply into the manuals for his airplane, becoming intimate with the operating details of those subsystems. He must speculate both on the probability and the impact of any failure, taking nothing for granted, searching for the weakest link.

Unless the business pilot is willing to make this effort, then develop meaningful alternate plans, and test them, flying for business is not an activity of well-considered risks. Instead, it is simply a matter of gambling. And this is certainly the "big gamble," since the ante is your life.

A WORD ON WEATHER

There was a time when I felt very strongly that owning an airplane which couldn't be turned upside down represented a total waste of money and indicated that the owner didn't really understand what flying was all about. Aerobatics and off-airport landings were the standard fare upon which I honed my developing stick-and-rudder skills, and low-level hammerhead turns were practiced to refine my sense of timing. Of course, I had come into general aviation by way of an extended apprenticeship as a skydiver, which most of my pilot acquaintances accepted as an excuse for my attitudes toward flying that the polite ones termed as "somewhat bizarre."

During that period of time before mandatory transponders and terminal control areas (TCAs), I often flew across the entire United States without ever seeing or talking to an employee of the FAA. Weather briefings were taken from the sky beyond the windshield. If it looked poor ahead, I would either turn to a heading which offered a more pleasant view or land to ponder cosmic questions until the skies had cleared. No one was waiting. There were no appointments to keep, so it really didn't matter where I went or what time it was when I got there. And the total utility of my airplane was assessed in terms of the personal pleasures provided and the lessons learned.

Business flying makes different demands. There *are* appointments to keep and there *are* people waiting. The aircraft required is larger, faster, and far more sophisticated. It would not be at home in a farmer's field. It is an expensive corporate asset which must earn its keep. This type of equipment is just too costly to sit unproductively on the ground while its pilot chews upon a straw and contemplates the heavens. A business aircraft only makes money when it is flying, so it must, within reason, fly in fair weather or foul.

Even when the business pilot is a current and well-qualified instrument pilot, there are still times when he will be wise to tarry on the ground and ponder those cosmic questions. For me this occurs when the reports are calling for embedded thunderstorms. There are few things more frightening than the thought of flying along in the clouds and unexpectedly blundering into a mature thunderstorm cell. This happened to me once during an instrument flight from Opa Locka to Savannah, and the experience was sufficiently impactful to leave a negative attitude toward thunderstorms, which I'm certain will remain with me for the rest of my life.

It is extremely difficult for the business pilot to be faced with the decision *to not go* when an appointment has been set for weeks in advance. It makes it even more difficult if he had been trying for months to get that appointment in the first place, but sometimes there is no other choice. Usually, if you have been following the general weather pictures, you will know in advance that there will be the possibility you may be forced to keep your appointment by using an alternate form of transportation.

During August 1977, a high-pressure area east of the Rockies created a situation which pushed Tropical Storm Doreen up the California coast, spawning areas of low ceilings, torrential rains, and embedded thunderstorms in the clouds obscuring the coastal mountains. Precipitation static made it all but impossible to understand the continuous weather broadcast on the LF/MF band, but the storm was forecast to break up on the morning of our planned flight.

Joyce had an eight-thirty appointment in Bakersfield (BFL), and Carolyn, our western sales manager, had one set for ten in Fresno. Normally, this would be an easy and pleasant flight, but Doreen added more complications than I was ready to cope with. The routine clearance from OXR to BFL would place 30 minutes of very rugged mountain tops a scant 2000 feet beneath the belly of the Lance. Considering the possibility of strong vertical currents along with the phlegmatic climb performance of our ponderous Piper, I decided this was one of those rare times when the compromises of Plan B seemed the better choice. The Lance would remain locked in the hangar, and the women could decide between airlines and automobiles.

While the women *drove* to their respective appointments, I agonized over my decision. Maybe we could have gone and encountered nothing more severe than moderate rain. The freezing level was well above the MEAs for the route, so there was no danger of ice. And maybe those "embedded thunderstorms" were a product of pessimistic forecasting rather than reality. Yet, the consequences of launching into that dark sky and finding that the forecasters were right could be an event of catastrophic proportions.

The danger of a thunderstorm does not lie in the frightening sound of the rain which beats so hard against the aircraft skin that it sometimes removes the paint from the wings. It is the enormous, mind-boggling power of the turbulent vertical gusts that endanger an airplane of *any* size which blunders into this maelstrom. Even the strength and structural integrity of an F-4 fighter which was used for thunderstorm penetration experiments proved an inadequate match for nature's most awesome demonstration of power. Inspection after one particular flight revealed that the wings were so twisted and battered and so many rivets had popped that the fighter was relegated to the scrap heap. In 1977, a DC-9 encountered a cell and reportedly suffered a complete loss of power from its two jet engines due to ingestion of hail. The resulting crash took seventy-two lives.

If a thunderstorm can destroy military fighters and jet transports, the business pilot in his Bonanza or Cessna 310 would be wise to steer clear of any confrontation with these towering monsters. The problem need not be the structural destruction of the aircraft. As pointed out by Bob Buck in *Weather Flying*, "a stalled airplane in a thunderstorm is in a desperate situation, and the cleaner the airplane, the more desperate." Buck goes on to caution that "we should never be on instruments when thunderstorms are nearby unless we have radar and know how to use it."

The message from this 30,000-hour pilot is extremely clear. But until recently airborne radar was very heavy, very expensive, failure-prone, and totally unavailable for single-engine aircraft. Now, it is still relatively heavy, expensive, failure-prone, but it is available for at least two models of single-engine airplanes. This fact demonstrates that the industry at last recognizes singles can and will be used to fly "hard weather." This recognition ultimately will create pressure to advance the technology required to overcome the current problems of weight, cost, and failure rates.

Radar is an *avoidance* tool which allows us to work around the critical problem of embedded thunderstorms. Since the prime danger in thunderstorms is turbulence, not the rain, and since the areas of the greatest precipitation and greatest turbulence don't necessarily coincide, the use of radar, which only depicts the precipitation, requires training and experience for effective interpretation. It is not a device which an affluent pilot can have installed in his airplane and then successfully go out to probe for a "soft" spot in a squall line.

High on the list of priorities for the business pilot is the avoidance of thunderstorm cells. Radar is the usual tool for determining a route around active cells. Until recently, airborne radar was available only to the pilot of a twin. Now, radar can be installed in several models of single-engine machines. An alternative storm-avoidance tool is the Ryan Stormscope, which was recently installed in Joyce Jewelry's Piper Lance. The Stormscope is usable in *any* twin- or single-engine aircraft.

Another tool for thunderstorm avoidance has just recently become available—the Ryan Stormscope. It is *not* a radar type of device, and it functions on a different basic assumption. Whereas radar assumes a correlation between rain and turbulence, the Stormscope assumes a correlation between atmospheric discharges of static electricity and turbulence. The system is comprised of three units and weighs about the same as many of the radar systems. It seems a more simple approach to the problem and reflects this in a lower price. At approximately $6000, the Stormscope is significantly less expensive than all but one of the current radar systems. When the total cost for the system installation is examined, however, the Ryan Stormscope remains the lowest cost system currently available.

Unlike radar, the Stormscope can be used on the ground to survey the surrounding situation *before* launching into the clouds. Where radar displays live weather as it happens, the Stormscope displays weather history. Using small green dots on a TV-like display, the Stormscope maps the occurrence of electrical discharges. Clusters of these dots would therefore indicate the area of greatest turbulence according to the theories of Paul Ryan, Stormscope's inventor.

Stormscope is a relatively new concept, but the first users of this system are very happy with it. Based on conversations with Stormscope owners and a test flight in a Texas-based Bonanza, we installed a Ryan Stormscope in our company's Lance. Now, with more than 600 trouble-free hours with this system, I am convinced that the Stormscope was an excellent investment in increased utility and safety. Every flight with the Stormscope increases my belief that Ryan's invention is not only a viable alternative to radar as a storm avoidance tool but it might just be superior.

Weather is the eternal variable in the aviator's world. It is the subject upon which any pilot can spend a lifetime of study. This visible manifestation of the hydrologic cycle bears on every human endeavor and in some way, great or small, affects the bottom line of every business enterprise. For the business pilot, weather is not only a source of occasional frustration but it also provides opportunities for rewards beyond those which can be measured on the balance sheet or operating statement.

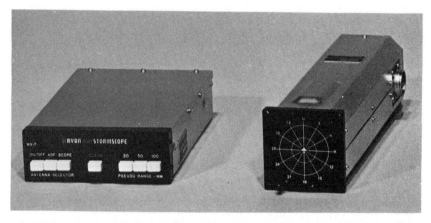

Pictured here are the Ryan Stormscope receiver (left) and the Stormscope display screen (right) which mount in the aircraft instrument panel. The receiver is used in selecting range settings of 40, 100, or 200 nautical miles that will indicate direction and distance of a storm center on the display screen. The range setting of 200 nautical miles permits the pilot to actually look at weather conditions in excess of 200 nautical miles in every direction around his aircraft. The shorter range settings are used for navigating around adverse weather conditions. The Ryan Stormscope works as well on the ground as it does in the air. (Courtesy of Ryan Stormscope.)

In a world of plastic virtues, governmentally guaranteed success, and rewards on the basis of simple existence, there is a beauty and rare delight to be found in making an instrument approach down to minimums, watching as the gray-cloud nothingness is split by the sequential strobes.

In a matter of seconds the scene materializes before your eyes. The approach lights flash a ball of brilliance pointing the way to the runway's end. This is a sight without equal.

The transition from the bright, blue skies above into the strange and alien world of instrument flight in the clouds and ending with the squeak of rubber tires against the rain-soaked runway is an experience which defies comparison. It is unique unto itself. There is a real sense of accomplishment here, of having met a challenging task, and knowing you have done the job well.

Suggested Reading

Buck, Robert N.: *Flying Know-How*, Delacorte, New York, 1975.

———: *Weather Flying*, Macmillan, New York, 1970.

Cagle, Malcolm W., and C. G. Halpine: *A Pilot's Meteorology*, Van Nostrand, New York, 1970.

Collins, Richard L.: *Flying Safely*, Delacorte, New York, 1977.

Donn, William L.: *Meteorology*, McGraw-Hill, New York, 1975.

Foster, Timothy R. V.: *Aircraft Owner's Handbook*, Van Nostrand, New York, 1978.

Garrison, Peter: *Flying Airplanes, The First Hundred Hours*, Doubleday, Garden City, N.Y., 1980.

Hoyt, John R.: *As the Pro Flies*, McGraw-Hill, New York, 1959.

Langewiesche, Wolfgang: *Stick and Rudder*, McGraw-Hill, New York, 1944.

Larson, George: *Fly on Instruments*, Doubleday, Garden City, N.Y., 1980.

Mauriello, Joseph A.: *Businessman's Federal Tax Guide*, Dow Jones-Irwin, Homewood, Ill., 1971.

Myer, John N.: *Accounting for Non-Accountants*, Hawthorn, New York, 1967.

Petzoldt, Paul: *The Wilderness Handbook*, Norton, New York, 1974.

Reichard, Robert S.: *The Figure Finaglers*, McGraw-Hill, New York, 1974.

Taylor, Richard L.: *Instrument Flying*, Macmillan, New York, 1972.

———: *Understanding Flying*, Delacorte, New York, 1977.

Pertinent Names and Addresses

AVIATION ORGANIZATIONS

Aerobatic Club of America
2400 W. Seventh Street·
Ft. Worth, TX 76107

Aerospace Education Foundation
1750 Pennsylvania Avenue, N.W.
Washington, DC 20006

Air Traffic Control Association
Suite 409, ARBA Building
525 School Street, S.W.
Washington, DC 20024

Air Transport Association of
America (ATA)
1709 New York Avenue, N.W.
Washington, DC 20006

Aircraft Electronics Association, Inc.
P.O. Box 1981
Independence, MO 64055

Aircraft Owners & Pilots
Association (AOPA)
7315 Wisconsin Avenue
Bethesda, MD
Mailing Address: Box 5800
Washington, DC 20014

Airport Operators Council
International, Inc. (AOCI)
1700 K Street, N.W.
Washington, DC 20006

American Bonanza Society
Chemung County Airport
Horseheads, NY 14845

American Helicopter Society
30 E. 42d Street, Suite 1405
New York, NY 10017

Antique Airplane Association
P.O. Box H
Ottumwa, IA 52501

Aviation Distributors &
Manufacturers Association
Management Office
1900 Arch Street
Philadelphia, PA 19103

Aviation/Space Writers Association
c/o William F. Kaiser
Cliffwood Road
Chester, NJ 07930

Civil Aviation Medical Association
801 Green Bay Road
Lake Bluff, IL 60044

Experimental Aircraft Association
11311 W. Forest Home Avenue
Franklin, WI 53130

Flight Safety Foundation
1800 N. Kent Street
Arlington, VA 22209

Flying Chiropractors Association
215 Belmont Street
Johnstown, PA 15904

Flying Dentists Association
Dr. James H. Cooper
President, 1974
3130 Maple Drive, NE
Atlanta, GA 30305

Flying Funeral Directors of America
811 Grant Street
Akron, OH 44311

Flying Physicians Association
801 Green Bay Road
Lake Bluff, IL 60044

General Aviation Association of
  America
8755 112th Way, North
Seminole, FL 33542

General Aviation Manufacturers
  Association (GAMA)
Suite 1215
1025 Connecticut Avenue, N.W.
Washington, DC 20036

Helicopter Association of America
Suite 610
1156 15th Street, N.W.
Washington, DC 20005

International Flying Bankers
  Association
Box 17
Downers Grove, IL 60515

International Flying Farmers
Mid-Continent Airport
Wichita, KS 67209

National Aero Club
16740 Highway 281S.
San Antonio, TX 78221

National Aeronautics Association
Suite 610, Shoreham Building
806 15th Street, N.W.
Washington, DC 20005

National Aerospace Education
  Council
806 15th Street, N.W.
Washington, DC 20005

National Air Transportation
  Associations
1156 Fifteenth Street, N.W.
Suite 515
Washington, DC 20005

National Business Aircraft
  Association
Suite 401
425 13th Street, N.W.
Washington, DC 20006

National Intercollegiate Flying
  Association (NIFA)
Parks College
St. Louis University
Cahokia, IL 62206

Ninety-Nines
Will Rogers World Airport
Oklahoma City, OK 73159

Professional Air Traffic Controllers
  Organization (PATCO)
Suite 706
2100 M Street, N.W.
Washington, DC 20037

Soaring Society of America
Box 66071
Los Angeles, CA 90066

Society of Experimental Test Pilots
44814 N. Elm Avenue
(Mail: P.O. Box 986)
Lancaster, CA 93534

University Aviation Association
c/o Parks College
St. Louis University
Parks Airport
Cahokia, IL 62206

Whirly Girls (Women Helicopter
    Pilots)
Suite 700
1725 DeSales Street, N.W.
Washington, DC 20036

GENERAL AVIATION MANUFACTURERS

Analog Training Computers, Inc.
189 Monmouth Parkway
W. Long Branch, NJ 07764

Avco Corporation
Avco Lycoming Division
652 Oliver Street
Williamsport, PA 17701

Beech Aircraft Corporation
9709 E. Central
Wichita, KS 67201

The Bendix Corporation
The Bendix Center
Southfield, MI 48075

Cessna Aircraft Company
P.O. Box 1521
Wichita, KS 67201

Champion Spark Plug Company
P.O. Box 910
Toledo, OH 43601

Collins Radio Company
400 Collins Road, N.E.
Cedar Rapids, IA 52406

Edo Corporation
Edo-Aire Division
216 Passaic Avenue
Fairfield, NJ 07006

The Garrett Corporation
9851 Sepulveda Boulevard
Los Angeles, CA 90009

Gates Learjet Corporation
P.O. Box 1280
Wichita, KS 67201

Grumman American Aviation
    Corporation
P.O. Box 2206
Savannah, GA 31402

Hartzell Propeller, Inc.
350 Washington Avenue
Piqua, OH 45356

Jeppesen Sanderson
8025 East 40th Avenue
Denver, CO 80207

King Radio Corporation
400 North Rogers Road
Olathe, KS 66061

Mooney Aircraft Corporation
Sub-Republic Steel Corp.
P.O. Box 72
Louis Schreiner Field
Kerrville, TX 78028

Piper Aerostar Corporation
2560 Skyway Drive
Santa Maria, CA 93454

Piper Aircraft Corporation
Lock Haven, PA 17745

RCA Corporation
Aviation Equipment Department
8500 Balboa Boulevard
Van Nuys, CA 91409

Rockwell International Corporation
5001 N. Rockwell Avenue
Bethany, OK 73008

Sperry Rand Corporation
Flight Systems Division
Box 21111
Phoenix, AZ 85036

Teledyne Continental Motors
Box 90
Mobile, AL 36601

FEDERAL AVIATION ADMINISTRATION

FAA HEADQUARTERS

Director of Public Affairs
Federal Aviation Administration
Department of Transportation
800 Independence Avenue, S.W.
Washington, DC 20590

FAA REGIONAL OFFICES

Alaskan Region
Public Affairs Officer
Hill Building
623 Sixth Avenue
Anchorage, AK 99501

Central Region
Public Affairs Officer
601 East 12th Street
Kansas City, MO 64106

Eastern Region
Public Affairs Officer
Federal Building
JFK International Airport
Jamaica, NY 11430

Great Lakes Region
Public Affairs Officer
2300 E. Devon Avenue
Des Plaines, IL 60018

New England Region
Public Affairs Officer
12 New England Executive Park
Burlington, MA 01803

Northwest Region
Public Affairs Officer
FAA Building, Boeing Field
Seattle, WA 98108

Pacific Region
Public Affairs Officer
P.O. Box 4009
Honolulu, HI 96813

Rocky Mountain Region
Public Affairs Officer
P.O. Box 7213, Park Hill Station
Denver, CO 80207

Southern Region
Public Affairs Officer
P.O. Box 20636
Atlanta, GA 30320

Southwest Region
Public Affairs Officer
4400 Blue Mound Road
P.O. Box 1689
Fort Worth, TX 76101

Western Region
Public Affairs Officer
5651 West Manchester Avenue
P.O. Box 92007, Worldway Postal
 Center
Los Angeles, CA 90009

NATIONAL TRANSPORTATION SAFETY BOARD

NTSB HEADQUARTERS

Director of Public Affairs
National Transportation Safety Board
800 Independence Avenue, S.W.
Washington, DC 20591

NTSB FIELD OFFICES

Anchorage, Alaska
Hill Building, Room 454
632 Sixth Avenue
Anchorage, AK 99501

Chicago, Illinois
2300 E. Devon Avenue
Room 208
Des Plaines, IL 60018

Denver, Colorado
10255 East 25th Avenue
Suite 14
Aurora, CO 80010

Fort Worth, Texas
Federal Building, Room 7A07
819 Taylor Street
Fort Worth, TX 76102

Kansas City, Missouri
Federal Building, Room 625
601 East 12th Street
Kansas City, MO 64106

Los Angeles, California
8939 S. Sepulveda Boulevard
Suite 426
Los Angeles, CA 90045

Miami, Florida
P.O. Box 1245
Miami International Airport
Miami, FL 33148

New York, New York
Federal Building, Room 102
JFK International Airport
Jamaica, NY 11430

Oakland, California
7700 Edgewater Drive
Suite 748
Oakland, CA 94621

Seattle, Washington
9010 E. Marginal Way
King County Airport
South Seattle, WA 98108

Washington, D.C.
P.O. Box 17226
Gateway Building #1
Dulles International Airport
Washington, DC 20041

MISCELLANEOUS

Aviation Consumer Magazine
P.O. Box 4327
Greenwich, CT 06830

Business and Commercial Aviation
Hangar C-1
Westchester County Airport
White Plains, NY 10604

National Rifle Association
1600 Rhode Island Avenue, N.W.
Washington, DC 20036

Professional Pilot Magazine
225 East Street, Box M
Winchester, MA 01890

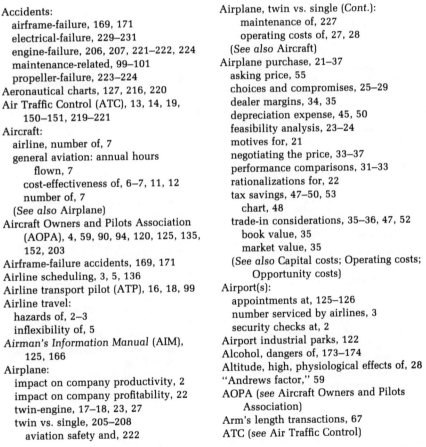

INDEX

Accidents:
  airframe-failure, 169, 171
  electrical-failure, 229–231
  engine-failure, 206, 207, 221–222, 224
  maintenance-related, 99–101
  propeller-failure, 223–224
Aeronautical charts, 127, 216, 220
Air Traffic Control (ATC), 13, 14, 19,
    150–151, 219–221
Aircraft:
  airline, number of, 7
  general aviation: annual hours
      flown, 7
    cost-effectiveness of, 6–7, 11, 12
    number of, 7
  (See also Airplane)
Aircraft Owners and Pilots Association
    (AOPA), 4, 59, 90, 94, 120, 125, 135,
    152, 203
Airframe-failure accidents, 169, 171
Airline scheduling, 3, 5, 136
Airline transport pilot (ATP), 16, 18, 99
Airline travel:
  hazards of, 2–3
  inflexibility of, 5
Airman's Information Manual (AIM),
    125, 166
Airplane:
  impact on company productivity, 2
  impact on company profitability, 22
  twin-engine, 17–18, 23, 27
  twin vs. single, 205–208
    aviation safety and, 222

Airplane, twin vs. single (Cont.):
  maintenance of, 227
  operating costs of, 27, 28
  (See also Aircraft)
Airplane purchase, 21–37
  asking price, 55
  choices and compromises, 25–29
  dealer margins, 34, 35
  depreciation expense, 45, 50
  feasibility analysis, 23–24
  motives for, 21
  negotiating the price, 33–37
  performance comparisons, 31–33
  rationalizations for, 22
  tax savings, 47–50, 53
    chart, 48
  trade-in considerations, 35–36, 47, 52
    book value, 35
    market value, 35
  (See also Capital costs; Operating costs;
    Opportunity costs)
Airport(s):
  appointments at, 125–126
  number serviced by airlines, 3
  security checks at, 2
Airport industrial parks, 122
Alcohol, dangers of, 173–174
Altitude, high, physiological effects of, 28
"Andrews factor," 59
AOPA (see Aircraft Owners and Pilots
    Association)
Arm's length transactions, 67
ATC (see Air Traffic Control)

Paul E. Hansen is the president of Joyce Jewelry, Inc., a West Coast manufacturer and distributor of costume jewelry. Once a free-lance photographer, Hansen became involved in general aviation when *Flying* gave him an assignment to cover a story with their staff writer Richard Bach, author of *Jonathan Livingston Seagull.* That encounter led to an intense and continuing involvement with flying. Today, he is a multithousand-hour commercial-instrument pilot and CFI.
(*Photo by Joyce Hansen.*)